"Boz's story is gripping. What start   redemption. I remember our first mee.   I would occasionally sing for the inmates—he wanted to talk up his music business connections. I liked Boz right away and I knew that our meeting wasn't about the music business; I could sense God's call on his life. It was only a matter of time until he surrendered himself to Jesus's voice of love speaking to him. His life and this book are powerful reminders of what God can do with any of us who surrender our will and choose to serve and live God's way wherever we are."

—**Brian Doerksen**, Christian singer-songwriter

"'When our soul is thirsty, we can dig our own wells ... [but] we want to learn what it means to pant after God, to come to Jesus as thirsty people. Only thirsty people pant ... We must discover how we can become aware of our deepest thirst. Facing confusion is one way. Feeling disappointment is another' (Larry Crabb, *Inside Out* [Colorado: NavPress, 2013]). The gripping story you are about to read reveals a very thirsty 'well digger' who encountered deep confusion and disappointment. To his surprise, the pain and fear of those traumatic experiences led him to the quenching satisfaction of vibrant life in Jesus Christ.

"Since first meeting Bosco some ten years ago—during some of his darkest days in prison—I have seen a young man blossom and grow. I have witnessed the birthing of a dynamic ministry vision. I have grown to love and appreciate a man of deep humility and boundless passion for reaching the younger generation. I have had the honour and privilege of mentoring a man of gifted creativity and uncompromising focus. Though this book in itself is complete, it marks just the beginning of many more chapters of an exciting adventure upon which, by God's grace, Bosco has embarked."

—**Rev. Tom Rathjen**, former chaplain at Mission Institution

"I am very grateful to have known Boz for six years and in that time become his friend, hear the detailed account of his testimony, and see Christ Jesus's amazing and miraculous work in his life. The beauty of Bosco Poon's story is not only the radical transformation in his character but also the fact that there is a very public media and legal record testifying that he was once a gang member and criminal but is now a pastor and man of God. I would encourage the skeptic to read the 2006 newspaper articles detailing the crime that landed him in jail and to compare the story of the man who once was to the man who is now: the one born of Zion's hope."

—**Daniel T. Holmes**, MD, Vancouver, BC

"Boz's story is our story. We have all been imprisoned. Pride, unforgiveness, ignorance, prejudice, and a hard heart have led us to foolish decisions and broken relationships. We've been separated from God. As Boz writes of the prison inmates, 'All of our hearts had the same deep yearning for something that could set our souls free. We all wanted forgiveness and a second chance.' In these pages, Boz finds true freedom through the only one who is the Way, the Truth, and the Life. As you read this story, may you allow your heart to be set free and to find its home in Christ."
— **Marina H. Hofman**, PhD, award-winning writer, Old Testament scholar

"God's ability to transform a person is unmistakable in the life of Boz. This narrative is gripping, awe-inspiring, and filled with unexpected plot twists. The grace of God is sufficient to forgive and cleanse all human transgression. Boz's life is a vivid testimony of spiritual, emotional, and physical transformation. This is a must read!"
— **Rev. Kenneth A. Russell**, district superintendent, Pentecostal Assemblies of Canada–BC/Yukon

"Boz articulates with rich poetic descriptors a life that was hungry for acceptance. He shares with the reader how as a young Asian immigrant to Canada, he faced a new culture, a new social hierarchy, leaving him feeling isolated and alone. The need to be needed is innate in each of us, and Boz takes on a journey of choices leading to his willingness to give himself to people who would accept him not for who he was but for what he could do for them. His choices eventually cost him his personal freedom. The isolation that separated him from the society that he so much desired to be a part of brings him into the presence of the God of redemption, Jesus. This encounter validates the value, worth, and purpose God had for Boz from the beginning of time.

"I have known this young man for the last few years, and I am witness to his call into ministry and how he embraces his new life. God has taken the talents and gifts He gave Boz, who had planned to rise to the top of the Asian world of entertainment. His choices changed that plan, and God has redeemed the person of Bosco Poon, placing him in the front lines in His plan to reach the world. This book is a beautiful picture of love, acceptance, forgiveness, and redemption. Everyone who takes time to read the transforming love of God in this young man's life will be blessed, encouraged, and reminded of the love of God for each of us."
— **Rev. Jim Caruso**, DMin, author of *Spiritual Sinkholes*

RISEN FROM PRISON

BEYOND MY WILDEST IMAGINATION

Uncle Chris

God's love for you is so deep!

BOSCO H.C. POON

RISEN FROM PRISON: BEYOND MY WILDEST IMAGINATION
Copyright ©2020 Bosco H. C. Poon
All rights reserved
Printed in Canada
International Standard Book Number 978-1-988928-25-8 soft cover
ISBN 978-1-988928-26-5 EPUB

Published by: Castle Quay Books
Burlington, ON, Canada | Riviera Beach, FL, USA
Tel: (416) 573-3249
E-mail: info@castlequaybooks.com | www.castlequaybooks.com

Edited by Marina Hofman Willard
Book cover illustration by Minnie Chau
Book interior by Burst Impressions
Printed in Canada

Winner of Castle Quay Books and the Word Guild's Best New Manuscript in 2019

All rights reserved. This book or parts thereof may not be reproduced in any form without prior written permission of the publishers.

Some names have been changed to protect the privacy of individuals.

Unless otherwise marked, Scripture is taken from the Holy Bible, New International Version®, NIV® Copyright ©1973, 1978, 1984, 2011 by Biblica, Inc.® Used by permission. All rights reserved worldwide. • Scripture marked (ESV) is taken from the ESV® Bible (The Holy Bible, English Standard Version®). ESV® Text Edition: 2016. Copyright © 2001 by Crossway, a publishing ministry of Good News Publishers. The ESV® text has been reproduced in cooperation with and by permission of Good News Publishers. All rights reserved. • Scripture marked NLT is taken from Holy Bible, New Living Translation, copyright © 1996, 2004, 2015 by Tyndale House Foundation. Used by permission of Tyndale House Publishers, Inc., Carol Stream, Illinois 60188. All rights reserved. • Scripture quotations marked (NKJV) or "New King James Version" are taken from the New King James Version / Thomas Nelson Publishers, Nashville: Thomas Nelson Publishers, Copyright ©1982. Used by permission. All rights reserved. • Scripture marked (AMPC) is taken from Amplified Bible, Classic Edition Copyright © 1954, 1958, 1962, 1964, 1965, 1987 by The Lockman Foundation.

Library and Archives Canada Cataloguing in Publication

Title: Risen from prison : beyond my wildest imagination / Bosco H.C. Poon.

Names: Poon, Bosco H. C., author.
Identifiers: Canadiana 2019021368X | ISBN 9781988928258 (softcover)

Subjects: LCSH: Poon, Bosco H. C. | LCSH: Poon, Bosco H. C—Imprisonment. | LCSH: Christian converts—
   Canada—Biography. | LCSH: Prisoners—Canada—Biography. | LCSH: Ex-convicts—Canada—Biography. |
   LCSH: Clergy—Canada—Biography. | LCSH: Christian biography—Canada. | LCGFT: Autobiographies.

Classification: LCC BV4935.P66 A3 2019 | DDC 277.108/3092—dc23

CONTENTS

CHAPTER 1
NIGHTMARE   7

CHAPTER 2
IN THE BEGINNING   17

CHAPTER 3
CHANGES   27

CHAPTER 4
JUST A DREAM   35

CHAPTER 5
I MET A GIRL   45

CHAPTER 6
KEEP FIGHTING   53

CHAPTER 7
SO IT BEGAN   65

CHAPTER 8
BEHIND THE BARS   75

CHAPTER 9
SANCTUARY 87

CHAPTER 10
AWAKENING 101

CHAPTER 11
ONE LAST TIME 111

CHAPTER 12
UNEXPECTED DEPARTURE 121

CHAPTER 13
THE TRUTH 131

CHAPTER 14
SERVANTHOOD 141

CHAPTER 15
FORGIVENESS 153

CHAPTER 16
A HINT OF FREEDOM 165

CHAPTER 17
TIME TO MOVE ON 177

CHAPTER 18
A STEP CLOSER 187

CHAPTER 19
A BITTERSWEET GOODBYE 197

CHAPTER 20
TELLING MY STORY 207

CHAPTER 21
THE NEXT CHAPTER 215

CHAPTER 1
NIGHTMARE

"No, no, NOOOOO … stay away from me!" I screamed, accidentally falling off the couch like a startled cat, but, unlike a cat, I didn't land on my feet. My shoulder hit the carpet with a thud, and the side of my head followed. "Ouch, that hurt! Whoa … how long have I been sleeping?" I mumbled to myself—still half-asleep. I was drenched in sweat. It was another bad dream. Seems they were coming fast and furious these days, given the mess I had gotten myself tangled in.

I rubbed my forehead and struggled to recall what I had been doing when I fell asleep. Through the crack between the curtains I could see that it was already dark, and judging by where the moon was, I guessed it was about midnight. As I strained to survey the dark empty room—my computer room—I suddenly had a flash of intense memories of all of the things that had happened there. They came like a little slide show.

I remembered our first day in this house. It was just as empty then as it was now and with just as many nail holes in the drywall, dust bunnies on the floor, dead bugs between the windows, and cobwebs in the corners. Piece by piece, my family had cobbled together enough money to furnish the place and make it seem like a home.

In this room I had parked my first desktop computer—the kind that came in a huge case and occupied half of the workspace. I had smoked my first cigarette with my head sticking out the window so my mom wouldn't bust me. I had my first private guitar lesson, practised for my first public performance, and composed my first song—all of this on the very same wood-framed couch. It was a room of firsts—like a treasure box of my teenagehood. And now, in the same manner I had first seen it, it was empty again. We were moving, and the house was up for sale.

Bosco H. C. Poon

I was enjoying all of these fond memories until I heard a hoarse and emotional voice yelling from the basement: "Help me! Please! Please, let me go! Is anybody up there? Someone, please help!"

All of a sudden, stark reality shattered my reverie, and I recalled exactly why I was here. Oh no! This can't be happening, I thought. This was way beyond playing Grand Theft Auto on PlayStation or watching *Alpha Dog* on the big screen.

What a mess, I thought, *what a horrible mistake!* Some innocent kid was tied up in the basement of my parents' house. I didn't know why Blade had picked this guy to kidnap. It seemed more or less random to me.

What have I become? I berated myself. I knew there was a risk that this could all go sideways, but I never dreamed it would end up in a tailspin so quickly. If I recall correctly, it had begun two weeks prior.

———

With the "For Sale" sign planted on the front lawn, my parents' house had been vacant for eight weeks. It was built on a hillside at the edge of a neighbourhood called Westwood Plateau, which is in the north end of the city of Coquitlam in British Columbia, Canada. My family had lived here ever since we arrived in Canada from Hong Kong, but we had recently moved to Richmond, BC, a suburb of Vancouver that was a lot closer to the recording studios I was working with. Blade and a few other old schoolmates of mine told me they wanted to "throw a party" and asked if I would let them use the empty house as a venue. I was hesitant, but they kept pressuring me to say yes to the idea. It got more awkward as Blade kept changing the story when it came to the purpose of using my house. I knew something was fishy and tried to avoid his calls. Then he showed up at the front door of my Richmond home.

"Hey, brother, why don't you pick up my calls?" Blade greeted me with a big smile.

"Hey, man, I'm so busy these days. You are always calling at a bad time. I can't pick up in the middle of meetings, you know."

"Well, you're not in a meeting now, are you?"

"Yeah … I can talk now … What's up?"

"Yo, listen, I know what you're thinking, 'cause you know me too well. And you're right; I need a favour again."

"Oh man … Again? I knew it!"

"You gotta help your brother out. I'm in some deep sh*t … and you're the only one that can get me out. A couple weeks back, I was gonna triple my chips at the casino, but man, I lost it all—10Gs, man! I needed it back big time! My girlfriend's money was in there too. So I talked to my buddy, and he helped me out. He lent me some chips. I went back in. The second round was good, and I made it all back. But gosh, I was too greedy! I just didn't know when to stop."

"Come on, don't tell me you lost it all again!?"

"Yeah, 30Gs including interest, man!"

"No way! You can't be serious. That's a car worth of money!"

"I'm dead serious, no joke! And the loan shark doesn't play around. He sent people to chase after me already. Luckily I'm still on good terms with them, but now I have less than a month to fix this."

"Your buddy was a loan shark?! Why get yourself into this kinda situation over and over?"

"I know I screwed up again, but man, this is no time for lecturing. I need your help. You don't wanna see me being chopped in half, do you?

"I ain't got no 30Gs, man!"

"But you have a house. I'm gonna do a run, just need a place to store the stuff. I'll be fine after this run. Lend me the house key for a few days, and I'll make sure to pay you your cut."

"The house is my parents', not mine. I can't just let you use it for a few days."

"Come on, bro, you wanna see me die? Make up some stories, man. Right, tell them I'm doing a music project and I need the basement to do some recordings. I'll pay them good rent. Trust me, it'll work. You'll get some money to upgrade your wardrobe too. Some new T-shirts and jeans, you know. Just help me, please."

"Why do you have to put me through this kinda crap? I'm already super stressed. I hate this. Umm … let me see what I can do. I'll give you a call later."

"I have your word? Don't play me, man. Remember, the loan shark is after me. I got no time to waste."

"You really ain't making my life easier, man … all right—"

"You're the best bro ever! What do I do without you? I'll be waiting for your call. Thanks!"

Looking back, I'm not sure why I even considered helping him out, but I guess I didn't want to see him being sliced into pieces by the loan shark. So I lied to my parents and got their permission to rent out the house. With an over-occupied mind, I didn't bother to think what Blade was going to do with the house that could net him 30Gs in a few days. Obviously something illegal. Maybe trunkloads of cigarettes from Mexico. Or boxes of ecstasy from some home lab. I didn't care. All I wanted was to do him one more favour so that he would leave me alone and keep his troubles away from me. A week later, during a social gathering, I handed over the house key to Blade.

I overheard a conversation about "kidnapping" someone and setting a ransom to generate some quick cash. I had a bad feeling about it, but I was busy writing and producing music, and my time was all occupied. Besides, I didn't really believe he'd follow through on such a stupid plan.

Little did I know I would regret my deliberate ignorance, because it was about to turn really ugly.

Bosco H. C. Poon

The colours of spring had arrived, and blooms were everywhere. I'd be walking down the street and find myself in a pocket of warm air laced with the beautiful smell of hyacinth. As I strolled around that spring, every time a plane flew overhead I would imagine myself heading out on tour. Some local production houses were hiring my music crew "Syndicate" to perform at local events throughout the coming summer, and two different overseas record labels, EMI and Universal Music Taiwan, were interviewing us about the possibility of an album. It was promising to be the best season yet, and I was really looking forward to the experience. I felt my time had arrived.

There would be no such luck. Although I had caught snippets of ominous-sounding conversations, all along I thought that Blade and his buddies were just blowing smoke. *They wouldn't really do anything that stupid, would they? They're just trying to get attention from each other*, I thought. They had bragged about all kinds of stuff they never had the guts to follow through with ... lots of times. Why would this be any different? When they were high they would even plan stunts like you'd see in the movie *Jackass* or on the TV show *The Dudesons*—but nothing ever came of it. Besides, there was a lot going on in my world. I had a ton of stuff on my mind and no time to burden myself trying to crawl into *their* heads. I just hoped that they would stop bothering me after I did them this one favour.

To my surprise, a few days later Blade phoned me. "Hey, Boz, how you doing, bro?" There was no indication of any urgency in the greeting.

"Fine. What do you want? I'm kinda busy right now," I replied.

"Oh, nothing terribly important ... just thought you'd like to know that we've got our 'package' stored in your basement, that's all."

Package? What does he mean, a person? They went through with it? I felt panic rising in my heart. My knees started to shake. With a swallow I took a deep breath and gathered enough composure to ask, "Why ... why are you telling me this?" Maybe I was still hoping that this whole thing was just another one of their puerile jokes. "And what do you want me to do about it?"

"Well, you know, it's like this. We need you to keep your folks away from the house for couple more days. Understand? They can't go over for any reason. Just make sure of it, okay?"

"What are you trying to say?" I blurted, still not fully accepting what I was hearing.

"You heard me," he said. "Just come to the house right now and I'll show you what we mean—in person."

He didn't have to say any more. I got it. I was now an accomplice to kidnapping. This was not good.

I was in the studio at the time. One of my music partners shot a glance in my direction as I hung up. They must have seen me going pale or noticed the sweat accumulating on my forehead—and now running down my eyebrows. The look on their faces told me that they knew something was dreadfully wrong. Silently I waited for them to finish the session. I then got in my car, started the engine, and let it idle while I thought about what I should do. Coming after me, Julian knocked on the passenger side window to see if I was all right. I was so confused that I couldn't even respond. All I cared about at that moment was to get my parents' house back. I turned to give him a half-hearted smile and a peace sign, then stepped on the gas. That was the last I saw of any of them for a while.

My heart was bouncing around in my chest as I sped out to Coquitlam. Every time I saw a cop car my hands would tremble so terribly I would have to grip the steering wheel just to keep them still. After 40 minutes, I arrived at the house. As I pulled into the driveway Blade was waiting for me at the door, and he immediately stepped outside to greet me. He was flanked by two of his men. One was a tall dark-haired muscular Caucasian wearing black-rimmed glasses, and the other one was a skinny short-haired Asian with the butt of a handgun peering out of his left pocket. I didn't know either of them, and I didn't like what I was seeing.

"Ahh, there you are! The MAN is finally here!"

"What's going on, Blade? This is way beyond what I can handle."

"What? You want to chicken out now? Relax, buddy, everything is gonna be fine. We'll get our money, and *you'll* get your cut as promised. We won't hurt him. All we want is cash. That's all!"

"But Blade, what if—"

"Shh! Help us get this job done, and we'll all walk away! I need the money! You know that. We'll get what we want, and you'll get your house back plus a little bonus in your pocket. It's a win-win. Now get in the house!" He was getting impatient.

The two men escorted me inside, filling me in on the rest of the plan as we went. I just marched along, silently stunned. They weren't calm. Everyone involved was very much on edge, like hungry jackals prowling for a meal: aggressive and anxious. It felt like they were going to do anything they needed to. They made it very clear to me that I had no choice but to comply with their wishes.

They spent the ensuing hours on the phone and made arrangements with the other wing of the operation, cussing incessantly, cigarette after cigarette. Blade gave me orders to guard the front door while they took care of business. He also warned me of the consequences if I did anything stupid. The other guys in the room seemed amused by my agitation, snickering and almost looking down their noses at me. *Who are these people anyway? Where did Blade find these nutcases?*

At about 9:00 p.m. everyone went outside to their vehicles, leaving me alone in the house. Knowing that the victim was in the basement, I decided to hold out as far away from him as I could. So I went upstairs to the old computer room.

Should I untie him and take him to the police station, or should I run out the back door and then call the cops? But what would happen if I left the house? Would they come after me? Maybe they'd come after me and my family too. No matter which way I looked at it, I saw no way out. Ultimately, paralyzed by my fears, I did nothing but lie on the couch, and ever so gradually, I fell asleep.

Bosco H. C. Poon

———

Why did I get myself involved in this? Was it because I didn't know how to say no? Probably. But I treasured Blade's friendship. He'd rescued me from being a nerdy outcast back in high school and his gang members had protected me from bullying. So I had a sense of loyalty to him. Did I need the money? No, not really. My parents had promised to support my musical projects until the end of that year. However, I didn't mind the prospect of some extra cash. For that matter, it's not as if Blade didn't owe *me* anything. For years I had been lending him money to supply his gambling addiction and wild partying. There were many nights when I handed over my food money for the whole week to get him out of one debt or another. Not even once had he managed to pay me back—at least not in full. To my mind, it would only be fair if I was able to cash in on any windfall that came his way. But I never thought that things could go so wrong.

The next morning I was sent to pick up breakfast at McDonald's on Barnet Highway in Coquitlam. I used the opportunity to call my Aunt Tina, my mom's sister-in-law, who also happened to be our realtor. "Auntie, my friends are done using the house. You can go take a look. If you need someone to help clean up, just let me know and I'll come over."

"All right, sweetheart, I'll go check it in a couple of hours. Don't worry about the cleaning. I can take care of it myself. Thanks for the call. I'll probably put it back up for showing tomorrow. There's quite a lineup for it. Say 'Hi' to your mom and dad!"

"Sure thing, Auntie. I'll do that. Talk to you soon."

I hung up and took a breath. I deliberately lied to my aunt, hoping that she would discover what was going on by going into the house. As a result, Blade would be forced to let his victim go or my aunt would call the police, and the whole thing would fall apart. In retrospect, I placed my aunt in a rather dangerous position. What if the guys hurt her too? I don't know. I was so exhausted and befuddled, I could not come up with a better plan in the middle of my Egg McMuffin run. I considered it a calculated risk—but it was poorly calculated, and it did not proceed as planned.

Blade apparently managed to stop my aunt right at the front door. Because I had lied to my family, telling them that we were using the empty house as a recording studio, Blade was able to quickly come up with the story that the recording sessions were not done and they needed a couple more days. He also assured her that he would pay her extra rent. To my surprise, my aunt believed the whole thing and said this was not a problem, even apologizing for the miscommunication.

My heart sank as I realized that, one, my plan had entirely failed, and two, I now had to go back to the house and explain to Blade why my aunt had shown up unexpectedly. My cellphone started getting flooded with calls from all of them. When you bat a hornets' nest, you hear a lot of buzzing. I dragged myself back to the house, hotcakes and sausages in tow. Blade was rightly suspicious that I had sent my aunt over in an attempt to sabotage things, but at length I managed to convince him that it was a coincidence. In any case, I still got a long and threatening lecture about how I must ensure that no one from my family would come by until the ransom was secured or the "package" was moved to another secure location. After that, I was not allowed to leave their sight until the completion of the operation.

I don't remember the exact sequence of the events that followed because I had only slept a few hours over the course of several days, and I was completely strung out. Blade and the others were demanding $130,000, and evidently there had been some progress in making that transaction happen. Blade commissioned me with cleaning up the basement and wiping everything down with cleaning solutions while they took the victim away and collected the ransom elsewhere. I'm not sure where this was supposed to occur, but it didn't matter.

Red and blue lights panned outside the house. It was the afternoon of April 10, 2004. With that I knew that this misadventure was over, and I was strangely relieved, but I also knew that I was in a heap of trouble. We were not sophisticated criminals, I have to say, and I suppose that has something to do with how quickly this all came to a screeching halt—that and the fact that 60 police officers had been involved in the investigation. According to the police press release, they had spent $400,000 in overtime monitoring our phone calls. I guess Blade had underestimated the Vancouver Police Department.

As I was being handcuffed by the police, one of the officers informed me that Blade and two others had been apprehended in Vancouver and that more arrests might ensue. The victim had been rescued unharmed and was to be soon released to his family. I was actually happy about this. On the one hand, I was glad to know that he was alive and well, but on the other I was extremely fearful about my own future. Curious neighbours trickled out of their houses one by one. Their lives now seemed attractively boring—the preparation of dinner, the changing of motor oil, the making of tea—interrupted briefly to watch me being thrown into the back of the paddy wagon. I wonder what they were saying. "I told his mom I didn't like the boys he was hanging around," or "That's what the music industry does to people."

My mom, dad, and aunt were standing in the driveway, all of them sobbing. I'm an only child, and I knew what this was doing to them. I was so ashamed of myself, and I felt absolutely wretched for having dishonoured them so terribly. I didn't know how I would be able to face anyone I knew ever again. I leaned up against the steel wall of the police van and stared down at my feet. It was a bumpy ride to the station.

Everything I had on my person, including my underwear, was confiscated. In exchange, I got to wear a scratchy white paper jumpsuit and a pair of shoe covers like the ones patients wear in the hospital. Before I was taken to the interrogation room, where I would spend the rest of the evening, two officers fingerprinted me and had me sign a pile of forms. As each of my fingers was pressed into the wet spongy black inkpad and then onto paper, I felt like I was signing my life away. Then, as you see in every crime movie, I was asked to stand against a wall and pose for a mugshot and two profile shots.

Bosco H. C. Poon

I was escorted by two uniformed police officers from the holding cell behind Vancouver Criminal Court on 222 Main Street in Vancouver to the Vancouver Police Department. As I crossed East Cordova Street handcuffed in my white jumpsuit, the homeless folks from the downtown eastside mocked and catcalled me. After entering the VPD building we ascended a long flight of stairs and ended up in a room with one window, one coffee table, and two chairs facing each other. I was left alone in the room for about 20 minutes before an investigator in normal dress walked in.

"Okay, Mr. Poon, I'm going to tell you this straight up. I'm a very experienced investigator. It's what I do for living. My job here is to get information from you, so that I can report it to my boss. Why don't we work together, and it'll make both of our lives easier? After all, it's getting late. I'm tired, and I'm sure you are too. If you co-operate and tell me the truth, you'll be home in no time. So let's not beat around the bush, all right?"

"You're right. I am extremely tired... What do you mean by I'll be home in no time?" I hesitated.

"That means if you tell me everything, no lies, no BS, then I can probably get you out of here before this long weekend is finished. Okay? You want to go home, right?"

"Of course I want to go home—"

"I know. I hear you. So why waste more time? Let's get going!"

At first I thought he was there to help me. He seemed friendly, even gentle, but after a while he changed his approach, becoming more and more aggressive with me, particularly when it didn't appear that he was getting what he wanted or if he thought I was withholding something from him.

Sitting closer and closer to me, he stared me right in the face and asked the same question the fifth time. "Tell me where you were on the night of April 2. You were at an underground parking lot in Vancouver, right? You and your buddy were looking for someone, right?"

"How many times do I have to repeat myself? I told you already! I was in a recording session at the studio! Go ahead and talk to the guys in my group. Call them."

"You sure you didn't get the date mixed up? It was a Friday night. You were at the parking lot. Think again."

"I'm sure I was at the studio. Call the owner of the studio."

"You sure?"

"Yes, I am!"

"How sure?"

"Very sure!"

"How come you are so sure?"

"Because I was at the studio! How many times do I have to repeat myself?"

The investigator then dropped his pen. "Mr. Poon, you know damn well why you're here! This is not a random chit-chat. This is something very serious, very very serious! We've been after you for a whole week. We have stacks of pictures of you and your buddies. We know everything. So go over it again. Did you kidnap the victim on April 2 at the parking lot?"

He tried to box me into one corner and then into another. If things were not proceeding the way that he liked, he would circle back and start with the same set of questions all over again. You can't really understand how frustrating this is until you're in the middle of it, but I guess it must work, because he did not relent.

I had been awake for over 24 hours, my lips were cracking, and my mouth was dry. I knew that however tired I had ever felt in all my life, I had no understanding of "tired" until now. All I wanted was to go home and to collapse into bed, but that wouldn't happen for a while.

After the questioning ended, I was tossed into a dirty holding cell: three walls of concrete, one steel door, and, naturally, no window. It reminded me of a horror flick called *Saw* that came out that year. Staring at the light coming from the fluorescent bulbs on the ceiling, I wondered how long I would have to stay in there. It was the Easter long weekend, but there would be no celebrating. This was just the beginning of a long, dark nightmare.

> "My son, if sinful men entice you, do not give in to them … These men lie in wait for their own blood; they ambush only themselves!"
> (Prov. 1:10, 18)

CHAPTER 2
IN THE BEGINNING

When most kids are little, their parents are their heroes. While this is not always true, it usually is. So being a child is simple: you look up to your parents and follow their example. Hopefully things just work out. You don't really worry, because life just seems to be something that happens to you—not something you can shape and control.

For me things were a little bit different. While I loved my parents and did look up to them, ever since I can remember I had a fascination with superstars performing on stage. The things that attracted me about the celebrity lifestyle are the ones you'd expect: the adulation, the recognition, the massive sphere of influence. I wanted it all—I wanted to be a star. I wanted to impact people with my voice and the message of my music. But most of all, I just wanted to be famous—camera flashes, fancy hotels, and nice cars. The problem was I didn't know where to start. For years, I quietly kept the dream tucked away in the back of my mind. After all, why invest so much hope in something that might not come true? In my more conservative moments, I dismissed it all as a pipe dream.

But in my last year of high school, I decided that those who do not try cannot succeed. So, if I didn't take a crack at stardom now, in the window of my youth, it was never going to happen. I would end up as just another grey suit working a desk job in a cubicle somewhere, typing away under fluorescent lights and giggling at the daily wisdom of Dilbert cartoons—not that there's anything wrong with that.

Back in those days I was a diehard partygoer, and by chance I was introduced to a Chinese vocal trainer, Miss Mary, by a friend whom I'd met at an outdoor rave. It had been a three-day party held at some remote area east of Langley, BC. The organizer provided school buses to pick us up from the Willowbrook Shopping Centre parking lot. After a short 15 or 20 minute ride, we got dropped off at an entrance to a muddy trail walled with tall trees on both sides. As we walked deeper into the woods, my heart pounded harder and harder as the music got a bit louder with each step we marched forward. The moment we exited the trail, we saw a wonderland with many tents set right in front of a huge stage with lasers and colourful lights. After some of our guys finished setting up our tent, we went inside to put on some gear for the party: white gloves, visors, glow sticks, plastic bead bracelets, and necklaces. Before we headed outside to join the growing crowd, each person got to choose a favourite kind of candy from the goody bag. The one that always gave me the right boost of energy to dance the whole night was a custom-made capsule containing the perfect proportion of MDMA (ecstasy) and speed.

As soon as the drugs kicked in, my body movements seemed to flow to the music. Like a robot with new batteries, I danced six hours straight non-stop that evening. When the sun came out I realized just how much I'd exerted myself. All my joints were swollen up and in pain. Resting in the tent after taking some Advil, I talked to Andrew about our lives and my dreams. We carried on discussing the same topic for a couple of hours.

While we were on the school bus heading back to the mall parkade, Andrew said, "Since you want to have a music career, why don't I hook you up with my vocal trainer? She is quite well-known in the local music scene, and she's a good friend of my dad. They both used to be singers in Asia. She doesn't accept just anyone as a student. But since she knows my dad, I'm sure she'll help you out."

"Really? That would be awesome! I would love to meet her. Thanks so much, man!"

Within a week, Andrew had arranged for me to meet Miss Mary. After the initial audition at her home studio, she frowned and said, "To be honest with you, there's tons of work we need to do before you can go on the stage to perform professionally. You have a long way to go. But don't be discouraged; if you are determined and not afraid of hard work, I can train you to be at that level. Unlike traditional music schools in North America, you don't need all these musical qualifications to enter my program, just a passionate heart and a commitment to follow my instructions. I act as a private coach. My vocal master in Hong Kong trained me since I was a little girl. Many famous singers from the '80s and '90s are my personal friends. In our tradition, we're not allowed to pass our knowledge and skills to anyone until we receive the approval from our master-teacher. When I decided to move to Canada, she then finally approved me to be a teacher for others. The same condition would apply to you when you become my student."

I nodded as I hung on every word that came out from her mouth, not wanting to miss anything. She then pointed to a wall full of photos and posters. "Many of my students have won singing contests, some of which were hosted by Sony Music Taiwan and other big name companies from overseas. Two of my students were signed by record labels in Taiwan. You can see their pictures and signed posters in this collage."

Looking at the people inside the photos with trophies in their hands, smiling so happily, I instantly wanted to be one of them. The beautifully made posters of the two famous recording artists mesmerized me. Miss Mary continued, "Once you have the agreement from your parents about the tuition, we can get started. I'll base my fee on a thorough evaluation to tailor a program just for you. Towards the end, I'll use my connections in the music business back in Asia to set up meetings with agents and record label representatives. Though there's no guarantee, I'll help you to get into the business as best that I can. In between, you'll have to go to a lot of competitions to gain live performance experience. It's not going to be an easy road; hard work is required. Now you go think about it, and then let me know your decision."

After talking to Miss Mary, I felt like there was a beacon of light shining down upon my path. I finally got a sense of direction after wandering for so many years. She showed me an avenue to the music industry that I so desperately wanted to be part of. I was stoked. That was it. I was going to go for it. I made a decision to pursue a music career full time with the help of Miss Mary after graduating high school. Without a whole lot of musical background besides the violin lessons that I took in primary school, I was definitely going to be swimming upstream. Since I wasn't going into any recognized music college, most people thought the whole thing was a joke.

However, my parents responded differently. They were ecstatic that I was distancing myself from the rough crowd I'd been hanging around with at the end of high school and was setting my sights on a concrete goal. While many parents would consider shooting for a career in the music industry a longshot—like trying to make the NHL or something—from my parents' perspective, it was way healthier than hanging out with guys who spent their time organizing parties and getting high, so they were very supportive. They decided that they would provide for me financially for the full duration of the 18-month program that Miss Mary had tailored. The program included vocal training; body gesture and modelling training; physical training; dancing and on-stage training; and audition training.

In order to focus on my work, I would have to completely withdraw from the party scene, which, at the time, represented a sacrifice because I knew that this would alienate me from my closest friends. But I had to do it—this was my one chance, and there may never be another window of opportunity. Furthermore, I needed to sober up and embrace a fairly disciplined lifestyle because I would have to get up early and work all day in the years to come. I needed to look good too, so this meant exercising regularly as part of a physical training program. There was no room for goofing off anymore.

At first it seemed to be a huge personal sacrifice to miss all the fun. For a while, my friends would continue to call and ask me to join them, but after I had said "No thanks" a few too many times, the calls petered out, and the phone was pretty much silent. Compared to my former life, I felt like I had entered a monastery or something—to bed early, up early, working all day, structure, discipline, and practice—and all this while daydreaming about getting high, especially on the weekends, when I knew all my buddies were out clubbing. I would stare at the microphone on its stand, the symbol of all that I wanted to be and become, and with that meditation I would find strength to resist the party scene. Gradually I overcame it completely and defeated the feelings of loneliness by fixating on the promise of a brighter day ahead.

Even though I wasn't endowed with the kind of undiscovered angelic voice you might see on a viral YouTube video, I strived to learn how to become a professional performer and to create a unique style that would capture the interest of my audience. During that time, not only was I working on music, but I was also working very hard on physical fitness because it is part of the work of a live stage performer. I woke up bright and early in the morning to run laps and went swimming in the afternoon. I took dance classes, went to stage performance boot camp, and three times a week worked out in the gym. I had vocal lessons once a week with Miss Mary and practised vocals all week at home. I worked fairly unrelentingly, and there were many days when I just wanted to sleep in 'cause it was pouring rain outside. But every time a voice from within would pull me out of bed and remind me that I had a goal and I wanted to achieve it. My imagination was not going to make my career. I had to do it.

Everyone around me knew about my plans too—because it was nearly all I talked about—and I wanted to show them that I wasn't all talk. I wanted them to see my drive in the efforts that I was making. In the back of my head, I would hear all of those questions of self-doubt: *Who do you think you are, some kind of prodigy? Do you really think you're going to be able to do this? What if you're a total failure? You will have wasted all this time and energy, and you'll look like some kind of idiot wannabe to all your friends.*

I struggled a lot. While many of my schoolmates were either studying at college or finding a job that could provide a substantial living, I was chasing after my dream without an income. But I would tell myself that if I didn't try, I wouldn't succeed, and somehow I just kept chipping away at it. Training myself day after day, fixing my eyes on the goal, hoping that one day it'd all pay off.

Eventually, Miss Mary thought I should give a crack at a public performance. It was a talent show hosted by the Yaohan Centre in Richmond, BC, and the radio station AM1470. All the local Chinese media were advertising this event, so my master-teacher Mary wanted to put my newly acquired skills to the test. I was so nervous!

"Listen, kid, don't let it get into your head. There are going to be a lot of people there, but the more aware that you become of them, the more they will be aware that you are nervous. Audiences like confidence, not nerves. Even though you may be trembling inside, never show it on your face. Remember everything that I taught you."

"Yeah ... but how do I make myself confident when I'm not?" I replied.

"Are you nervous in the studio?"

"No."

"So you have to make yourself feel like you are in the studio. The way to do that is to imagine the people as just part of a backdrop—like they were painted on a big tapestry or something. They are just scenery. You need to turn them into scenery in your head."

"I'm not sure it's that easy."

"Trust me, you will get there, and the more confident you are, the better time your audience will be having and the better time you will be having. Remember, this is what you want to do. This is your dream, so go get it!"

The pep talk didn't really work. My hands were shaking so badly that I ended up stuffing them in the pockets of my yellow hoodie. Not only that; I was just soaked in sweat. It was dripping down my forehead, and I could feel the beads piling up and running down the small of my back. I'm just glad I wasn't wearing a dress shirt, because it would have been soaking wet and sticking to my skin. No surprise, I didn't place in the competition, but I had conquered my first public performance, and that gave me some sense of accomplishment.

As time passed, I got to perform more often. What used to be a very nerve-racking experience began to feel quite comfortable, and as this happened, I began to fall in love with the stage. The whole thing became addictive—the spotlights on me, the sound of applause, the larger-than-life feeling. I loved it all.

Sitting by the windows of the Fairways Grill & Patio up at the Westwood Plateau Golf Club on a hot summer day, I felt a dark cloud hovering over our table. We had just received a call early that morning from our management overseas to arrange an emergency meeting. Our downcast faces stood in contrast to the spectacular view of the sunlit ridge visible from our seats. After months of training and relentless practice, our record deal had all but evaporated.

"What's going on? This is crazy! I thought we were going to sign the contracts next month? I thought everything was in place." Joe was getting really angry.

"I know! What the heck? He promised us everything. First album coming out before Christmas … all lies! All this work we've done—all for nothing? This is BS!" James lit up his smoke.

"This is ridiculous! I can't believe it …" I was trying to digest what I'd just heard over the phone.

"He even told me I should drop out of university. Good thing I didn't listen to him. I'd be so screwed otherwise!" Joe hit the table with his fist.

"And luckily I still have my business running. He told me to give up everything here too. Well, what are we going to do with this group now? It's over, right?" James picked up his lemonade.

Bosco H. C. Poon

"I don't know, man ... We still need to tell the other three what's going on. I wonder how they're gonna react. But before we do anything, let me make a follow-up call and see if this deal is really over. Maybe there's still hope." I sighed.

In 2001, an agent from MTV Taiwan came to Vancouver in search of young talent for a new boy band. They wanted to form a Chinese version of NSYNC. I was selected at the interview along with Joe, Kenny, Abraham, Wilson, and James—all my music friends. This experience gave me confidence that we were really going to make something of ourselves.

The agent promised us a lot of things. However, after six months of working with us as their prospective boy band, management decided to drop us because they had a better opportunity with some guys from LA. They were not going to fund two projects. That put an end to this chapter of my dream.

I felt like a loser and spent weeks feeling completely dejected. I had a terrible time coming to terms with the experience. Yet in my heart I didn't believe that the dream was dead, so I began to think about far more pragmatic career backup plans. I had to prepare for the possibility that I was never going to make it in music, but I wanted a job where I could have a little artistic outlet. After chatting with my grandpa, I decided to apply to a hairstyling college to earn my hairstylist licence while I continued to seek ways to enter the music industry. That way, I could earn a little money and would have something I could fall back on for a while if nothing came of music.

Another year went by—lots of practising, lots of training, lots of sweeping hair clippings from the floor—and then another big-name record label, Warner Music Taiwan, came to North America to scout talent in view of forming a hip-hop group. With the help of my new-found friend Yuen, a young music producer, I entered the competition with a song I had co-written. It was held inside Radisson Hotel, Richmond. Some big name producers and artists' agents and two regional department heads of the record label in Hong Kong and Taiwan were among the panel of judges. Apparently, I hadn't been selected in the first round of auditions at Fairchild TV Station, Vancouver, four weeks earlier. Somehow when the judges reviewed all the video footage in Taipei, they spotted my performance and picked me as one of the 12 final contestants. They had high expectations. Later I was glad that I didn't know all these details until after the competition or I probably would have been under so much pressure that I wouldn't be able to give my best shot on the stage.

In the green room everyone was busy getting in some last-minute practice, while I lay down on the couch to rest. My theory was that since I had spent countless hours practising at the dance studio for the past four weeks, if I still didn't remember my routine, there would be nothing else I could do at this point. So I chose to reserve my energy.

"Boz, you're up in 10 minutes!" The stage manager woke me up from my rest. I stood up slowly and did my last stretch. In front of the mirror, I looked into my eyes, tapped my face lightly, and said to myself, "This is your dream; now go get it!"

Risen From Prison

The moment I entered the stage, all spotlights were on me. The panel of judges was at eye level. Lights flashed from all corners of the auditorium. Some friends of mine, including Joe and Kenny, were there cheering for me. I could hear them yelling my name somewhere in the crowd. Audiences didn't bother me anymore. I had mastered the skill of treating them as a backdrop. Once the music kicked in, I was on autopilot because of all my practising, and the performance went very smoothly. I had a great time on stage. After I finished singing the last line and had my ending post, I bowed my head, greeting everyone, then headed back to the green room. Not wanting to think too much about the outcome, I lay back down on the couch to rest.

An hour passed by before all the contestants were called back up to the stage for the final result. Standing up there, I didn't know what to expect. The judges announced the second runner-up, then the first runner-up. In the midst of all the cheering and applause, my mind went completely blank. I snapped myself back and turned my focus to the two contestants who were holding their trophies, and I wondered how it'd feel to hold one myself.

Suddenly, the MC asked everyone to quiet down as Sam, the regional department head of Warner Music Taiwan, came up to the stage. He spent a couple of minutes giving the audience a short story about the next-superstar search and how they ended up in Vancouver. He went on to list all the successful stars of their company. Unexpectedly, after his speech, he turned to me and said, "And I'm happy to announce that Bosco Poon, B.O.Z, is now part of our family! He is our winner! He is the next superstar of Warner Music."

In front of everyone there, Sam announced to the Chinese media that they were going to make me the next mega hit in Asia. I was overwhelmed with camera flashes and clamouring entertainment reporters. To be honest, as happy as I was, I wasn't really prepared for so much attention. It happened way too fast. All that I was sure of was that I should smile, but I was so tense that I probably acted a little like a robot. While I was still answering reporters' questions, I was escorted from the main lobby to the second-floor meeting room of the hotel. While I was waiting for the introduction meeting to begin, I excused myself to the hallway and made a quick call home. As soon as someone picked up, I screamed, "Aaaaaaah, I made it! I WON!"

"Hey, you're hurting my ear! What? You serious? You won as in—" my dad questioned.

"First place, Dad. Can you believe it?!"

"Yay! He won, he won!" He was yelling the good news to my mom. I could hear both of them clapping together. After letting them calm down a little I continued, "Please go dress up. I'll come pick you guys up for dinner in two hours, after our meeting is done here. They want to meet you in person. I have to hurry back. I just snuck out to give you the news. See you in a bit."

Later that evening, the company took my family to a high-end Japanese restaurant nearby Radisson Hotel to celebrate in a private dining room. Everyone

Bosco H. C. Poon

was treating me like a king. During dinner Sam promised me just about anything you can imagine: personal assistant, private vehicle, apartment in downtown Taipei, an expense allowance, access to the top recording studios, VIP access to the major clubs, etc. I was overwhelmed by everything. Just listening to what lay before me, I was starting to feel like a celebrity already.

The next day I woke up to see my face plastered over the Canadian Chinese newspapers, and the Chinese TV stations were running the interviews that had taken place at the hotel. I could barely contain myself. I was absolutely bursting with excitement—my heart was racing all the time—but in a good way. I was a ball of nerves one minute and cockily self-assured the next. I spent the next couple of days calling all my relatives and friends to tell them that I had finally made it.

Page by page, I combed through the preliminary artist contract to make sure that this was not some kind of hoax. It wasn't. This was really happening. Gazing up in the sky I would see airplanes pass and envision myself sitting in executive class—or maybe even on a private jet—on one adventure after the next. New cities, new venues, new fans, and a new life. My head was so far into the clouds, I even practised scribbling my signature hundreds of times in preparation for all the upcoming signing events. It was such an amazing feeling, I have to say. For years, countless people in my life had pointed their finger squarely at my forehead and chided me for having set my sights on such an ephemeral goal. Chinese kids are supposed to become accountants or go to medical school or something. This contract would shut all their mouths. I would finally be vindicated.

"Those who exalt themselves will be humbled." (Matt. 23:12)

While I was walking by an urban accessory store in Richmond Centre, the passport cases caught my attention. There were over 50 different designs. I combed through them to find the one that would suit my new image. *Strawberries ... ummm ... no. Hello Kitty ... no. Handguns ... too violent.* After I picked around for five minutes, one of the cases caught my eye. *What's this one? This is pretty cool.* It was decorated with a pattern of steel-grey airplanes and had a glossy black lining. There was a bold silver airplane icon stamped in the bottom right-hand corner. *That's the one*, I thought. *It has the right look.*

Smiling joyfully, I strutted up to the cashier to pay. *In a year,* I figured, *she'll know me by name, and I'll be so famous, someone will be picking out my accessories for me.* As she dropped the change into my hand, my cellphone rang. *Hmmm, I don't recognize that number. Better pick up.*

"Hello, who's this?" I asked.

"Hey, uh ... it's me, Boz. I'm calling from Taiwan," a familiar female voice replied.

"Oh! Hi, Linda! I've been waiting for your call. How are you?"

"I'm doing okay. Thank you. And you?"

"Oh yeah. I'm doing great—practising non-stop. I'm totally ready to start recording. As a matter of fact, I'm buying a passport case as we speak. I can be in Taipei on a day's notice as soon as you give the green light!"

"Uh … it's like this … The reason I called today is to update you with the progress of your contract. There's so much going on. Listen, this is nothing against you personally. It's just the business side of things, you know. I hate to tell you this, but our deal got turned down. Warner Music has signed off our project's budget to a new hip-hop group made up of the former LA Boyz. It's a decision made by upper management. We're terribly sorry for what this means for you. Your written agreement with the company will be terminated automatically after one year. So basically you'll be free to sign with other companies after that. Son, you're talented. There are many other ways—" she said in a deep tone.

"What? This is a joke, right? I … I don't understand. This is impossible! I won the competition fair and square, and they pumped it up in the media. You were there. You saw it. They can't do this to me, can they?" I accidentally dropped my shopping bag.

"Unfortunately, this is not a matter for negotiation. It's a decision that has already been made. No one was going to tell you all this. They were just going to let you flounder in the dark until your agreement expired. I felt sorry for you, so I decided to call and fill you in. The deal is over. I'm sorry. It was good meeting you in Canada. I wish you all the best. Listen, I have to go. Take care." She hung up before I could ask another question.

No way. She must be confused about something. I'm sure that this is just a misunderstanding. I had a hard time believing what I had heard. Fumbling through my wallet, I found Sam's business card. I dialed his number in haste. I was so agitated that I dropped my phone twice before I successfully made the call. *Answering machine? Got to be kidding me!* I dialed again. *Same? All right, I've had enough! This joke has gotta stop right now!* Standing in the middle of the mall, I felt tears start to well up in my eyes.

I tried all the numbers on his business card: personal mobile phone, Taipei head office, Hong Kong head office. I couldn't reach him. Different receptionists just kept sending me to his voicemail. I must have left a dozen messages. Sitting in front of my phone, I waited and waited. The phone was silent.

Months went by. Every morning I woke up in total misery. I would sit still and stare at the preliminary contract. I simply could not face reality. Then Warner Music Taiwan announced the debut of a new hip-hop group, Machi, to all the major media outlets in Asia. This was the group that Linda had told me about. Their faces were plastered all over the front page of the Chinese newspaper my dad brought home. I immediately tore it into pieces. Whenever their music came on the radio, I'd turn it off right away. Every time someone picked one of their songs at a karaoke bar, I'd storm off to have a smoke to calm myself down. No matter where I went, they seemed to be following me. My dreams were shattered—and reshattered. Jealousy, anger, and feelings of betrayal gradually overwhelmed me. I lost to bands from LA, not once but twice. First, seeing a boy band and now a hip-hop group taking *my rightful place* was totally infuriating. To rub salt in my wounds, I had to constantly see them on all the Asian music channels.

Just in case that wasn't enough grief to bear, all kinds of people kept calling me to ask about my music career news. They'd want to know when my album was coming out *and* where I would be touring *and* whether they could get backstage passes *and* this, *and* that, *and* anything-imaginable-that-would-result-in-further-humiliation. I had no idea how to answer. *Why would the record label do that to me? Why would they launch me into the media stratosphere only to let me catastrophically slam back down to the Earth? Why bother awarding me a prize at all?* From whatever angle I looked at it, it seemed completely senseless.

"Son," my dad pleaded, "this is a testing from above. And when you come out of it, you'll become stronger and wiser. Not everything will go your way. In fact there will always be things that won't happen exactly the way you want. There's no way to escape disappointment. But that's okay. It's just the cycle of life. You win some and you lose some. Don't let these failures defeat you. You can get back up from where you fell, you know. This is not the end." I got this speech in various forms day after day.

Dad's words were extremely difficult to swallow at first, but as I chewed on them, I slowly understood the wisdom in them. There was really no point dwelling on the past, since I had absolutely no power to change the situation with Warner. I gradually concluded that I should turn this experience into an asset of experience and keep moving forward. At the very least, my talent had been recognized, not once but twice, by two major music companies. That had to mean something. I should have taken this as an encouragement. My only way to repay the unconditional support from my family was to get up, wipe off the dust, and try again. Right there and then, I swore to create my own promise of a brighter day—a promise to put my past behind me and to make it into the music business, no matter what the cost. I determined to prove to the world that I was worthy.

CHAPTER 3
CHANGES

"Baby, whatcha lookin' at?" Amanda tried to catch my attention. She could see me occasionally craning as I tried to catch a glimpse of a stranger who was about a block ahead of us in the mall. She swung my arm playfully as we walked together—trying to get my attention—but she could see that I was clearly distracted.

"Nothing really ... I think I just saw an old friend that I haven't seen for a long time. Let me go say 'Hi.' Why don't you wait for me back there at the food court? Grab us something to drink at the bubble-tea stand. You know what I want. I'll meet you there in a minute, all right?"

I gave a quick look both ways as Amanda disappeared around a corner and dodged my way through the mall traffic to catch up to Cheri and a couple of her friends. When she saw me, her eyes lit up. "Hey, baby! What're you doing here?" she asked. "You stalking me?" She cocked her head and squinted her eyes coyly at me.

"Yeah, totally! I'm watching you, so you'd better be good! Nah, I'm just here with another friend." I leaned over and kissed her on the cheek. She smiled and looked me in the eye with a hint of suspicion. Man, she was pretty. Cheri introduced me to her friends, though I'm sure I had seen them before at a party or something.

"A 'friend,' eh? Better not be another girlfriend! You're not allowed to mess around with other girls. You promised me that!" Cheri punched me gently square in the middle of my chest. I didn't feel guilty, but I *was* a little nervous that I was going to get busted.

"Yeah, yeah, yeah ... don't worry. What are you doing here—just shopping?" I tried to change the topic.

"Yes, in fact, we are here to shop. Tanya and Brenda are helping me pick out something."

"Well in that case, I better let you continue your mission. I need to get going too. Don't stay out too late. See you tomorrow?"

"All right. Of course you're gonna see me tomorrow! Call me before you go to bed. Love you!" She threw her arms around me and pressed her whole torso against mine. I could smell her hair and a gentle waft of perfume rising from her blouse. She really liked me—it was obvious. Over time, being a two-timing jerk was bothering me less and less. I was addicted to the feeling of finding someone new, and my conscience gradually faded behind the fog of my own desires.

I burned through girlfriend after girlfriend—I needed the rush of new feelings to keep me excited about life. Different types of girls attracted me in different ways. If they were taller than me or had money to flaunt, I didn't let it intimidate me. All it represented was another challenge in a game that I was getting pretty good at—for a guy who used to be a geek, that is.

Some of my guy friends thought I was some kind of hero, but the truth of the matter is that maintaining the deception and constantly lying were completely exhausting. The exhilaration would keep me going for a while, but eventually I would long for a calmer and more honest reality. This I am certain of: a lot of this was overcompensation for my days as a social outcast. It was what you might call an "evil nerd syndrome": high-school loser is suddenly popular and becomes a megalomaniac.

I still remember my first impressions of Pinetree Secondary School in Coquitlam, BC, Canada. It was a beautifully built modern school surrounded by stands of West Coast fir trees and overlooking Lafarge Lake. I was very grateful to be able to attend such a great school in a beautiful part of greater Vancouver. The natural beauty of north Coquitlam—the mountains and the constantly fresh air blowing through the valley—stood in sharp contradistinction to the place of my birth, Hong Kong. All I remembered is the concrete. Never before had I seen so many living things (other than humans, that is). Real trees and plants everywhere I looked. For a city kid from Hong Kong, this seemed pretty exotic.

The educational system in Hong Kong was very stressful and competitive. Students were forced by their parents to have tutoring in almost every subject, just to make it to the top tier. My parents wanted to shield me from that environment. Further, Hong Kong was scheduled to be handed over from the United Kingdom to the government of China in 1997. This created a lot of uncertainty as to what Hong Kong would become. For all these reasons, my parents decided to move to Canada.

At the age of 15, I had a lot of anticipation about senior high. Feel free to call me naive, but I thought it would be something lifted out of a scene from *High School Musical* and *My Super Sweet 16*. Everything I had learned about Western teen culture had come from TV and movies, so I was certain that the formula for social success was (athletic + good-looking + fashionable + eloq' girlfriend + happily ever after. Notice that I took the time to factu 9 was not completely wasted on me.

To my horror, high school was not at all like a Disney movie, a. reason, I had received none of the variables on the left-hand side of the e. *First, I wasn't athletic.* As a matter of fact, I was kind of a wimp. There I was, skinny legs in gym shorts that didn't fit right, doing the old 12-minute run ... dying. *I wasn't good-looking.* I knew very little about how to live in my skin, so to speak. No grooming skills. No confidence in my stride. And then there was my haircut—skillfully supplied for 10 dollars cash by some neighbour-lady who had a barber chair in her basement. *I wasn't fashionable.* My entire wardrobe was from Wal-Mart. *I wasn't eloquent.* My English was broken and heavily accented. I could never even finish an English phrase without punctuating it with so many "umms" and "uhhhs" that people did not want to take the time to listen.

Lacking all of the necessary ingredients for popularity, not surprisingly, I wasn't popular. All of this led to a paralyzing self-consciousness and the complete inability to engage *any* girl, never mind the pretty ones, in *any* form of meaningful conversation.

Moving to Canada was like moving to another planet, except on this planet. Culturally it was so different. Even the Asian kids did not act like they did back home. They had been "bananified," as they say. They still held on to some aspects of Asian culture, but they seemed to blend in pretty seamlessly with Western culture also. I didn't know how to interface with people. It was like having the wrong power cable for your cellphone: it just did not work. In my primary school in Hong Kong, things had not been this way. I had friends, and I was not the quiet one. I seemed to be able to make friends with everyone. Even the principal seemed to like me, and I was the prefect for my grade level and had been nominated for head prefect before my departure.

Being able to express yourself in your native tongue imparts a confidence that you can't appreciate until you have been parachuted into a place where you barely understand a word. Back in Hong Kong I had it all together—fearlessly ready to conquer the world each day. Each morning I'd show up early for school in my neatly ironed uniform, proudly displaying my prefect patch on my lapel. I was like a little hall monitor, and I wasn't afraid to confront troublemakers, even ones from a higher grade. Although there was the odd person who didn't like me that much, they still had to show me some respect because of my title. Generally I was liked by my fellow students, and, I have to admit, between the popularity and the fact that I was an only child on whom my parents doted, I had a bit of a swollen head. My parents tended to heap praise on me for my every achievement, which eventually turned me into an overconfident brat.

But that world came to a rapid demise after we moved to Vancouver. I was now a victim of culture shock, just another one of thousands of clueless Asian kids trying to figure out how to be in a place that had an entirely different set of rules. Despite fact that there were lots of kids in my situation, I felt totally alone. My support network had bid me a final farewell at Hong Kong International Airport. In this new land, nobody knew who I was, and no one particularly cared.

As I mentioned, the language barrier was a big blow to the precocious Poon ego. Nothing that I said would come out smoothly, and every English-speaking listener would ask me to repeat it three or four times. It was completely debilitating—all of this social isolation was simply because my first language was Cantonese. The part that quietly irritated me the most was that my teachers would treat me like a kindergartener and give me Walt Disney books for homework—all this in front of the class. The other kids would snicker while I died the same thousand deaths many other Asian immigrant kids had died before me. Only, I did not know any of my fellow martyrs, so I just swam around in my tears and felt pity for myself.

Even choosing my clothes was a big deal. In Hong Kong I wore a uniform, but in Canada I had to pick my own outfits five days a week. Even this small task intimidated me. Bosco Poon, former grade six socialite, graduates to the status of mute loner. Even though eventually I strived to maintain really good marks in school, I still couldn't completely adapt to the Western culture. I was desperately homesick for my former life.

Everything changed the day I met Blade in the English as a Second Language (ESL) class in senior high. He was about my height (which is kinda short) and came from Hong Kong, just like I did. He was built like a tank and had a big black dragon tattoo on his right arm. Against the backdrop of quiet, demur, studious-looking Asian immigrants, Blade really stood out. I watched him interact with his friends. They were all pretty cool looking: stylish clothes, edgy haircuts, and boisterous confidence.

Even though Blade had a strong Cantonese accent, like I did, the Caucasian kids didn't laugh at him. They actually seemed to respect him. Wherever he walked, he was flanked by at least two guys—like a pair of bodyguards but without the earpieces and billy clubs. Blade exuded authority. It seemed to me that Blade had all the elements of the formula–and whatever he had, I wanted it! Quietly, over the course of a few weeks, Blade became my role model.

Despite all the social turmoil, my grades were good, and I was actually excelling in school. In fact, I was on the honour roll and remained there from Grade 9 up until the second semester of Grade 11. That was the point when Blade and his friends fully brought me under their wings. In addition to the cool factor, Blade offered me something very practical: protection from the bullies. I got to take advantage of the bodyguard types.

One of the many reasons for my intrinsic trust of him is that we both spoke Cantonese—I knew he understood all the things that I had gone through during the prior three years. This created a special bond between us. I started to hang out with him and his friends at the smoke pit, and then after school we would go to the arcade. Recognizing that I lacked a certain *je ne sais quoi* in the fashion department, they dyed my hair blond—well, that kinda orangey blond that dark-haired people get when they use peroxide. Then they took me to the mall for their impromptu version of *What Not to Wear*. They were systematically purging me of my nerdiness like some kind of upside-down version of *My Fair Lady*. House parties, rave parties, hip-hop, cigarettes, booze, weed, and ecstasy.

Twelve months later, the old Boz was gone, and the new Boz was suddenly surrounded by friends of all nationalities. And, at long last, girls finally started to show an interest, and just about everyone at school was treating me like someone who mattered. I was no longer an immigrant geek. The formula had worked. Though it had taken longer than I anticipated, I had successful engineered my social life back to something I was happy with, with the help of Blade and his friends.

While my social life was soaring, what with all the partying and dating, my marks were really tanking. Not surprisingly, my parents, being Asian parents, were doing the usual Asian-parent-flip-out about getting into university and becoming a professional. *Professional* was a secret code word for any one of the following: doctor, lawyer, accountant, businessman—in order of relative importance.

They warned me over and over about my friends, who were never going to amount to anything, and begged me to get serious about my studies. "Son, birds of a feather flock together. You are who you hang around with. Those friends of yours are no-good company. Look at your marks, and look at your hair! You've changed for the worse! Wake up, please. Don't waste your time on useless things." My mom cried every time I headed outside to party.

"Blah blah blah. Whatever, Mom. I know my future ain't becoming a boring nerdy accountant like you always wanted me to become. I hold my own future, not you, not Dad, not anyone else! I'm heading to my future right now as I speak: to live LIFE!" I would slam the front door as I stormed out of my house in anger.

Naturally, I ignored them and proceeded to spend every weekend partying and getting high with friends from all over the city. Popularity was no longer a problem. When it came to the decision to pursue my grades or my social life, I always chose the latter. I kept hanging out with the same gang of guys, and I was very content to do so. But as time passed, I understood more and more that it was not just a gang of guys; it was actually a gang.

That fall, Blade revealed to me that he was a member of an Asian gang called the Cat-Walk, a branch of a well-known local organization called the Lotus. For reasons inscrutable to me at the time, he made a decision to introduce me to his boss, Fury, a local underground Chinese boxer. He was one of the very few Asians who could hold their own in the underground boxing tournaments that went on in British Columbia. The tournaments were really just an excuse for illegal gambling—like dog fights or cock fights. Fury's followers were bidding high money on him every time he was in a match. At the time I figured Blade just wanted to show me how much he trusted me.

It never gets terribly cold in the fall in Vancouver. It's not like other parts of Canada. Most of the trees here are evergreens, so we don't have the beautiful fall colours of the east. But in the city parks, isolated stands of deciduous trees create the familiar sound of dry leaves crackling in the breeze before they are shaken free and drift to the ground, blanketing walking trails and filling them with the scent of their gradual return to the earth.

It was a typical fall day, an overcast Friday afternoon, when Blade decided to fill me in on the details of his extracurricular activities.

The car speakers were blasting hip-hop. I was crammed into the back seat of a white two-door Mustang GT. Blade was in the front passenger seat, having a cigarette, flicking the ashes out the window intermittently, as another friend drove us down Barnet Highway. We were on our way to the headquarters of Lotus. Gradually the scenery of the North Shore mountains was swallowed by the concrete of Vancouver's east end, the griminess of the downtown east side, and eventually Chinatown. We parked on the sidewalk in front of a two-story building with a huge yellow sign displaying two red Chinese characters: 天下 "Tian Xia" (Dynasty).

"This is the home base of many major players in this city. Don't say anything stupid. I want you to leave in one piece! I'll handle all the talking," Blade warned me sternly.

His comment sent a chill down my spine. As we entered the front doors, I heard the pounding of a heavy bag coming from the left. Pumph … thump … pump-thump! I turned to the left and saw couple of guys sparring in a ring—sweat beading up on their faces only to fly off in a spray when each blow connected. We walked past and continued our way up the stairs to the second floor. The upper floor was separated into two spaces by a bar counter in the middle of the room. Half of the room was devoted to a half dozen snooker tables, and the other half was a dance floor, with multiple private meeting rooms at the very end. The lights were dimmed because we had arrived during off-hours.

Blade led us to a corner of the room, where I could see the silhouette of a man seated by the window. He bowed his head in deference and respectfully addressed the man as he turned toward us. "Boss, we're here!"

I could now make out his face with the help of the track lighting behind me. Fury was a five-foot, eleven-inch man in his late thirties who had broad shoulders and looked like he could bench press 300 pounds. He was wearing a black muscle shirt and tight jeans. I don't quite know how to put this, but he gave off an angry and wrathful vibe—you could just feel the cloud of menace around him, and I knew immediately that he was not one to mess with.

"Welcome, boys! I've been hearing excellent reports from Blade about your team in Coquitlam."

Team? I thought. *Am I part of a team that I didn't know about?*

"I'm well pleased with the expansion of our territory in that area," he continued. "Well done."

"Thanks, boss." Blade seemed pleased with the affirmation.

"Come on, let's have a shot! It's on me!" Fury snapped his fingers, and a waitress brought a half dozen shots of tequila.

As I downed the tequila and reached for a lemon wedge, I listened intently to the conversation, carefully trying to infer what exactly was going on. It seemed to me that I was in the middle of a strategy meeting of sorts. I turned to Blade and gave him a subtle "Why am I here?" look. He stared back and whispered, "Just keep your calm, everything is fine. You're with me. We're gonna party hard later tonight, all right? But let me deal with some business first."

They spent another hour discussing how to recruit more members and increase membership dues. I was not in any way interested in the topic of conversation, and, probably to my own peril, I didn't keep that fact a secret, constantly gazing out the windows.

How did I end up in this place? I thought. *I didn't think that being popular would have anything to do with ending up at a gang headquarters in Chinatown.*

After their meeting was over, Fury called a troop of five guys to escort him out of the building to his vehicle, a heavily modified street-racing silver Honda. The others gave me a cue to bow my head until he disappeared down the stairs. Though I was somewhat resentful about it, I didn't have any other choice. I bowed my head, all the while feeling extremely uncomfortable.

Then I took Blade aside. "Blade, did I miss something? Am I being forced to join this gang?"

"Well, not forced, really," he said, "but I will need you to assist us in a few things."

"So, I am being forced."

"No, no, no … relax, man. Just chill out for a sec. Look, if we're going to get access to Fury's people and money, I'm going to need you to play along. You don't need to go through any initiation or anything. I don't need you to be 'official,' but I need you act like a member of the Cat-Walk."

"But I'm not technically a member, right?"

"No, not technically, but if anyone asks you about it the last thing I need you to do is say you're not one of us. Just act like you fit in, and no one will start wondering."

While I was relieved on the one hand, I wondered what the implications of "playing along" were, exactly. Even though I was never pledged to be part of the Cat-Walk, most of the members thought that I was. Only Blade and I knew the truth, but I wasn't sure that it made a great deal of difference. The expectations of me seemed more or less the same.

As the evening wore on, more and more people appeared on the dance floor as the lineup around the bar counter gradually grew. Blade introduced me to all kinds of people. Fortunately, there were enough girls there that I actually maxed out my phone's memory (ahh, the flip phone) gathering their phone numbers. So I selectively deleted the old girls from my phone and put the new ones in. In those days, there was only one thing on my mind: fun. The concept of faithfulness didn't even cross my mind. I didn't care about hurt feelings, lies, broken promises, or betrayal. I just did what made me happy, and as long as I was happy, nothing else mattered.

In the middle of the dance floor with my new friends, I was totally revelling in the moment. The DJ was spinning hot, and laser light filled the room. The mixture of booze and the smoke coming out of the fog machine created a very sensual, almost pornographic, mood. When the high came down at the end of one party, I'd just go to the next one, seeking another high. In quiet moments, I knew I had changed. I was not the same person I once was. I didn't care about my school, my future, or even my family. Consequently, everything except the party scene was coming apart at the seams. Problems were piling up in reality. Not willing to deal with any of them, I chose to escape. Bottle after bottle, joint after joint, Blade and the gang were taking me farther and farther away from the place where they had found me. Without thinking about responsibilities or consequences, I continue this style of living until my high school graduation.

> **"Do not be so deceived and misled! Evil companionships (communion, associations) corrupt and deprave good manners and morals and character." (1 Cor. 15:33 AMPC)**

CHAPTER 4
JUST A DREAM

The sun was making a cameo appearance. It always rains in Vancouver, but not on that day—the sun was shining out of a perfect cloudless blue. If you looked carefully, you'd notice that the sky right above you was a slightly darker shade than on the horizon. But it was all blue—a beautiful silky blue. It was the kind of day when Vancouverites rollerblade on the seawall or ride their bikes on the dike that protects Richmond from being submerged by seawater.

Scattered light illuminated even the dark corners of the alley we'd been ushered into, but that didn't make it any more pleasant. It stunk of garbage and urine, and if you scanned the edges, you'd inevitably see a used syringe or some other discarded evidence of the unsavoury things that go on in dark places.

I tightened up my black bandana, closed my eyes, and took a deep breath. After tossing my flimsy plastic water bottle into a dumpster, I gently tapped my cheeks to loosen my tense facial muscles. I walked towards the others, who were already positioned in front of a long two-storey wall that was years before surrendered to graffiti artists by shop owners too exasperated to repaint it yet again.

"All right. Everyone ready? Let's roll! I need you all to look into the lens of the camera. I need attitude. Yeah, that's right! Julian, tilt your hat to the left a little. Good! Girl, chest up, look straight. Give me that sexy look. Come on! Boz, point your finger at me. Act cool! Good. Fabulous! I'm feeling it." The shutter went off in bursts of three or four shots per second. We were shooting profile pictures for our press kit. The session went on for 30 or 40 minutes. When it was all done, I had a self-satisfied assurance that things were finally really coming together.

Instead of diving headlong into the crevasse of my self-pity, I made a decision to turn my anger into artistic passion. For the year following the Warner Music debacle, I worked as a junior hairstylist in a Vancouver salon while completing a ten-song demo CD with my newly formed hip-hop crew. We named ourselves Syndicate. There were four of us: Yuen, our talented producer; Rita, our powerhouse of a female lead vocal; Julian, our handsome ladies' man; and of course, me. We worked out of our basements producing songs with our own unique sound. We used English in the verses and stirred in Mandarin and Cantonese rapping—a sort of West meets East Asian fusion. The result was an innovative and refreshing style that no one had heard before—a sound considered especially cool by the Chinese community.

It took us about six months to feel and present ourselves like an official group. By that time our music was finding airtime at local college events and radio stations. Door after door of opportunity kept opening up. More and more people started recognizing us at the nightclubs. Requests for copies of our demo album kept coming, and it was very encouraging to see our efforts recognized.

Eventually, our music found its way overseas, and calls started rolling in from Taiwan. Different management agencies approached us for partnering relationships, and my schedule was jammed with online meetings and email correspondence.

An agent called my cellphone. "We think you guys are extremely talented and have a great chance with the Taiwan music industry. After years, we're finally hearing a sound none of us has heard before. With a little more polish, you guys are ready for a launch. Our company has the ability to take you there. A draft of our contract has been sent to your email. Take a look and get back to us ASAP. We really want to work with you guys."

"Thank you very much for your interest. We'll take a look at the contract and will get back to you soon," I replied with excitement but also with caution.

I started to learn how to deal with the business side of things. By now I had already read a few of these contracts, and there were many tricky lines hiding within blocks of boring legalese. From my past experience of dealing with people in the music industry, I learned not to trust anyone easily. After all, I had been burned by MTV Asia and Warner Music Taiwan already.

All the while we had to finish a full-length album in the studio during our spare time. We were getting so busy it felt like we didn't even have time to eat or sleep some days. Our dream of reaching the top of the billboard chart no longer seemed an impossibility. Every time we went shopping for outfits as a group, we were showered with attention by giddy store clerks, some even suggesting sponsorship of our stage appearances. Of course, Julian was always the one who got spotted first since he was the tallest and best looking. "You have a great look, man. Are you a model or something?" a hip-hop clothing shop manager asked Julian in front of the mirror.

"Thanks! Nah, I'm not. I'm a local Chinese rapper. And this is my crew!" Julian pointed his finger towards us three.

"An Asian hip-hop crew? That's fresh! I like it. You guys look sharp. Doing any gigs around?"

"Yeah. Yeah, we perform here and there. Got one coming up at one of the clubs on Richards Street. That's why we're shopping for outfits."

"Nice, nice. Seems like you guys are doing pretty good. Got yourself a clothing sponsor?"

"It's all right. We do have more gigs coming up. No official clothing sponsorship yet. We're still local, you know. Still finalizing our demos and trying to get the word out."

"Good stuff. Let me listen to your tracks. I see potential. If things are going good for you guys, maybe we can work something out together for your next gig. Bring your CD in, and then I can have a listen, and maybe we can talk further."

Posing in front of the mirror we fantasized about modelling for our own clothing line one day, as many in Hollywood do. With everything seeming to fall into place, it was easy for us to believe we would make it. As our "stock" rose, so also did our pride, and as always, pride goes before a fall.

"Well who do we have here? Since when does the *superstar* have time for us small potatoes?" The gang was really making fun of me as I stepped into the restaurant.

"Come on, guys. I'm totally baked. I don't need this right now. Have you guys ordered yet? I'm starving." I sat down at the only empty seat at the table.

One of the guys turned to me. "What you need, Boz, my good man, is to smoke a big fat joint with us. We just picked up some really good stuff yesterday, BC's finest. It's gonna make you feel so much better. You'll forget all the BS you're worrying your little head about. Guaranteed! Besides, it's been quite some time since we all smoked up together. We had so much fun back in the day. Remember?"

"Yeah, those were some good times, guys. I remember them well. But things have changed now. Haven't we had this conversation a few times before? You guys go ahead and have fun without me. I still need to head back to the studio when we're done eating. It's gonna be another long night. I still have loads of work to do." I rejected the offer as gently as I could.

"Man, you're no fun! What's happened to you? No time for your friends anymore. Whatever. You're the one missing out." The guys turned and continued their conversation without me.

Three years had passed since my personal exit from the party scene. My cellphone contacts used to be almost entirely comprised of party animals, but now those contacts were nearly all replaced by music industry people. This was in the dark ages of flip phones that had limited memory, so I had to delete contacts to add new ones. Only a handful of old friends were still on my phone, and most of them were sitting at the table in front of me. These were the guys who were closest to me.

Bosco H. C. Poon

After my graduation, while pursuing my music career, I continued to meet with Blade every month to maintain my relationship with him. However, I was careful to avoid drugs and excessive use of alcohol because of my need to stay focused on my career and to maintain the public image that had become important to me. Despite the fact that I knew they were a bad influence on me, Blade and the other guys from this group always held a special spot in my heart because they had rescued me from my general social ineptitude in high school. If not because of them, I would never have graduated from my bowl cut, blue dress shorts, and white tube socks. This was the reason I felt so much loyalty towards them and why the boundaries I had set were relatively low.

Recognizing my weakness, Blade and a couple of the others would constantly take advantage of me: asking favours, borrowing money, etc. Against my will and better judgment, somehow I would always accommodate them, in part to repay the protection and acceptance they had afforded me in high school.

"Copy that, we've got him here with us." A uniformed police officer set his walkie-talkie down in the car, adjusted his sunglasses, and walked toward me slowly. "Mr. Poon, you're now officially under arrest. You're being charged for kidnapping and extortion. Do you understand?"

"Yes," I choked out. It was almost like someone else was saying the words and I was watching a bad dream from somewhere down the street.

"You have the right to talk to a lawyer. We'll give you an opportunity to arrange for legal counsel if you don't have a lawyer already. Be aware that anything you say from now on can be used in court as evidence. Do you understand?"

"Yes."

"We can do it the easy way or the hard way. Please extend your arms towards me."

I was handcuffed, cold and tight. They felt like they were crushing my wrists—a metaphor for the crushing of every dream I'd ever had. I caught glimpses of my neighbours emerging from their houses to gawk at me and to whisper in each other's ears, while my family wept in the driveway at the sight of me being arrested.

Why is this happening? What have I done?

They tossed me into the back of the paddy wagon, known affectionately as the "meat wagon" by those who pay it frequent visits. I sat down onto the cold metal floor.

After a few mind-numbing days between the interrogation room and the holding cell, I was scheduled to transfer to the pretrial detention centre from the former Vancouver jail behind the provincial court. By that time, I was exhausted beyond anything I'd ever imagined possible. I could smell the reek of my body odour wafting up from my white jumpsuit. I'm sure I smelled a lot like the downtown eastside folks who'd mocked and catcalled me as I was escorted into the station. I was sat down to wait for my ride at 7:00 a.m. The bus came to get me at about 3:00 p.m.

While we were on the road, scenes of what had transpired in the last few days flooded my mind in slow motion. I played and replayed all that I had lost: the singing career, the beautiful girl, the cover of a magazine. Now all I could confidently say I possessed was a throbbing headache.

I couldn't eat. I had no appetite. But even if I had, the dry baloney sandwiches they slid through the door slot were only sustenance at best. I was completely overcome by the anxiety and uncertainty of what lay ahead of me. I know this sounds a bit strange, but I literally pinched my thighs over and over again to make sure that I wasn't just having a bad dream.

Suddenly the vehicle took a sharp turn to the right, and I was thrown across the cab, hitting my head on the left wall. The shackles prevented me from bracing myself properly with my arms and legs.

Ouch! That hurt.

Reality was validated again.

After two hours of driving east, the vehicle came to a stop, and the officers came around to the back of the wagon. The door opened with an annoying high-pitched creak, and I was ordered to step out. My feet hit the ground, and I shuffled up to the gates.

Surveillance cameras protected by a bubble of bulletproof glass were in every corner. Lifeless tall grey concrete walls were everywhere. I was at the North Fraser Pretrial Centre in Port Coquitlam. They led me into the building and down a sterile looking corridor lit by the irritating glow of bad fluorescent lighting, unlocked my shackles in front of a door, and ordered me into the holding tank with room for about six to ten detainees.

"ARRRGGH! I'm gonna kill you all!" A bald prisoner exploded from the bench as we entered the room, making a run at the correctional officer who was escorting me. Smack, SMACK! I heard the sound of fists connecting with flesh. Within 20 seconds a backup squad rushed into the room and subdued him. They pinned his head to the tile floor, his face contorted, red, panting, and sputtering. Between breaths he would spew profanity and abuse at them. He was entirely undeterred. My heart was pounding while witnessing this whole thing that happened before my eyes.

What kind of place is this? What just happened? I kept asking myself.

"Pigs! Let go of me! SH*T! ARRRRRGGGH!" The guy was using all his might trying to prevent the officers from cuffing his hands behind his back, but it was no use. His strength was no match against four of them. To my surprise, they left the guy on the ground, walked out the door, and locked it behind us. I was left behind with my new best buddy.

What I observed next was so disturbing to me. While screaming at the top of his lungs, he made his way onto his feet without using his arms. He was beet red and looked entirely possessed. Running to the door, he head-butted the metal bars full force over and over. He was like a malfunctioning robot from *Terminator* who'd gone into self-destruct mode. I couldn't believe what was happening. For over 15 minutes he kept banging his head on the door, screaming from the top of his lungs, before someone came and took him away. Releasing my fingers from my ears, I sat there entirely speechless. This was my introduction to prison life, and "frightened" didn't begin to describe it.

Time seemed to stop behind bars. I was under 24-7 surveillance and always wearing the bright red two-piece uniform. My world came to a complete standstill. I was moved to a concrete cell with a double bunk and a toilet, a single roll of thin scratchy toilet paper, and a musty smelling uncomfortable wool blanket—the kind people toss in their trunks for emergencies.

I slept on the upper bunk. My roommate was a tall Caucasian teen who was all tattooed up and very proud of his gang activity and drug life. The room was dark, always dark. Every day we had a few hours to go out of our cell to the mess hall in the middle of the unit where meals were served, and we'd get locked up again shortly after eating. When we were out of the cell, the lights were on. Once we were called to go back to our cells, the lights went off and stayed off. There was a small courtyard beside the mess hall with four tall concrete walls and fencing at the top to prevent escape. There were showers, and we could ask for a tiny square of soap from the guard station. At night we got locked up around 7:45 p.m. until 7:00 a.m. the next day for breakfast.

After a week or so, the door opened at an uncharacteristically early hour, and two guards were waiting for me to get out of bed. They told me I had a bail hearing that day. After I made my bed, I was escorted to the holding tank. Waited there for another few hours until all the paperwork was done. Then the guards came into the room to shackle my hands and feet and took me along with a few other inmates to the vehicle. We then headed off to the provincial court on Main Street.

Upon my arrival, I was dumped into the holding cell as usual. By then I was accustomed to this procedure. After about an hour, the judge's secretary called me in. An officer escorted me into the courtroom.

In the booth for the accused, I was put beside Blade and the rest of the gang. I was the last one to arrive. My parents and my aunt and uncle were there, and from a distance, I could tell that they had all been crying. My heart sank. I felt entirely helpless.

The process took about two hours because the lawyers kept going back and forth with the judge. The language they used was so specialized and formal that its meaning was lost on me. Once the pretrial hearing was over, my parents put their house up as collateral for my bail, which was about $200,000. As promised by the judge, I was released that same day after surrendering my passport.

Sitting in my parents' sedan, I started to gain perspective of the scope of what I had involved myself in. It wasn't just me who was affected but my whole family. They had put their house on the line. I only knew one thing for sure: I had no idea where to begin starting to mend the damage I had caused.

When I was out on bail I treasured the temporary freedom. People who have never been incarcerated don't realize how wonderful freedom is. The most boring day as a civilian is filled with excitement compared to a day alone staring at a cell wall. The other challenge was the way I felt inside. I was carrying baggage so heavy that I could hardly bear it.

Of course, the music came to a screeching halt again. My music crew was justifiably angry with me. I had been extremely unwise in my decision making, and all of their careers would be affected by my bad choices.

Ironically and painfully enough, while I was away, EMI Music Taiwan was offering us, as a group, a record deal. They promised to make us the next megahit group in Asia. They played it up like we would be the Chinese Black Eyed Peas. When I heard this, I knew I would again be like Tantalus from Greek mythology, the food coming down to my mouth and the water just coming up to my lips, and as I reached for it, it would vanish. There was no way that EMI would be willing to pen a deal for us while I was being tried for kidnapping and extortion. Going through the details of the group contract they had emailed me only made things worse. I sat there running my fingers through my hair and sobbing into my hands.

Why is this happening to me?

After many sleepless nights and seemingly interminable consultation with my lawyer, I was left with no other options but to accept reality. My bail conditions forbade me from leaving the country, and I was left with no choice but to withdraw from the group. In the hopes that I could mitigate the damage and prevent the dissolution of the contract offer, I personally called the record label manager to apologize and to beg her to sign with the group without me. I made up a story, telling her that my parents didn't want me to enter this business and wanted me to focus on going to university instead. She was obviously disappointed and saw my decision as nonsense: "I don't understand. What's wrong with you?! Do you know how many demos we receive at the front desk every day? Over a thousand! Most of them go to the garbage can before even crossing the threshold of my office. Come on, this is a once-in-a-lifetime opportunity! Just get yourself to Taipei with all the crew within the next few days. Don't play games with me. I want to work with you as a group—all of you!"

At this I couldn't control myself and broke into tears on the phone. I had no idea how to negotiate this without ruining it for everyone. I just wanted to blurt out the truth to her, but I knew that if she knew the seriousness of the situation she might drop me like a hot potato. Eventually, I was able to convince her that I was not exaggerating and I really could not leave Canada, but I had to do it in a manner that did not reveal the seriousness of the matter.

Bosco H. C. Poon

With a lot of telephone negotiations over the next two months, we came to an agreement that I'd kind of act as an agent for my crew until such a time that I was free to travel. I managed to give the company enough of an excuse without telling them the whole truth of my trial: "I'm sorry, I'm so sorry … Thank you so much for giving us a chance. I'd *love* to work with you alongside my crew. I'd die for this opportunity! You have no idea. But, you see, I'm in the middle of some very serious personal problems, and I can't leave the country. I'm terribly sorry … it's all my fault! Please work with the group even without me. Every single one of them is very talented. They'll be just fine. You won't regret signing them. I can guarantee you."

To sincerely put the interests of others before my own was a new and humbling but strangely gratifying decision. Even though it hurt like hell, my heart was telling me that it was the right thing to do. In the end EMI accepted my convoluted explanation, leaving me an option to sign with them when my problems were resolved. I was deeply touched by this offer.

"I guess this is it. Man, what a shame that you can't come with us! After all the hard times we've been through together … This sucks!" Julian was picking up his backpack.

"It's all good. Just make it big there for me! Share our music, our spirit, all right?" I helped him with his luggage.

"Yeah, B, we won't forget you! Get your things done here and come meet us ASAP. We'll reserve your spot. No one can replace you!" Yuen was giving me a very firm handshake.

"That's right, you hang in there, all right? We'll give you a call right after we arrive. We'll miss you." Rita hugged me tightly.

There at the airport, in front of everyone—the group and their friends and family—I forced a plastic smile onto my face and waved goodbye to them. Watching them heading to customs one by one, I felt my heart tear in half. It was by far the most painful thing that I had ever experienced. The passport case that I'd bought for the last record deal was still sitting in my drawer.

Two days after my group-mates' arrival to Taipei city, a contract negotiation meeting was scheduled. EMI included me in that meeting by conference call. I did my best to make my voice sound cheerful on the phone, but I felt like a violin string pulled taut and about to snap. Every chuckle, every friendly exchange, every scrap of happiness exchanged in that meeting was like lye poured onto an open wound. I didn't want to be bitter, but I couldn't suppress my feelings. Clenching my teeth, I held back my tears for five long hours until the meeting was over. By the end I was so exhausted I just lay down on the carpet by my desk instead of taking 30 seconds to make it to the couch.

This was the third time a record deal had slipped through my fingers. Was it some sort of cruel divine joke? Didn't I have a unique calling that I was simply following? If I had been noticed by three major music companies, didn't I have some genuine talent? Why did I get into these situations where there was so much promise, only to see it vanish at the last minute? Was this punishment? Was I such a horrible person? I needed some answers! If life was trying to destroy my spirit, it was doing a very fine job! I was crushed, and it felt like I would never recover. Slowly I stopped believing in hope, stopped believing in a brighter day. Maybe this was all just foolishness—just a dream.

"Even in laughter the heart may ache, and the end of joy may be grief." (Prov. 14:13 ESV)

CHAPTER 5
I MET A GIRL

Maybe it was the lyrics and maybe it was the catchy melody, but every time I heard "Stickwitu" by The Pussycat Dolls, I'd crank my radio to full blast. The song had something that made my heart melt. I'm sure this sounds cheesy, but as I sang along I would always dream about my future wedding day. Lost in my romantic dream, I'd be belting out the song and grinning ear to ear in the car as I drove along, the music blaring and inevitably annoying people at the stoplights. After many years of singleness, my soul yearned for someone who would be my match.

Up until this point in my life I had never been in a super-serious relationship. It's not as if I had never dated anyone during my days as a "player," but, in retrospect, they were all pretty much puppy-love situations. At times I had felt as if no relationship could be deeper and more intense than what I was feeling right at that moment. Only later would I realize that this destructive view of relationships was leftover teen angst—angst that now I was happily finished with. On the other hand, numerous relationships were selfish and not terribly innocent in nature. Unfortunately, I have to live with the regret of those past decisions.

Eventually I got sick of how having so many regrets made me feel. I wanted a more meaningful relationship with someone whom I actually loved—not just someone I thought was "hot." When I made up my mind to pursue a music career after high school, I focused all of my attention on that goal and didn't really have any time for a girlfriend. Even though the club-and-music scene was crawling with good-looking girls and all of my bandmates were in relationships, I didn't want the distraction. I had learned it is impossible to avoid drama when you are with someone, and I couldn't afford this on top of all that was already on my plate, which was brimming up to the edge and sometimes spilling over.

Bosco H. C. Poon

"Hey, handsome, why not get some balloons and roses for your girlfriend? I guarantee she's gonna love them. Trust me!" A saleswoman stopped me in the middle of the sidewalk with a big smile on her face.

"No, thank you. I don't have a girlfriend," I replied sulkily.

"No way! You? Come on, it's Valentine's Day! You gotta have someone you like a little, don't you? Get something for *her*." She wasn't ready to lose a sale so easily.

"I, uhh … don't have anyone to be honest." I was embarrassed.

"Oh, okay, all right. Sorry about that. I didn't know. Well, have a good day, sir." She walked away to accost another pedestrian.

I glanced back at her fistful of heart-shaped Mylar balloons bouncing back and forth in the breeze. There were vases and pails filled with fresh roses: pink, white, classic red. The odd rose looked a little tired on the edges, though—bruised, wilted. You'd probably ask them to replace it if you got caught buying your roses too late in the day to have your pick. Those bruised roses, the tired ones: I felt like them. My heart ached.

Wherever I went that day, all I noticed were the couples, love songs, and red banners in the windows. All the chocolate stores and coffee shops downtown had Valentine's Day specials, and the theatres were showing the yearly string of romance movies. Everything reminded me of my loneliness. Love was in the air, evidently, but I was just window-shopping on the street all by myself because everyone else was busy dating each other and loving or being loved. Deep down inside I had this void, like a hole in my heart. I closed my eyes, drew a breath, and looked up to the sky. It was not often sunny in February, but that day it was. I looked up to the sky and made a wish in silence.

Being in and out of the courthouse week after week left me despondent. *Is this ever going to be over?*

I knew that I had to find something to do to get my mind off my trouble with the law. Since I had been single for so long, I thought it might be a pleasant distraction to start hanging around with girls again. One day as I was flipping through magazines, thumbing through the glossy pages of beautiful women, I thought, *How could I meet someone who looks like this? Maybe if I worked in some facet of the fashion industry I could find someone.*

After my bandmates moved to Taiwan to begin their journey with EMI music, I had this bright idea that if I wanted to meet a beautiful girl, I could just go to where they are rather than waiting for them to come to me. So I enrolled in a makeup artistry program from the Blanche Macdonald Centre, a small college in Vancouver named after a Canadian Métis fashion icon. I also got a job working weekends at Backstage Hair Salon in Richmond, BC. So, in a few short months, I had managed to literally surround myself with beautiful women, doing their makeup, cutting their hair, kibitzing with them all day long. But it didn't work. I still felt so empty inside.

When it came down to my careerism—no matter in music, hair design, or makeup—I went full throttle. Immediately after I graduated from Blanche Macdonald, I gathered some talented friends to form a small freelance image design firm for individual clients and media events. We were hired for jobs such as model photo shoots and small fashion events. Despite my mandatory 11:00 p.m. curfew (one of my bail conditions), I managed to become very active in the local fashion scene. My team took on the promotion of different Asian fashion event projects within the Lower Mainland and worked very hard to rapidly build a reputation. During one of the shows, I met a local Chinese fashion model and had an instant crush.

It had been years since I had been so distracted by a girl. Maybe it was her suntanned complexion and her hazelnut locks, her intoxicating perfume, or maybe it was the way she smiled. I couldn't take my eyes off her all evening. As soon as my co-worker finished her makeup, I walked up and introduced myself with my business card. She extended her immaculately manicured hand to shake mine. "Hi, I'm Allie."

Our eyes locked, and it felt totally magical. I could barely get words out of my mouth because my head was spinning with excitement. I had to manage two conversations at once—my ongoing commentary to myself about how attractive she was and my ongoing conversation with her, which was running a serious risk of being filled with non sequiturs if I didn't get hold of myself.

I was enjoying the moment so much that I forgot that I was going to turn into a pumpkin at midnight—well, one hour before midnight—11:00 p.m. It was my own little Cinderella moment. Alas, it was time for another awkward departure when I had to distract someone from the reality that I was being tried for kidnapping. I cut Allie off as politely as I could, making up some lame excuse why I had to leave. On my way out the door I gave my image team a wink, letting them know they had to handle the rest of the show without me. *Why would any girl want a guy like me? I'm in such a terrible situation.* I needed a fairy godmother and, you know, a bunch of singing mice or something.

"Junk, junk, more junk mail." Going through my email account, I was doing the daily routine of trying to wear out the delete key. There were fifty-something messages, and none of them got my attention except for the one with this subject line: "It's Allie, I met you the other night." *Whoa! I can't believe it.* She wanted to continue the conversation where we'd left off. *I didn't think that would happen.*

Within days, we were on our first date. It was a bright sunny day. I went to pick her up from her place in Vancouver's west end. Upon my arrival she came outside and took a look at me beside my car, then ran back into the house in haste without saying a word. *What on earth?* I scratched my head, wondering what she was up to.

A full 20 minutes later she came back out wearing a pink tank top and a greyish white camouflage miniskirt, which matched my dark-green camouflage hoodie and light-grey jeans. She wanted to impress me by matching my outfit. Such was the world of fashion sense in which we lived.

That evening, we spent hours talking about our dreams and passions at a fusion Japanese restaurant in downtown Vancouver. The more we talked, the more I wanted to hold her in my arms. She laughed at all my jokes—including the humourless ones—that's how you can spot devotion. It was a wonderful evening that came to a rapid close at 11:00 p.m., as usual.

In the back of my mind, I thought my curfew and bail conditions would be a major roadblock for our budding romance. Ironically, in this scenario, however, it had the opposite effect. By not going out late at night, she thought that I was different from the other guys. It was interpreted as gentlemanly and chivalrous to have her home well before midnight and to always have to vanish before 11:00 p.m. She seemed to find this mysterious, and it actually made for more frequent dates.

Eventually, I had to divulge the nature of my situation. To my surprise she didn't flip out. Instead, she showed me compassion. She listened to my music and was impressed by my passion for the arts. On the miserable days I spent in the courthouse, she would cheer me up in the evening by picking a movie for us to go to or arranging dinner reservations.

Moreover, she even started coming to some of the boring hearings with me. I was thoroughly touched. She was a real angel to me in this dark and tumultuous time in my life. I felt like I could go on because I had her to look forward to. My bitterness towards the people who had gotten me mixed up in this mess gradually began to dissipate. Was Allie the answer to my deepest longing—the long awaited promise of a brighter day?

"Hey, would you like to get some flowers to celebrate Valentine's?" I passed by the same spot from the previous year.

"Wow, a year has passed. Yeah, I would like to get something today."

"You interested in some roses?" the saleswoman asked.

"Sure. Please make me a bouquet of roses to match this Gucci wallet that I got for her." I reached into my pocket to get my credit card. After a few minutes of picking, arranging, and adorning with paper and a card, she returned with my purchase and a couple of those little packets you are supposed to put into the water to keep the flowers fresh.

"Here you go! I guarantee she's gonna love it! Happy Valentine's Day." She handed me the bouquet over the counter.

Just the thought of Allie filled my heart with excitement. Was this love? Maybe. That's sure the way it felt. Undoubtedly, her presence in my life added a dimension that was totally absent before. Instead of pouring every bit of my energy into the salon and courthouse, I was able to have some fun and take refuge in a relationship.

Risen From Prison

Whatever I did and wherever I went, as long as she was beside me, there were fireworks. That's the way new relationships are—and I was loving it. However, after the honeymoon period, we had to face some harsh reality.

Allie was 20, young and ambitious. In this great big world, there was so much out there waiting for her to explore. She wasn't anywhere close to settling down. Louis Vuitton handbags, Gucci wallets, Chanel jewellery, the glamorous Hollywood lifestyle was what she was after. All of her previous rich boyfriends were able to supply her with top designers' brands, meals at high-end restaurants, and rides in expensive vehicles. I was a broke artist who was in and out of court.

It took me a great deal of effort just to save up for that Valentine's Day present. For other guys, this kind of purchase was a trifle—something they could do any day of the week. Allie realized that I wasn't going to be able to lavish her with gifts and struggled to see reasons that she should stick with me. I was living in a shallow world, and I was seeing the fruit of it.

I recommended sincerely that she try a different style of living to gain a different perspective towards life. After considering my suggestion, she was willing to give it a try.

"What's wrong, baby girl?" I picked up the cushion Allie had thrown to the floor.

"I'm bored! I'm not happy! I don't like this life!" She was acting particularly petulant that day.

"Okay, okay, just chill. What do you want? You just got your Gucci wallet. You were very happy the other day, weren't you?"

"That was the other day! Today I'm *not* happy. I need new things. I need to go shopping!"

"Really? Do you really think more new things would make you happy? You have received many new things before, and how long did the happiness last? Listen, you don't need more new things. What you need is a new way of living."

"What do you mean?"

"You need to have a purpose to live for. Going from party to party to get drunk does not give you a healthy purpose. When you wake up in the morning, you still have to face the problems of this world. I've been there. As a matter of fact, it nearly ruined my life. I went from being an honour roll student to a kid with failing grades. You see, music saved me. It gave me a purpose and a goal to strive for. It gave me the energy to keep moving forward. You need to find your art like I have so you'll have something to commit to yourself too."

"My art? Oh, I've always loved drawing. As a kid, I used to draw comic book characters and dreamed of publishing my own comic one day. I still have some of my old drawings around. Let me find them!" She ran to her closet and dug out some boxes. There was a folder filled with her drawings. Her eyes lit up with passion as she explained each of them to me.

"These are beautiful. I see it in you. You should become an artist. You need to share your inner world with your drawings and artistic endeavours."

"Now that you mentioned it, I actually did some research before. I wanted to go to the Emily Carr Institute of Art and Design."

"That's great! What's the holdup? You should do it!"

"But ... I haven't even finished high school yet—"

"No problem; finish it! That should be your goal. It'll give you purpose and energy. This is good!"

"What ... really?" Allie looked skeptical.

"Come on, trust me. Your mom would be so happy to see you have a goal in life. And it's your dream too. One day when you see your dreams come true, you'll be so happy. It's the kind of happiness that 'new things' won't be able to give you."

"Wow, really? I want that. Okay, I'll give it a try."

"Now you have some work to do. Don't worry, you're not doing this on your own. I'll do whatever I can to help you get there."

In order to get into Emily Carr Institute, she needed to finish off her high school diploma. We tried out different adult schools, but it was literally impossible to get her up in the morning. I kept a tube of tennis balls in my trunk. When she didn't answer the doorbell in the morning, I'd toss tennis balls at her bedroom window until I'd see her groggy eyes peering out with some combination of affection and resentment—mostly the latter. By the time she was finally dressed, classes were usually over.

We eventually decided that night classes were the way to go. The ensuing challenge was homework. With the intention to create a distraction-free study environment, I assumed many of her daily errands, including taking care of her dog—a white toy Pomeranian. Little by little, I slowly became Allie's personal assistant and general domestic. Even though it wasn't at all easy, I was thoroughly invested in making a respectable career woman out of her somehow.

In addition to arranging for Allie to attend adult high school, we found a student who was already studying at Emily Carr to be Allie's personal tutor to help her prepare an admission portfolio. She had to spend at least 12 hours per week over eight months to learn all the different techniques required to create the twelve required projects. This was the toughest challenge of the process because each project was a lot of work—something to which she was not accustomed. The projects were a kind of mandatory rehabilitation from the laziness she'd developed after dropping out of high school. I would see glimmers of hope and some change in her behaviour, but because I was the primary motivator, she was prone to relapses of indolence. It was too easy to party, exploit her looks to get what she wanted, and generally be a "taker." She desperately missed the fun and attention she garnered at parties.

A quarrelsome relationship was the last thing I needed in the middle of my long and emotionally draining trial. I'd go to trial all day long, only to find myself in an all-evening-long battle with Allie. I was no longer "living the dream" with my high-maintenance girlfriend. What started as a fairy tale had turned into the most stifling, frustrating, and unfulfilling relationship I had ever had, fight after fight, insult after insult. I should have ended the relationship months before, but something inside me just wouldn't give up. I wasn't ready to let it go, but circumstances soon forced the matter.

The final chapter of this love story was not the making of a Disney feature. It's very difficult to date from behind bars. One evening prior to receiving my sentence I was watching an episode of *Prison Break* with Allie. In that episode, a prisoner was meeting his girlfriend in the visitation room. He was so happy to see her, but the feelings were not being reciprocated. She told him that she was pregnant, and while the guy was jumping up and down cheering, she delivered the cruel news that he was not the father. He went crazy, and the prison guards swarmed him and took him back to his cell. The cigarette in my hand dropped into the ashtray. *This could easily be me.*

After my sentencing, it was nearly impossible to maintain the relationship with Allie. After all, I could no longer function as her personal assistant. When she needed me to help her solve problems, I wasn't there. Whenever she wanted to talk to me, there was no way for her to call me. When she wanted to cry, there was no shoulder to lean on, and vice versa. My going-away gift for her was to pen the admission essay required for her portfolio submission. I spent days doing the research and putting the essay together while she slept beside me on the couch. While I knew I should not spoil her to this extent, I wanted her to have a better future than the one she was headed for.

After a year of hard work, it finally paid off. Allie got accepted by the Emily Carr Institute a month after my imprisonment. I had a sense of achievement for keeping my promise to get her there. After so many failures, this made me feel useful, though in retrospect this was not a healthy way for me to bolster my self-image. Eventually we had more and more arguments during our very rare phone calls with one another. Loneliness slowly gnawed away at the frayed cord that held us together. It inevitably broke. Within six months, Allie had met someone else.

Why does every good thing in my life turn bad? I desperately wanted an answer, so I pondered the situation with Allie at length. When I looked back to the beginning of the relationship, I realized that I was focusing on all the wrong things. The type of girls I found attractive were the ones with a hot body and a pretty face. I learned that relationships based on superficialities were a form of candy-coated poison, and in time I understood that inward beauty was far more important. I could have seen this on my first meeting with Allie had I the maturity to look for the signs. Fake eyelashes, lip gloss, foundation, and concealer can hide physical blemishes. In a similar way, Allie's beauty itself had distracted me from her *character* blemishes, but with time they inevitably rose in the same manner that physical blemishes can be exposed by soap and water. I could have avoided a lot of hurt by applying a little wisdom.

Bosco H. C. Poon

"For the lips of an immoral woman are as sweet as honey, and her mouth is smoother than oil. But in the end she is as bitter as poison, as dangerous as a double-edged sword." (Prov. 5:3–4 NLT)

CHAPTER 6
KEEP FIGHTING

"Well Mr. Poon, can you tell me how you occupy your time each day?" My bail supervisor, Marcus, peered at me with my file sitting open on his desk. His demeanour and tone betrayed his skepticism, but I sensed his genuine desire to help me get back on the right track.

I responded in a somewhat dejected tone but tried to make myself sound productive. "Well, I'm in court from Monday to Thursday, so I can't do much then. I do work at a salon on Fridays and the weekends. Sometimes I get hired on a freelance basis to do makeup for models at local fashion events."

"Really? You get fashion work? That's pretty interesting, but I have to say, you don't look too excited, kid."

"Well—the trial is taking a lot out of me. What do you expect?" I was far too familiar in my way of speaking to him. "Plus, I have a curfew. I have to rush home like a madman from work most nights. How excited should I be?"

"Boz, you seem passionate about what you're doing, and you are getting opportunities to work. Despite the circumstances, I think you ought to be a little happier." He seemed to actually care about me.

"What's your dream?" he continued.

"Don't talk to me about dreams ..." I sighed. The truth was, I wanted to talk about dreams. I had them—in spades. But I was feeling pretty petulant about everything at this point, and I was playing the part.

"Why not? Everyone has dream. Tell me. What's yours?" He leaned forward, and his forearms slid onto the table. He looked me in the eye and waited. I snubbed him as long as I could.

Bosco H. C. Poon

"You've got to be kidding me ..." I sat silent for 30 seconds. "I spent over four years chasing after my so-called dream, and look where it's landed me. You have no idea how much time I spent and how much energy I wasted."

"What was it? What were you working on?"

"I was a recording artist."

"What? You? When?"

"Yes. And I've had two record deals slip through my fingers. A third one is on hold right now as we speak."

"C'mon."

"Yes, and my group and I—I'm completely trapped waiting for this situation to resolve so I can release our first album with them in Taipei. So tell me, can I go fulfill my dreams now? No, I can't leave the country, so I'm going to lose this deal too. What is there left to talk about? My dreams are evaporating." I clenched my fists to keep myself from showing a lack of self-control.

"Wow, really? That's really unfortunate. If that's your passion, why are you doing all these other things then—the fashion stuff, I mean? Why don't you focus on the music if that's what really brings you satisfaction?"

"Do I have a choice? Hair and makeup have always been a backup plan. I don't love them, but it is work, and I need to eat. If the music thing never happens, at least I will be able to seek out a living. But the way things are looking right now, I'm going to be cutting lots of hair. God only knows when this trial's gonna end or if I'll just get tossed into prison—"

"It's still up in the air. The case isn't settled yet. There's still a chance that you'll be released. Why not think about channelling your energy toward your music? I mean, maybe not full time, but give yourself a little freedom to do something you love. There are many aspects of your situation you can't change, but there are things that you can do to help make yourself feel better," he suggested.

I sat silent.

"Well, I'll let you think about that on your own. Let's book our next appointment. Does next Friday at this time work for you?" I gave a barely perceptible nod and a begrudging approval. He smiled and jotted it into his calendar.

"All right, sir, I'll see you next week." I placed my hands on the desk, pushed myself up to my feet, and shuffled towards the door.

"Remember to stay out of trouble, okay?" He'd barely finished his sentence when the door clicked shut behind me.

Walking down the stairs of Richmond Community Corrections Office, I was fuming—not at any one person. I was angry at my circumstances, angry at Blade, and angry at myself. How did I get myself into this terrible mess and lose everything that I had strived for? I thought I had buried all of my feelings of loss, and Marcus had brought them to the surface again. I had managed to dull some of my pain over the preceding year by putting my nose to the grindstone, but with one five-minute conversation it was as if it had all happened yesterday.

Risen From Prison

Despair boiled up from some dark place in my chest and swallowed me from head to toe. I grabbed the metal handle of the main entrance door. Wind poured through from the blustery weather outside, causing me to squint. As I stepped into the weather, whether my eyes were wet with tears from sadness or the wind, I'm not sure, but I looked up to a cloud-filled dreary winter sky and yelled at the top of my lungs, "What do you want from me?!"

It was a cool day in April. The cherry blossoms had come into full bloom and had begun to fall from the trees, creating sidewalks bespeckled with pink petals. For two glorious weeks, the streets were lined with fragrant pink.

That day, I had booked a Caucasian model named Michelle for a photo shoot for my image-consulting website. I had to take her through a head-to-toe makeover before the sun set. I had invited my buddy Yuen to watch the whole process. He'd been in Taipei for a while but had run into a disagreement with EMI and had abandoned the process of getting signed and returned home.

The minute he walked into my workshop, he looked bewildered at what he saw and shook his head. He pulled me aside to another room and with both of his hands on my shoulders whispered, "Man, I wasn't expecting America's next top model or anything, but I wasn't expecting someone as homely as this chick! What are you thinking? I thought this girl was going to be hot. Are you losing your standards, B? I mean, better looking girls were selling cigarettes in the corner stores in Taipei." Yuen went on and on.

"Waiwaiwait, Yuen, wait!" I composed myself and then got a curl at the corner of my mouth. "You don't know what you're talking about. What you see in the magazines is all fake. Every girl starts looking pretty ho-hum. Trust me. Even when you see a beautiful woman on the street, a lot of what you're seeing is the illusion created by confidence and makeup. It's a temporary swindle that disappears at the end of each day, and I, my friend, am going to show you how it all works. I want you to witness the magic of makeup. Trust me, you'll see a total transformation, and by the end of the day you'll be wanting to ask her out. Just go relax for a bit. Go online or whatever. Feel free to use the Wi-Fi."

The night before, to speed up the process, I had had her come to my small home studio to get the cut and colour out of the way. I was looking to create a stark colour contrast, so I intentionally separated the colouring sections into two parts: medium hazelnut brown from the ears and below and light ash blonde for the upper part of the head. Cutting wise I gave her a mid-length layer cut using a combination of three different texturizing techniques and finished it off with wide straight V-shape bangs. With that out of the way, now I only needed to focus on the makeup and styling.

I carefully tied her hair back and looking at her in the mirror asked, "So, you ready to get started?" She nodded and closed her eyes.

So I turned on the music and stretched my fingers to loosen up my hands. After quickly picking out the right brushes from my makeup kit, I got going. I started off applying the first layer of foundation to balance out her complexion. I covered visible blemishes with a colour concealer. It is said that "the eyes are the window to the soul," so I always spent a lot of time on my clients' eyes. On the eyelids, I did four layers of eyeshadow in different shades to create dimension. I enhanced both top and bottom eyelashes with two heavy coats of mascara and finished with eyeliner. I used a lighter shade of concealer under her eyes and eyebrows to cause her eyes to really shine. With a fine brush, I outlined her lips in light pink, and I used a darker, milkier shade of pink for the fleshy part of her lips. For a finishing touch, I carefully painted on a thick layer of lip gloss and highlighted the edge of her lower lip with a light shade concealer using an angle sponge. After contouring her face with proper highlighting and lowlighting, I added a cream peach blush to both sides of her cheeks.

"Look up and blow me a kiss, Michelle." She pursed her lips at me. "Oh yeah, that's sexy! Time to do your hair." As I plugged in my blow-dryer and flat iron, out of the corner of my left eye I caught a look at the smile on Yuen's face. He'd started to get curious about what was taking so long. He was suddenly no longer chagrined.

I turned to him and snapped, "Get lost, man! We're not done yet." He giggled and tried to redirect his attention to his laptop.

I returned to my work. I needed her hair to have more volume, so I blow-dried the roots with a medium round hairbrush. To get colour contrast, I blow-dried the bottom portion of her hair outward and flat ironed the top. From start to finish the styling took about 30 minutes. Letting the last portion of her bangs slide through my left index and middle finger as the flat iron followed, I finished her bangs with a V-shape that conformed to the arch of her eyebrows. It was a cool look. I sprayed on the last layer of hairspray, and it was officially finished.

"Ta-da, you're done! What do you think?" I asked, placing the canister of hairspray on the table and stretching out my back.

"Whoa—this is so good. I look amazing!" She was grinning.

From the giddy expression on her face I knew that she was very pleased, so I continued, "All right! Now let's dress you up and head outside for some photos." On the table beside us was large white cloth I'd purchased from Fabricana. I wrapped it around her, strategically securing it with safety pins to accentuate her figure. In a photo shoot, this looked like an expensive dress, and no one knew that it cost me just a few bucks.

Looking into the mirror at her, I was happy with what I saw—it was a chic, clean, modern look. It had turned out just as I had imagined.

Taking Yuen aside I whispered smugly, "So, my friend, what do you have to say now?"

"Well, I gotta hand it to you, Boz, that's a transformation. She looks like she came right of the pages of *Vogue*. I love the whole look, man. If I hadn't watched the whole thing I would not have believed that this was the same girl. I take back what I said ealier." He couldn't take his eyes off her.

"Ha—I told ya so! Well, would you like to be my assistant for the photo shoot, or should I look for someone else?" I started packing my stuff.

"No, no, I'm in! Whatever you say, boss. I'm eager to see the whole thing now. I'm expecting more surprises!" Yuen grabbed my bag and the reflector, and we headed outside.

"Well, we'll find out soon enough." I gave both of them a wink.

It was about an hour before sunset, and we were about to get perfect light for the shoot. With the cherry blossoms in full bloom, we were going to get some spectacular photos. Michelle was bathed in golden light while standing under a banner of fragrant pink. For the next 30 minutes, I struggled to find the perfect angle while Yuen ran back and forth with the reflector doing my bidding. Finally, we were ready to get rolling.

"Okay, girl, look at me with some passion. I know it's been a long day, but this is the moment that we've been waiting for. Time to shine. I want you to think of me as the long-distance love you haven't seen in years—the one you've been pining for. Good! Hold that emotion. Yeah, that's it! Give me that again."

The noise from the camera shutter was like a machine gun. I was firing off hundreds of photos. "Yuen, a little to the right, okay? No, that's too much, come back a little. Good, stop right there!" I captured every angle I could think of—left to right, top to bottom. Beams of light shone through the petals creating a gently moving display of dappled light on and around her.

An hour slipped away without us noticing, and as suddenly as it started, our delicious golden light disappeared as the clouds over the Gulf Islands took on their final shades of red and orange and fuchsia before night descended. We were exhausted, but the giddiness lasted for hours because we knew it had gone better than we could have hoped for.

Mandarin pop songs were playing in the background—unintelligible in the ears of Westerners except for the occasional English word dropped in because there was no cool-sounding Chinese equivalent. We were at the Pearl Castle bubble-tea café. About a week had passed since the photo shoot. Yuen and I were having a lunch meeting together, discussing the photo edits and the first draft of my soon-to-be website just as a waitress interrupted our conversation. "Here's your dried-plum green tea."

"Thank you, you can put it right here." I gestured to the space beside my laptop. "That's great. Thanks," I said as she placed it on the table.

"How come you don't ever have pearls in your bubble tea, man? It's not *bubble* tea without pearls, you know?" Yuen tried to tease me.

"Sometimes I just like to keep it simple. My life is already complicated enough. Just let me be." I took a sip of my drink.

"Ha, I'm just saying I love my pearls." He spooned a bunch of big brown tapioca into his mouth.

Yuen swallowed the snot balls as I continued, "All right, enough about bubble tea. Back to business. So what do you think of the whole fashion photo shoot experience? Have you changed your mind at all?" I was formulating a rebuttal to any criticism before a word passed his lips.

"Well, I have to admit that I overlooked your ability."

Oooh, success. I have a convert, I thought.

"When you first invited me to check out your photo shoot, I didn't really know what to expect. I know you finished makeup school and all, but I didn't have much idea of what you could actually *do*. I mean, it's not really something I see a lot of guys interested in. Seeing you transform an ordinary plain Jane into something from a magazine, that really blew me away. Like really! I had so much doubt in the beginning."

"This is really good to hear, Yuen. I'm glad you feel this way. I guess it helps that I am making more beautiful girls in the world for you to daydream about."

"Yeah, I suppose that is an incentive to like what you do, and if you hadn't forced me to sit down and watch, I wouldn't have given you the time of day about this. I'm glad that you did. I hate to admit that I actually changed my mind. You got some mad talent there, Boz." He sat up and crossed his arms.

In my mind I was drumming my fingertips together while quietly crooning, *"Excellent."*

"Thank you. You know that's the whole reason I invited you, to show you what I can do now—all on my own. From hair and makeup to wardrobe and photography: concept to execution. Now that's what I can do alone. But can you imagine what we could achieve together if we combine our music with this package? We could literally do what a record label can do. The beauty of this is that if we do everything ourselves, we have full creative control. Here's what I have in mind. I want to establish an entertainment production company. We've been relying on others long enough. How many times did we get disappointed by these agencies and record labels? I mean, if we can do it all ourselves, then why do we need them?"

"Boz, I don't know if I can really get back into putting my hopes into music right now. I'm still so burned by my experience with EMI."

"I know, I know, but just hear me out. Believe me, I've tried to turn my attention to other things for the last year while I worked my ass off at the salon and offered myself as a volunteer to as many local fashion events as possible. Guess what, though? I haven't been satisfied. There's always a hole in my heart without being able to create music and perform. Like I wasn't really living—you know what I'm saying?" I paused to calm myself down.

Risen From Prison

"I understand what you are saying, B ... but listen, I think we need to forget music. There's no future in it. It's like high school sports. They seems really important at the time, but eventually you have to grow out of them. It's in our past now. It never paid the bills, and, to be honest, I'm getting kind of tired of it. I just want a normal life and a nine-to-five job with a stable income. Yes, we did get somewhere, but I think we got as far as we could go. Let's just be realistic. You have great talent in the beauty industry. Why don't you just invest your energy there?"

I cut him off without letting him finish his sentence. "Enough! Stop acting like everyone else. Stop lying to yourself. You know it's a shame to waste your musical talent like this. We worked so hard together for two years, and we actually got somewhere. We got so much further than everyone else. It was my bad to mess things up and let you guys down. I had no choice but to let you guys go to EMI without a full crew!"

"B, that's not really the point. I think we've missed our chance, man. We're not teenagers no more."

"I'm sorry. I wish things could turn out differently. But look at me. In spite of my lawsuit, curfew, and all the constraints on me, I'm still fighting hard for this dream. I have way more reasons to give up than any of you guys. All I'm saying is, if we did it once, we can do it again. We can band together and pull it off this time. This time we'll be bigger and better!"

Yuen was actually looking at me pretty intensely. I was giving this soliloquy my all.

"Wow, B ... you're actually serious, aren't you? You're still holding on to this stupid music dream. I'm speechless, man ... I dropped it in Taiwan before I flew back. I'm done with it. We're off chasing a fantasy, and we're constantly yearning and dissatisfied. Maybe all that I ever wanted was a regular life, B. Is that wrong?" He hesitated and looked away.

"It's all right; take your time. Just promise me one thing: be honest to yourself. Look into your heart and see what it's telling you. If you don't ever wanna touch music again, I'll respect that. But think about what I've said. What I'm offering is an opportunity to build an entertainment kingdom together. I believe in your ability as a producer, and I have the image, abilities, and connections to make our project work. I've got a lotta skin in this game. After all, if I lose my case and end up in prison next year, I want to have something waiting for me when I get out. Out of all my friends, you're the one that I can trust."

"I, uh ... well, I'll consider it, B." Based on the pensive look, he was not simply dismissing me.

"And that's all I'm asking for." I smiled.

After paying the bill, I took him to his car. I waited for him to leave the parking lot before lighting a cigarette. As Yuen drove off, I sat staring, and the frustration of my unfulfilled ambitions faded into the quiet of the evening. It wasn't peace that I found in those silent moments. No, as it had many times before, loneliness slowly bubbled up from within me. The quieter it got, the more I became aware of it, until I felt that it was nearly swallowing me. And my trial felt like being chained to a rock during the rising tide. I gasped for air above an ocean of inescapable emptiness.

Blowing out a cloud of smoke made thicker by the cool damp air, I quietly stared at a lamppost. *Will things get better?*

———

Usually the stars look dim from the city, but this night the stars were uncharacteristically bright. Under a clear sky I stood outside our home studio that we had built together in Abraham's basement a few blocks from Oakridge Mall in Vancouver. He was my bandmate from my MTV era, and now we were reunited to form a new music team. In the studio, we drew our cartoon avatars on the walls of the wooden recording booth we'd put together from materials purchased at Home Depot. It had now been two months since my meeting with Yuen. In the interim, Yuen had gradually been convinced to work with us, but the uncertainty of my legal fate was an ever-present gloom on the horizon.

We brought in extra talent to create some redundancy. This included a number of friends who could ensure that we would keep moving forward even if I had to bow out for a period of time.

We divided the production house into two wings. First was Phonic Architects, the music production arm of the company, which included Abraham, a five-foot, ten-inch bodybuilder and all-around ladies' man who'd been part of my very first band. He acted as both a recording artist and the sound engineer. Then there was A.C., a handsome muscular basketball player who had won a bunch of local singing competitions. He was a recording artist and our choreographer. Bonny had also jumped on board. She was a petite Asian with a gentle, caring disposition who had studied interactive art and technology at Simon Fraser University. She was in charge of the management of artists and our public relationships.

The other arm of the company was Bozconcepts. Angela, a very skillful hairstylist I had trained with at hair school, had the final say on our artists' hairstyles for each project and was notable for her ability to combine the latest Western and Eastern trends into her work. Heidi handled most aspects of makeup designs for our projects with her seemingly boundless creativity. She had earned the position of a chief makeup artist through her good reputation in the local Asian beauty industry. Finally, Gary was our photographer—skilled, knowledgeable, and experienced. He was an online junkie and knew all the right places to get what we needed for our photo shoots at the cheapest possible price. We didn't have cash flow, so this was a serious asset. Along with Yuen and myself, the whole crew was set. *Per aspera ad astra*, as they say.

"A man's heart plans his way, But the Lord directs his steps." (Prov. 16:9 NKJV)

"One two three four, two two three four. You gotta count your beat constant and stable—that's hip-hop 101—very important. Also, know where you want to emphasize your rhythm and rhyme, on the upbeat or on the downbeat. Think about how you wanna structure your sixteen bars, which normally would be one verse for, say, a song commercial. You can break down the structure to four bars at a time and then make some changes to the next four. Be careful that the transition is smooth. Don't make any drastic changes that create disconnects. It'll come to you more naturally over time. The key is practice, practice, practice. Let's do some exercises and try it out."

I was giving instruction to A.C. and Abraham in our song composition tutorials, passing on what I'd learned of music production to them. None of this had come easily to me. It had cost me years of hard work, research, money, failure, humiliation, and struggle. It felt a little like I was giving all my secrets away for free.

We worked countless hours in the studio, pouring our hearts into our first album. We were sacrificing a great deal. Whether after school or work or, speaking for myself, my trial hearing, we would meet daily or twice daily. There were many stressful days when everyone's patience was, shall we say, not at full bars. This made occasional conflicts inevitable, which was nothing new to me. Based on my previous experience, I knew that it would require a lot of patience and perseverance to make all of this happen on a budget of bubble tea.

From coming up with themes, to writing lyrics, to playing around with digital sounds in front of the computer, we were gradually formulating the concepts for each song. While everyone was longing to see immediate results and at times was very driven, there were days when the momentum seemed to just vanish.

"Man, we're stuck again ... how many days have we been working on this section? I'm running out of ideas." Abraham had his hands on his forehead.

"This is tough, man ... way more difficult that I thought. Are we going about this the right way?" A.C. threw himself on the couch.

"Guys, we gotta focus. We can do this. Remember what I said, it's all practice. Just keep at it. It'll work. I've done this so many times before. This is just how songwriting happens." I was busily fixing the verse A.C. had put together the previous night.

"Hey, why don't we try out something new, like something personal? Something we've never done before." Yuen looked exasperated and suddenly jumped from his chair and bolted outside.

"Where is he going?" A.C. lifted up his baseball cap.

"I dunno. We'll find out soon enough. In the meantime, let's just keep working on this." I was scribbling down changes.

Bosco H. C. Poon

"I'm just gonna go get myself a sandwich. Anyone want anything?" Abraham got up from his desk and went upstairs to the kitchen.

After 15 minutes, Yuen came back with a basketball. "A.C., let's play some ball. You go outside to shoot. I'll record the sound of your dribble. Let's make a beat out of it."

"Okay! That's a cool idea. It's about time you guys let me out of this room!" A.C. jumped up from the couch with a big smile.

"Hey, that's brilliant. Let's do it!" I put down my pen and went outside with them.

"Hey, hey, where are you guys going? Wait for me!" Abraham chased after us with a half-eaten sandwich in his hand while trying to talk with his mouth full.

There were always these fun moments during our song production. Whenever we came up with an innovative idea we'd be bursting with excitement. But there were many days when we were frustrated with the slow progress. Putting a song together so that it sounds professional and stands out is not easy. You can't force creativity. It has a mind of its own. Whenever it wants to, it'll flow spontaneously. Other times, it will hide and not be found.

This was a big struggle for me because I knew time was my unvanquishable foe. I looked at the calendar every day. My time was running short. I wanted to generate as much material as I could while I was still a free man since I might rapidly lose this privilege.

"Hey, you still remember the reason I asked you to join us, right?" I pulled Bonny aside while everyone was sketching ideas for an album cover.

"Of course; you said I had great potential in this industry as an agent and in management," she replied with a nod.

"And you can help me look after this company ... those guys in there, ya know, while I'm not here?"

"Well, you don't know for sure you're going to prison yet, right?"

"I'll find out next week. Anyway, just in case. Listen to me. The speed we're going is not good. It's not fast enough. If I lose my case, I'll be gone in an instant. I want you to promise me you'll do your best to manage this team and help them succeed."

"That's a big ask, Boz. I'm only a student. I'm still just learning, and these guys are pretty unmanageable sometimes."

"I know. But trust me, you can do it. You have it in you. I can see your potential. You have great management skills. Use them. Don't forget your dreams, Bonny."

"Yes, to be a great artist agent and have my own agency one day. Okay, I trust you. Don't you worry. I'll do my very best. I won't disappoint you!"

"Thank you. I appreciate it. Really."

I gave this production all the energy I had, and it slowly became part of me—the focus of my existence. No matter how rough of a day I had in the courthouse, when I came to the studio and saw the team, I could shake it off and keep going. Day after day, I laboured to make sure my dream would survive even if I could not be there for the whole process. We were going to make it big in the music industry. "*Am3ition,* yeah that's it! Ambition with a 3 instead of the b in the middle. That should be our name. A.C., Abraham, what do you think?" Yuen eagerly scrawled the name, in all of its dyslexic genius, across the whiteboard.

"Okay, okay, that sounds legit. What's the 3 in the middle stands for?" A.C. asked.

"A.C., Abraham, and any feature artists. 3 a's," Yuen answered.

"Ahhh—okay, I get it! Why not take it a little further? How about accept, absorb, and act on the message of our ambition," I suggested.

"Oooh, cool. I like that. Yes!" Abraham's eyes lit up.

"Sold!" A.C. agreed.

"Yeah, finally we have a name. Now we can shoot the album cover and get the graphic design finished." We were all very pumped up.

Inside Backstage hair salon in Richmond, A.C. and Abraham were getting their hair cut and coloured. The shop was closed for the entire afternoon for our album cover photo shoot. We had a sponsorship relationship with Backstage because of my working relationship with the owners on previous projects. Their whole team was there to assist us.

"Angela, you understand the look I am trying to achieve, right?" We had spent about an hour the night before planning for the day.

"Sure thing, Boz. Don't worry. You're going to love it." She was blow-drying Abraham's hair while giving instruction to other stylists for A.C.'s hair.

"Okay, Heidi. We need to highlight all those muscle groups. Let's use the airbrush to give definition to the chest, abs, shoulders, biceps, and triceps. Make them pop out." Sadly, though we were not in terrible shape, neither were we ripped, so we used the airbrush to, well, make ourselves look a little more cut.

"Got it. Leave it to me." Heidi was connecting the airbrush to the compressor.

"Do we have the wardrobe ready?"

"Yes, yes, everything is set right here." Bonny was putting all the clothes for the set together out on the table.

"Lights are ready, backdrop is set. Everything looks good. The photographer knows what he is doing … as usual. All right, boys and girls, listen up! We have four hours to work on this set. We are very grateful to Backstage for all their support. The clock is ticking, and we have a really tight schedule. We can't afford any mistakes or delays, so let's stick to the plan. If you're not sure about something, make sure to ask, all right? Let's get to it!"

I was directing that day. Yuen and all the rest of the team were sweating over the details, making sure the whole thing would go smoothly. Everyone was working really hard. There was no money in it for us at this stage, but we all had great ambitions and gave it our best. It was the last project I worked on with these guys before my trial came to a close.

CHAPTER 7
SO IT BEGAN

"Get me out of here! Get me out of here!"—the chorus would cycle through my head over and over. I'm sure all courtrooms are intimidating, but the Supreme Court of Canada is particularly intimidating when you're a kid accused of kidnapping and extortion. My palms were constantly soaking wet. The worst was when the judge would turn her attention to me, sternly glaring down from her bench while everyone else in the courtroom stared along with her. This was not the kind of limelight I had anticipated; it was one without any applause or adulation—quite the opposite. I felt like a soldier in a bunker constantly being shelled by the enemy—in this case, the prosecution. Their condemnation was relentless, and they painted the most ghastly image of my character.

Mind you, I was very much guilty of collaborating in the crime, but I was not quite the monster I was portrayed to be. They dealt blow after blow, and even though my counsel was doing his best to defend the remaining shreds of my honour, the whole thing took a terrible toll on me. When the Crown would finish its assault, the jury, seated on my right, would convene to discuss the case. This would send me into another tailspin of anxiety.

What are they saying about me? Do they really believe all this? If they knew me, they'd know I'm not such a bad guy. I just got mixed up with the wrong people. Oh, I wish I could just go back and hang out with a different crowd.

I ran to the restroom and vomited all over the counter, missing the sink. After splashing some water on my face, I looked in the mirror. I was trying to look my best by wearing a suit and tie, but I felt like the guy staring back at me was like a skeleton—dead man's bones—someone I no longer even recognized.

Bosco H. C. Poon

Who am I? What have I become? Where is BOZ? What am I now ... am I just a criminal?

"Mr. Poon, are you all right? You look pretty shaken." My lawyer had poked his head in the door of the men's restroom. I tried to flush the stench of my vomit down the sink.

"I really wanna tell you I'm fine, but I'm not. When is this gonna end? I can't stand it anymore. Two and a half years. This is sucking the life right out of me. Enough already." I leaned against the wall on my raised forearm, panting. I felt faint.

"I know, I know it's tough, but you need to hang in there. I'm doing my best to help you, and I think we have a good chance." To his credit, he was quite determined to calm me down and help me through the ordeal.

"You think? I hope you're right. But I'm not too hopeful given what's going on in there. Why are they withholding the evidence in my favour from the jury? They're never going to see my side of the story. Blade and the other guys went to the witness stand to testify against me ... against *me*! This is so ridiculous! He was actually pointing his finger at me saying I was one of them. Me and them? We're not the same! And worst of all I'm not allowed to even say a word to defend myself. Can't you do something about this?"

"You have to trust me. I know what I'm doing. None of Blade's testimony really matters. He's the bad guy, and everyone knows it. His words won't carry much weight. What's most important is that you have favour in the jury's eyes. And that is what you have. I can sense it." He tried to comfort me.

"I hope you're right ... my parents have spent more than the value of a new Mercedes convertible on me in legal fees, and there's almost nothing left in their bank account. If this thing goes down, my family is really hooped." At that stage in my life, the value I placed on everything was still measured against the superficial and frivolous—hence the benchmarking of my parents expenditures against a luxury car. That's how my mind worked then, but in all of these trials, this superficiality and immaturity were gradually being purged from me.

We made our way back to the courtroom. I looked over to my very distressed father standing at the entrance. That poor man had been there with me for every single hearing. This was such a humiliation for my parents, but they showed their unwavering love for me. My mom did not come to court. It was too much for her. So, for over two years, my dad sat patiently by himself in the public gallery. Some days he was accompanied by reporters, who dutifully recorded the case's progress on scratch pads. Other days there was no one but him.

The lawyers' uniforms reminded me of something out of the Harry Potter movies. They debated back and forth all day long, nitpicking about the minute details of each sequence of events, while the stern and emotionless judge presided from her bench. This torment was my daily routine. I felt like I was teetering on a cusp between two opposite fates and my fall could be in either direction. One was dark, descending into an abyss of misery; the other was filled with the light of freedom and hope.

Risen From Prison

Outside the courtroom, I filled up my time with tasks and projects that on one hand distracted me but on the other also exhausted me. That was my mechanism to cope with the pain and shame constantly bubbling up from within.

By doing everything from hairdressing at Backstage Salon to practising my makeup techniques at the Blanche Macdonald Centre to establishing a music production company with my friends to running errands for Allie, I kept myself distracted and as emotionless as possible. In retrospect I was totally lost, but I continued to furiously cast my nets at my career aspirations, hoping somehow I would catch some little treasure—a trinket to further distract me. All of it was vapour.

The annoyingly familiar high-pitched *nyi-nyi-nyi-nyi* of the alarm clock filled my bedroom at 7:00 a.m. I did not need to snooze it. I had been lying awake worrying for hours anyway. After having a smoke on the balcony, I put on my usual drab suit. Downstairs, my parents were already waiting in the living room. The house was deadly silent. Everybody looked teary-eyed. I was trying to choke out something to comfort them, but nothing came out. The corner of my eyes caught the calendar on the kitchen counter—November 14, 2006. Not a good day for Bosco Poon.

Ding dong! The doorbell broke the silence and awkwardness in the house. Bonny, Allie, Yuen, and A.C. came to escort my family to the Vancouver Supreme Court. We were driving in two cars. The rest of the team and some of my relatives were going to meet us at the courthouse. It was the day of my sentencing, and everyone knew what was going on except for one person—my grandpa. He was 84 years old, blind in one eye and deaf in one ear. Because he was elderly and somewhat infirm, my family didn't want to stress him out with my situation. Throughout the trial, we told him I was in college and going to classes each day. There were many days when he would compliment my suit before I headed out. Today was the same. "Look at how smart looking you are. You've grown up so much. I'm very proud of you. Now be good and study hard in Toronto, okay?" That's the line we had fed him. I was going off to Toronto to study. That way if I did not return home, there would be an explanation. My grandpa gave me a big hug at the door.

"I'll work hard. I won't disappoint you, Grandpa. Please take care of your health. I'm sure I will see you soon." I clenched my fists and felt a lump rising in my throat. I managed to hold back my tears.

"We gotta go. We have to get you there on time." Bonny sighed.

"Okay, thanks." I gave my grandpa a kiss on the cheek.

Yuen patted me on the shoulder as A.C. opened the door.

"No matter what, B, we'll always be here for you! Just promise us one thing—please come back in one piece. Hopefully we'll be successful in building our little empire, and it will be waiting for you the day you get out!"

"Thanks, I'll do my best." I nodded as I offered a half-hearted smile.

Bosco H. C. Poon

As I stepped into the passenger's side of Yuen's car, I had a flashback of the day I had been convicted about five months earlier.

"He's to blame too! He was with us for the whole thing. He's one of us! He gave us the house. No one put a gun to his head. He went right along with it." Blade shook his finger at me.

"We have concluded that Mr. Poon is guilty of all charges, Your Honour," a representative of the jury announced.

"Mr. Poon, you have been found guilty and you are charged on a four-count indictment with conspiracy to kidnap, conspiracy to extort, kidnapping with intent to confine, and extortion. You'll be scheduled on a separate date for your sentencing. Based on your consistent co-operation in this trial, I hereby grant you a period of three months' preparation before your imprisonment," the judge said calmly. Drops of sweat rolled down between my shoulders and pooled in the small of my back where my white dress shirt now clung to me.

When I finally gathered my thoughts and looked up, I realized that we were already halfway across the Granville Street Bridge—only five minutes from the Supreme Court. What was originally supposed to be a three-months' preparation time had turned out to be about five months due to delays in the judicial system. No matter now. The extra two months were gone, and here I was. I gave my head a shake, hoping that this terrible memory could somehow be flung off. Gazing at the skyline, I knew that I wouldn't see the fresh snow on the trees of the North Shore mountains again for a long time.

We followed closely behind my parents' car to the underground parking. I flipped over the lapel of my suit and put on my big black Elvis-style sunglasses to try to conceal my identity. Reporters had been clamouring for a good headshot of me throughout my trial, but I was always prepared for them. Ironically, in my budding, albeit brief, career as a pop music artist, I had dreamed of being pursued by paparazzi and had practised what I'd do to avoid them. I had no idea that my self-taught skills of photographer-evasion would be put to the test in such a humiliating way. Fortunately, none of them were able to get a good front-facing headshot. At one point, a reporter was getting so frustrated he yelled at me through the elevator doors as they closed, "You can't hide from me, pal. I will get your head at all costs. I promise!" With that warning in mind, I expected that this guy and some others would do their very best to get it today because this would be their last chance.

As expected, the moment we descended the ramp into the parkade, a reporter ran to my parents' car. Realizing that I was not in it, he immediately flew to Yuen's car as I was just stepping out.

"Hey, hey! Get out of here!" A.C. tried to beat him back. Shielding my face with my hand and looking down to the concrete below, all I could hear was camera flashes as I found my way by following Yuen's feet to the door.

My mom and Allie elbowed their way to create a path for us up ahead. When I got inside, I raced to the elevator, banging repeatedly on the button. When the elevator finally arrived, my mom urged me in and closed the doors behind us. She and I went up to the lobby alone while the others waited. She gripped my arm without uttering a word, and if she could have, I think she'd have never let go — I was her only child. She could not hear it, but inside I was begging her forgiveness: "Forgive me, Mom. Forgive me. Please, forgive me."

It was safe to take off my sunglasses. My parents, uncle, aunt, girlfriend, company team, and some close friends — altogether more than twenty people — came to support me and bid their farewell. I gave each one of them a hug before we headed into the courtroom. It was tense, and I was brimming with anxiety, making me feel as if I could hardly catch my breath. Some of my friends were already getting emotional, and I could hear their muffled sobs behind me. There was nothing they could say. I closed my eyes and took a deep breath, then took my place to hear the sentence.

After Judge Sunni Stromberg-Stein delivered some opening formalities in her authoritative but monotonous tone, she turned her attention to me specifically.

"Mr. Poon, you have committed a very serious crime." She paused to let that sink in and calmly moved her wire rim glasses down the bridge of her nose, looking at me over the brim of her lenses. "Your role in this operation may seem insignificant in comparison to your co-accused. However, your involvement and contribution to these crimes are just as concerning as those of the other young men. Without your supportive role in affording access to the home in which this played out, the kidnapping would have never been successful. You must understand the consequences of your actions. We, as the justice system of Canada, need to send a clear and unequivocal message to the public about how we handle these serious offences. This country will never tolerate behaviours such as yours. Therefore, I am issuing you a sentence of twelve years in prison." The gavel dropped, and the room echoed.

Time seemed to freeze while the words "twelve years" played over and over in my mind. A shroud of silence seemed to engulf me. Everything around me vanished from my attention. I now know that this is what they call "depersonalization" in psychology. The flurry of courtroom activities, the wailing of my mother, and the sobbing of my friends seemed somehow distant, as if I was looking at the scene the wrong way down a pair of binoculars. I was an observer of a distant silent film being played back at one-tenth speed. *"Twelve years."* Silence.

I'm not sure how long I remained unaware of the chaos around me. Maybe it was only a few seconds, but it seemed a long time. Then I felt something again: an ascending numbness in my legs, as if I was falling into ice-cold quicksand. I willed myself to look up toward my family and friends. Their faces, still in slow motion, were filled with disbelief and anguish. But this was not a film or dream. It was happening.

"Hey, buddy, we have to go." A guard broke me out of my time warp, putting his hand on my shoulder. With all my loved ones staring at me, I asked him to spare me the indignity of being handcuffed in front of them. He agreed. I struggled to my feet.

Bosco H. C. Poon

My legs were not obeying my commands. I grabbed the railing and pulled myself up, trying my best to just place one foot in front of the other. I felt as if someone had tied cement blocks to my ankles. Shuffling along, I willed myself forward, holding back my emotions and inching my way to the exit. My jaw clenched and the light dimmed as we entered the corridor. My legs gradually started to behave. I acknowledged to myself that I had heard correctly and that life would never be the same. I was now a prisoner.

I glanced back once more to smile at my loved ones and, with that, entered a world of grey bricks.

"Stay strong, son! We'll get the lawyer to contact you. Okay?" my dad called to me down the hall. His voice cracked.

The clanging of my chains echoed back from the narrow brick hallways of the Vancouver jail as I was led in shackles. The hall would dim as we passed under the characteristic flicker of fluorescent lamps needing replacement. This added to the creepy horror-movie ambience.

A solid metal door, rusty bunk beds, and the stench of stale urine greeted me as I returned to jail, but this time, it would not be a brief visit.

Later that day, a bus came to take me to the North Fraser Pretrial Centre. I was scheduled to stay there until my eventual transfer to Regional Reception and Assessment Centre (RRAC). On the loading deck where I was chained up with the other five inmates waiting to get on the bus, one guy quickly knelt down to pick up a few cigarette butts, probably left by the guards, and enthusiastically shoved them into his pocket. Looking at his smile and the pathetic way in which cigarette butts represented a treasure to him, I resigned myself that I might soon be similarly excited by similarly insignificant mercies. I determined that I had better get used to people and things like this.

At North Fraser, through the tiny dirt-splotched window of my cell, I saw a gauntlet of heavy barbed wire fences. *No chance of escape*, I thought. The window was so small that I couldn't see anything besides those fences. Graffiti of all different styles and colours disfigured the walls—the legacy of anger, frustration, sadness, and even evil of those who preceded me. I read the messages one by one. I had lots of time.

"F*ck it all," one chicken scratch said.

Then another: "I'm done, there's no hope!"

"I want vengeance! Kill, I want to kill."

"Take my soul! Take my soul!"

I was hypnotized by the narrative of enmity, violence, hopelessness, and rage that each line conveyed. On the far right, the scrawl of a demonic-looking skeleton caught my attention and glared squarely back at me. *Pretty lame drawing*, I thought.

I stared at the crude artwork for a while, but as I did something about it seemed to gradually change. This thing was not just a drawing anymore. *My mind's playing tricks on me.* But my dismissiveness did not alter what I was feeling and seeing—that somehow this drawing was alive. *Hey, wait. Did its mouth just move? Is it looking at me? What the heck? Why do those eyes look so dark?* In deep, guttural tones something in my head sneered, "There is no hope … no hope … no hope." At that moment I was completely gripped by fear as if fear had come to life in the netherworldly scrawl of a former inmate. Darkness seemed to open up like a cloud of thick black smoke behind it. I felt physically overpowered and fell backward, losing my balance like a drunk and falling sideways onto the bed. *What is going on?*

Sweat dripping from my forehead spilled into my eyes, stinging them and blurring my vision. Suddenly, I could not catch my breath—like something was choking me. The line between reality and my fears blurred in a waking nightmare. I writhed around the bed trying to get ahold of myself and pull air into my lungs. The cloud of darkness grew and seemed to swallow me into a lightless vortex of contempt, fear, and emptiness. Down, down, down I went, into a spiral of spiritual darkness manifesting in the physical realm. *Am I dying? What's happening? Where am I going?*

I opened my eyes once more to find that the sweat had cleared for a moment. My focus fell immediately on three small words I had not noticed, words that stood in stark but quiet contrast to the cacophony of blasphemies that littered the bricks. They were written in pencil on the opposite wall, illuminated by a ray of the small fluorescent bedside lamp.

"GOD help me."

Suddenly everything negative retreated like filthy water disappearing down a drain. My mind calmed, and the room seemed to brighten. The cell was suddenly quiet, very quiet—the kind of quiet of a calm winter night when there is a gentle, heavy snowfall. But through the silence I heard a very small voice speaking to me from a distance: "No. It is not over yet. There is still hope."

Trying to wrap my head around what had just happened, whether it was a waking dream or reality, I put my left hand against the wall and sat up in the bed. My heart was still pounding, and questions appeared in my head as if someone else placed them there: *God and the devil? Good and evil? What just happened?* It felt like I was a rope in some kind of cosmic tug of war between good and evil—two forces that my physical eyes couldn't fully perceive but my other senses could definitely feel.

———

I had a Roman Catholic upbringing. My whole family had been very devout prior to our immigration. I was an altar boy who helped the priest during mass back in our parish in Hong Kong. After we moved to Canada, due to the culture shock and the language barrier, we stopped going to church and slowly lost sight of our faith. In my teenage years, media tainted my perception, and my beliefs were influenced by different religions and philosophies. Over time, I became extremely superstitious and turned to various forms of fortune-telling for advice. Every morning I read the daily horoscopes. I read books about the Chinese zodiac and sought knowledge from predictions related to my sign. The anxieties of living in a foreign country had pushed me to find ways to buy and seek my fortune.

After the unexpected letdown by Warner Music Taiwan, my parents took me to see a well-known local feng shui master. "You have a calling to become a star in the realm of entertainment. That's the path of your destiny. However, for some reason you seem to have missed a few good opportunities. But don't worry; there's still hope. In order to get you back on that path, we have to increase luck's attraction to you." He was performing calculations from my birthdate with his hands. "First things first, we have to give you a new Chinese name, a new identity to have the right balance of all elements in your life. This practice is very common. Most artists in Asia have a well-calculated stage name to enhance their chances of success on the path of celebrity."

"Yes, we understand! We know how important it is to have the right name. Please help our son, master. He needs to have success getting into the music world," my mom said anxiously.

"Well now, the name is just the first step. It won't be enough. The 'qi' of your house will also play a big role. He needs to sleep in the perfect spot where he can absorb the positive energy, while the set-up of his surroundings must be arranged to deflect the negative energy. We'll need to do a thorough analysis of your house, then make a proper design for the interior."

"Okay, you're right! Let's fix up the house as well. We'll do whatever it takes. He's been through a lot. How much does this cost?"

"It's not an easy job. I have to put a lot of thought into this, because your son's success relies on it. Normally, I would charge $500 or more for a new name. Since you're doing the home environmental improvement as well, I'm going to give you a package price. Prep work plus one hour of on-site analysis is $1,000. I'll give you a 30 percent discount for the name, so altogether $1,350. Now if you require more of my service in other areas, I'll give you more discounts. Also, if you pay cash and don't require a receipt, then there's no tax."

"Hmm ... okay ... that's not cheap. But we came all the way out here to get your help, so we can't come away empty-handed. We've got to get this done. We don't need a receipt, and I can go to the bank and get cash."

"All right. Let me schedule you in. Please fill out this form and provide as much detail as you can about your son's situation. I'll start my calculation for the name."

A couple of days later he called my mom and gave me my new Chinese name. To be honest, it didn't sound very cool, so I wasn't very enthusiastic. It cost us $350 for a weird name that no fan would like and $1,000 for someone to come to our house with his "bagua" to detect spirits and energy for an hour. Seemed to me like he was making easy money. Perhaps more absurd is that we actually believed that all this hocus-pocus would bring us success. A few weeks later he gave us a statue-shopping list. We ended up spending another few thousands just to get statues of humans, dragons, and nian beasts in bronze. From my perspective, all this accomplished was to creep me out because strange faces were staring at me all the time. No "positive energy" came my way. As a matter of fact, my life ended up a complete mess. From the confines of my cell, I concluded that all of the superstitious practices didn't buy me any luck at all.

> **"And do not let your people practice fortune-telling, or use sorcery, or interpret omens, or engage in witchcraft, or cast spells, or function as mediums or psychics, or call forth the spirits of the dead. Anyone who does these things is detestable to the LORD." (Deut. 18:10–12 NLT)**

And so my twelve-year sentence began. I lost track of time in my cell. There was nothing to do except lie on the bed. Two weeks passed before some prison guards came to shackle me and escort me to an armoured vehicle. It was a whole day's journey travelling to different pit stops before I ended up at the federal inmates training centre—RRAC, in Abbotsford, BC. It was specifically designed to evaluate new inmates entering the federal prison system. Since my criminal status had been upgraded from provincial to federal, the colour of my inmate suit was now changed to navy blue and dark green. My name was also replaced by an FPS number—847631E.

Snowflakes slowly fell from the sky outside my new cell. The cold air blew in through a gap of the window. The thin blanket I was issued was not enough to keep me warm, and so I slept fitfully, shivering and repositioning all night. The next morning, I woke up with a terrible headache and a sore throat so bad I couldn't even swallow. Out of compassion, a female guard took pity on me and came into my cell to teach me the ins and outs of the paper-based request system used in the prison. She grabbed a form and helped me fill it out to request a visit from the nurse. I thanked her profusely. As she was locking up my cell door, she said, "Hang in there; you'll get used to it."

Twenty-four hours had passed before the on-site clinic received my written request. It took them another day to respond. Eventually, on the third morning two armed guards came to escort me to see a nurse. It was a five-minute walk from the living unit. After passing through gate after gate, we arrived at a two-storey building. From the outside it seemed like a psychiatric hospital, because there was an inmate screaming maniacally from the second-floor window, which kind of gave me the goosebumps. Walking through the door to the reception area, I saw a bunch of inmates, all looking sicker than me, waiting in line. After an hour wait, it was finally my turn. A nurse came, took me to a room, and gave me a three-minute once-over.

Bosco H. C. Poon

Then she turned to me. "It's nothing too serious. You've just got a bad cold. There's nothing we can do with it here. We're not even allowed to give you Tylenol. Just drink a lot of water, and you'll get better."

"What? How come? You mean there's nothing you can do? That's it? You're just gonna let me suffer? I can't swallow anything, and besides, where am I supposed to get extra water to drink?"

"I'm sorry, you'll just have to drink the water from the tap in your cell. Just press it and let the water run for a few minutes. Then it should be drinkable. You'll get used to it." She sent me back to the guards who were standing at the post.

It took another five days before I felt better. Between the mediocre food and feeling sick, I was getting pretty skinny. However, I did listen to the nurse and tried to drink more water. The pipes in the prison were pretty old, and the water tasted pretty horrible, but nothing bad happened. The nurse was right. I got used to it. I also adapted to the cold nights. All I had to do was wear my jacket and shoes to bed.

CHAPTER 8
BEHIND THE BARS

"Lock-up! Lock-up time! All inmates return to your cells immediately for count! Return to your cells immediately for count!" The PA system was so loud, I swear it could wake the dead.

The call for the head count came while I was standing in the telephone lineup. My heart sank, knowing that I wouldn't be able to get ahold of my family that night. With a disappointment now familiar, I dragged myself back to my cell. As I climbed the stairs to the second floor, the lights in the hallway started to turn off one by one, indicating that guards were coming to lock our doors.

"Count time! Come on now, guys, hurry up! Back to your cells, *now!*" Two guards were making a racket by hitting their batons against the iron staircase railing, sending clangs throughout the echoey concrete halls. I hustled my way back, not wanting any trouble.

The head count was a nightly ritual. After they stopped at the door and checked me off the list, they would lock me into my cell. My cell was about the size of a bathroom. My metal bed frame had a thin foam mattress on top. A metal toilet and sink unit were located right next to the bed, with a metal mirror screwed to the wall above. There was a push button on the sink to release water that worked like a drinking fountain. Across from the sink was a metal desk attached to the wall, which I could use for reading or writing. On the ceiling there was a utilitarian fluorescent light casting the usual dim, cold light. Across from the metal cell door was a window with bars where cold air constantly poured in. I spent a lot of time gazing out this window.

On the outside people were enjoying Starbucks peppermint lattes. Not us. No gingerbread houses. No Lindor chocolate balls. No roasted turkey with cranberry sauce. No Moet and Chandon champagne. No stockings above the fireplace. No tree, no tinsel, no presents, and no carols playing in the background.

Right at midnight, I gingerly took out a can of C-plus Orange Burst I'd bought from canteen and the fruit cream cookie I'd saved from dinner to celebrate my first Christmas behind bars. As that cookie passed my lips, I closed my eyes and imagined myself standing in the middle of a family Christmas party. Children were running across the living room while family members talked to each other, wine glasses in their hands. Colourful lights were shining through the needles of a fir tree while heaps of presents elaborately decorated with ribbons and bows lay beneath. "O Holy Night" played softly in the background. What a beautiful picture. I hummed the hymn—ironically clutching a can of orange soda.

With all my heart I was trying to wish that picture into reality and erase the depressing grey reality of prison life. How I longed for my family. I didn't have the strength to open my eyes. It all seemed too cruel. With no one else looking at me, it was safe to get emotional, so while the last of the cookie cream melted off my tongue, tears welled up and plopped out of the corners of my eyes onto my shirt. The loneliness was overwhelming, and on Christmas, it was naturally worse. I fell back on my bed, sobbing.

My memories of RRAC are of the concrete and the monotony. Everything I previously enjoyed was gone. No more internet. No music. No movies. No more comfy bed to sleep on. No freedom to go to a friend's place. My world had become one of "no longer," "no more," and "cannot." It was then that I realized how much I had taken for granted the many blessings I enjoyed as a free citizen. I'd been so fortunate without even realizing it. *Do the people buying hot chocolate and drinking it at English Bay know what a privilege they have?*

The rigid structure of our days and all the rules and regulations reminded me of going back to kindergarten—except a way more dangerous and dark version of kindergarten. There was no access to email, so any correspondence had to be with paper and pen—an art form my generation has lost. So, I had to get some stationary from the canteen. In prison, we were not allowed to carry any cash with us. Our money was tracked in a paper ledger in the prison system, recorded under our FPS number. To pay for things, we would fill out a paper form to transfer it from our ledger to the prison ledger. Once a week we could go to the canteen to purchase personal hygiene items, stamps, stationery, and snacks from the sparsely stocked shelves. With no money per se, these items became the de facto currency of the prison, used for gambling or drug debts. It was quite normal to see inmates using cans of tuna as poker chips.

Once we had all the tools needed to write and send a letter, we usually had to wait a few days to mail it. There were only two days of the week when our letters would be picked up to be transferred to the so-called V&C (Visits and Correspondence) department for screening before mailing. For this reason, local mail would take approximately one and a half weeks before arriving to the recipient because of the backlog in the screening process. While this may not seem like a huge inconvenience, I had become so accustomed to instant back-and-forth communication that I found the letter-writing process intensely frustrating. Getting my family members and friends onto my authorized telephone and visitor lists was equally annoying. After picking up the appropriate application forms, I had to send them to my loved ones along with accompanying instructions. The forms required them to obtain a passport photo, and after returning all the necessary paperwork, it would be another week or two before V&C would approve them. When my friend or family member had finally been added to my telephone list, I would then be permitted to call them on the prison phone system at a rate of 50 cents per minute, which, as you can imagine, added up quickly. My savings ledger was such that it would not survive many phone calls.

If my loved ones got approved for visitation, they were required to call V&C during their brief operating hours and log their request two to three days prior. Even if they called, there was no guarantee we'd have the visitation granted, and, of course, there was always the curveball of an unexpected lockdown. It was not unusual for visitors to get turned away at the gates. You might call it a process of "hurry up and wait"—once you scrambled to do your bit, you had to wait and wait and wait for the prison to let you in. Not surprisingly, many of my friends lost their patience and gave up on keeping in touch with me, and in time, most of my connections with the outside world faded from existence.

There were even more humiliating aspects to the restrictions placed on us. We were assigned to a living unit within the big building. Gates separated each of the units. During movement times, the gates would open, but we would be required to stay behind the yellow lines delineating the regions separated by the gates.

Guards constantly monitored our movements from the duty office, which was nicknamed "the bubble," a booth situated in the space connecting the units to one another. If we wanted to request anything from the guards, we had to wait behind the yellow lines for permission to approach, and if we violated this rule, we would get sent straight back to our cells. Everything required permission—even getting some extra toilet paper. On one occasion, for example, I had developed some pretty bad diarrhea, presumably from the food. The answer to my request for extra toilet paper for my *loose* bowel movements was a *firm* "no" because I had already been issued a roll that week. Holding my gut, I contemplated the available alternatives. Maybe I could find some scraps of paper. Luckily my good neighbour overheard the conversation and was kind enough to bail me out. Not all inmates were so kind.

"Hey Chinaman, hold up!" An inmate approached me outside the shower.

"What's up?" I paused from drying my hair with my towel.

"Did you just blow your nose in there?" He walked up to me threateningly.

"Maybe. I was having a shower. I don't remember. What's the big deal?" I was confused.

"Do *not* blow your nose in the shower!" he yelled.

"All right, buddy, chill out ... I never heard that rule before. Is that new? It's hard to keep up with these rules, but all right, I'll take notice." I tried to talk him down.

"Don't let me hear you do that again in there!" he yelled, and he walked away angrily.

So, in practice, there were two sets of rules, those from Corrections Canada, which were more or less predictable, and the *unwritten* code of conduct from the prison population, which varied from inmate to inmate and hour to hour with their respective moods. It was impossible to please everyone. I had to learn the balance and be careful not to cross the lines of either. The monotony, close quarters, and lack of freedom inevitably led to strained relations.

Guys would fight over almost anything: food, laundry, telephone, card games, showers, pillows, clothes—and most importantly, cigarettes and drugs. It didn't take me long to hear stories of how contraband materials were smuggled in, sometimes with surprising degrees of sophistication. Internally, inmates even managed to brew homemade alcohol with packaged coffee sugar and leftover fruit. What inmates managed to accomplish despite the constant monitoring never ceased to amaze and scare me. After all, I could easily end up on the wrong side of someone's shank if I made a wrong move or ended up in the wrong place at the wrong time.

I loved looking at the thick green grass on the other side of the fence—the way it flourished all on its own, it represented freedom to me. But I could never touch it. I could never lie down on a warm spring day and relish the distinctive smell of moist soil and a tended lawn. My daily practice during lock-up was to gaze longingly out the window to the nearby fields and imagine myself walking barefoot on the cool grass.

Towards the end of February 2007, my three-month assessment period at RRAC was over. I got called to the bubble in the early morning. I was handed a report indicating that my next destination was Mission Institution, a medium-security federal prison in Mission, B.C., and they gave me an hour to pack my things. As I was folding my jail clothes and setting them aside into a clear plastic garbage bag, I looked out the window at my favourite field and wondered what this new place was going to be like and how bad the inevitable hazing I'd receive would be.

About an hour later, two heavily armed guards escorted me to the checkout post. After finishing the paperwork and completing a strip search (another awful humiliating routine), they shackled my wrists and ankles once again. The ankle chain was short to prevent the prisoner from running away. It also had the effect of making me walk like a penguin while the shackles abraded the skin on my ankles.

"Listen. Don't think about your music anymore; you'll never make it! I knew it from the start. It was only just a dream! It's time to wake up now, bro. Face reality: you're just one of us ... one of us ..."

Blade's discouragement at the courthouse before I got my bail rattled around in my head all the time. That was the last time I saw him before our trial began, since he pleaded guilty in the very beginning. It had been a long time, and I still couldn't make his voice go away. Inside the boxy armoured transport wagon, I thought of him and was curious about where he was. I never saw him after he took the witness stand against us and thereby shortened his sentence to six years. He could have been out already if he was lucky enough to get his parole.

Thud ... thud. A speed bump broke my train of thought. Within five minutes the wagon came to a complete stop, the side door was unlocked, and a guard ordered me to step out. We had arrived at Mission Institution. A snowfall started just as my feet hit the ground—a suitable accompaniment to the loneliness I felt inside. Walking towards the administration building, I notice a bunch of inmates staring at me through the fence. I wasn't surprised. There were always sharks ready for a new fish. I was on high alert because inmates could go out of their way to make it hard for new prisoners.

I was assigned to Unit 4 and given a pillow and a blue blanket. I got my first tour of the gauntlet of danger and vices: guys tattooed from their fingers to their face doing chin-ups on a rusty water pipe hanging from the ceiling, drug deals going on under the stairs, poker games in the common area, and, of course, the long tracking stares of everyone as I passed. It felt a bit like walking down Vancouver's East Hastings Street at midnight with hundred dollar bills hanging out of my pockets.

Entering my cell, I met my new cellmate. He had the characteristically distant look I'd seen in addicts, and I concluded that he was likely high and that he might not be an easy guy to live with. Putting my pillow onto my upper bunk bed, I saw grass sticking out from the thin layer of snow on the field through the window. *Grass! They have a full field of grass in this prison!*

At the medium-security prison we had fewer restrictions than we had at RRAC. We had scheduled movement times each day that allowed us to walk to different parts of the prison. I was elated, and this joy overwhelmed any fear I had from being the fresh fish. At the first available opportunity, I hurried outside just for the privilege of walking on the grass—something I could only daydream about at RRAC. I'm not sure what the other prisoners made of me jumping up and down on a snow-covered field. Maybe they thought I was high, too. I could not have cared less. I was treasuring my alone time with the grass. I knelt down to touch it through the dusting of snow and then stroked it like a cat. I had never appreciated nature like this when I was a free man, but now it was such an incredible comfort. I was allowed outside in the snow for the rest of that evening until the PA system jarred us back to our living units for count.

Bosco H. C. Poon

Being an only child, I was pretty spoiled and well cared for by my parents. Even when I was working really hard in entertainment and fashion, I didn't have to do anything terribly physical, so I'd become a bit of a hothouse orchid. That was about to change. In a medium-security penitentiary, inmates work to earn a few dollars a day to buy items for personal hygiene, overpriced phone calls, and a miscellany of prison-approved items. Naturally, the vocations aren't chosen to suit the aptitudes and interest of the inmates, and so I became a dishwasher and a janitor.

This was an institutional kitchen in every way, and there was a lot of work to be done for every meal. The cookware and utensils were gargantuan, and my duty as a modern-day Chinese coolie was to wash out cauldrons that could literally hold three Bosco Poons, mop dirty, slippery floors, and haul enormous stinky bags of garbage to the alleyway dumpsters.

Not being accustomed to this kind of work and having gotten completely out of shape in my three months at RRAC, I was a little slow at first. This led to a fair bit of verbal abuse from the prison staff. Due to my inexperienced handling of cooking waste, my white uniform was always getting filthy from disgusting-smelling garbage runoff. On one occasion when I was taking out the waste cart in the rain, one of the bags broke in the air while I was swinging it into the dumpster. I was suddenly covered in a slimy mess from the waist down, and there was a heap of rotting chicken bones all over the pavement. I frantically swept the filthy waste back into the broken garbage bag with my bare hands. *How did I ever end up in this mess?*

I smelled like a garbage dump in midsummer and rushed into the shower, clothes and all, as soon my work was done. Even after we had washed up and changed into clean outfits, "jail-runners," as we were called, always carried with them an aroma reminiscent of vomit.

Every time we inmate workers entered and exited the kitchen, we were searched by the correctional officers, as kitchen food was forbidden in the living units. At the post, some guards gave us a hard time, humiliating us with nasty jokes in front of the others in the lineup. Some days they would even search you twice just to grind your gears.

"Oh, oh, oh, I think you have something in your pocket. I just have to make sure. You didn't steal anything, did you?" A South Asian guard was making things difficult for me.

"No sir, I don't steal."

"Ha, ha! Hey, guys, did you hear that! He said he doesn't steal. Oh, you so funny, Mista." He and his co-worker were giggling. "Everyone says that, boy, but it's kind of hard to believe. You know what. How about you turn around? I think I need to search you again. You're a pretty sneaky one."

"Okay …" I kept my head down.

"You *sure* you didn't steal anything? I just can't quite believe you."

"No, sir, I didn't. I just want to go back to my cell."

"Whoa whoa whoa! Was that attitude in your voice? Well, you better keep those Kung Fu hands to yourself, Jackie Chan. I'm just doing my job here. And by the way, it's a tough job. Not like you guys just eating and sleeping every day." He laughed out loud with the rest of the officers.

"Yep, that's all we do ..." I bit my tongue and squeezed my fists, something I had become practised at. Otherwise they could easily send me to the hole (segregation) if I reacted in any manner even suggestive of aggression. These kinds of experiences led to mounting inward resentment and even hatred towards some of the guards. Wasn't it enough that I had to go on for 12 years washing giant cauldrons, hauling garbage, eating tasteless food, and being cold at night? Not to mention the constant anxiety of run-ins with other prisoners.

"All right, I'll let you go this time. Lucky you, I couldn't find anything. Back to your cell."

Life seemed to get harder, not easier, as time went on. I'd gone from being an up and coming artist to an outcast in a chain gang. I had been fully disgraced. It seemed there was nothing in that place to help me secure a better future for when I finally got released. Sure, you could get a GED, but there were no opportunities for a decent post-secondary education. You could get some training in the trades, but as one might imagine, none of them suited me terribly well. Of course, there was no access to musical training. Day after day, I just mopped the same floors, dealt with the same cartloads of garbage, and got yelled at by the same prison staff. It didn't matter how hard I tried; my performance never seemed to be good enough, even when I worked overtime. My spirit was losing strength.

One day the supervising stewards were making small talk with us in the kitchen and asked me to share my aspirations. I was foolish enough to tell them about my music career—a decision I instantly regretted. Staring at my dirty kitchen outfit, one of them held his gut and laughed uproariously, mocking me like Blade had done.

"Come on, you ain't serious, are you? You're a f*cking criminal! You have no music future! What a joke. *You* performing on the stage? Gimme a break. Do me a favour, go perform with that mop and bucket. Tell you what. You can pretend it's a mike stand, and we can be your fans."

This was extremely hard to swallow, but deep down inside the repeated criticism had me convinced too. Maybe I'd end up in this kind of job for good. After all, by the time I got out, opportunities like the ones I'd enjoyed before would be long gone. *This might very well be my destiny.*

As soon as the clock hit 6:00 a.m., I quietly came down from the upper bunk while my cellmate continued to snore below. Mission Institution had a seniority system. All newbies had to double-bunk with a cellmate. Over time our names got moved up the seniority list as inmates moved out, and then we could request a single cell. Putting on my clean blue institutional clothes, I used the palm-size mirror above the sink to shave and fix my hair. Today, for a change, I wanted to look decent. When the cell door was finally unlocked an hour later, I ran towards the phone booth and inserted my identification access card. I dialed the number, and someone picked up on the other side. "Son, son, is it you?"

"Yes, Mom, it's me," I replied.

"*Happy birthday*, dear! I'm so glad that you could call. I love you so much, honey." My mom gave me a kiss over the phone.

"Thanks, Mom. Love you too! Is Dad still in bed?"

"Ha, yes, he is. Do you want me to get him?"

"Nah, it's okay. Let him sleep. Tell him that I called, and I miss him."

"He misses you too. So tell me, what are you going to do today?"

"I don't know … just gonna take it easy, I guess. There's not much to do here beside washing dishes in the kitchen." I sighed.

"Oh, I so wish I could get you a cake. Anyway, are you planning to call any of your friends? Call them. It'll make you feel better."

"Only couple of them have been approved to be on my phone list. Besides, it costs quite a bit. I don't know if I have enough in my account."

"Okay, well, maybe at least give Allie a call. I'm sure you want to hear her voice." She was trying to cheer me up.

"Uh … I'll try … but she hasn't been picking up the phone too much lately." I felt a bit upset since Allie hadn't taken my calls for about a week.

"All right, well, you're a big boy. You'll know what to do. I know it's tough, but try to enjoy the day. It's your special day!"

"Okay! I'll call you again soon. Bye, Mom. Love ya."

It was my first birthday behind bars, and it was completely demoralizing. Even though talking to Mom encouraged me, as soon as I hung up the phone I returned to my feelings of utter gloom. Further, I didn't have the courage to tell her that my relationship with Allie seemed to be deteriorating. Maybe I just didn't want her to worry.

Maintaining my relationship with Allie was getting tough. I couldn't afford to call her every day because of the phone rates. When I did manage to call her, I could sense that her heart was growing cooler. I knew that she didn't want me tying her down any more, and to be honest, I didn't blame her. We were living in two different worlds. When you're not present in a person's life, you can't share their triumphs and sorrows, and even if the cost were no object, it would still be so hard for her to get in touch with me. All I could do was record my feelings on paper and send them to her in the mail.

We received letters on Tuesdays and Thursdays at the living unit duty office. Week after week I'd get into the line, full of anticipation of receiving a reply from her, but every week I would come away empty-handed. She was probably too busy with her schooling and social life. It was a one-way commitment, but, of course, I really had nothing else to think about, while she had all the distractions of a college student.

Standing inside the phone booth, I hesitated. Something inside was telling me to make the call despite my apprehension that she would not bother to pick up. In the end I muscled up my courage and dialed the number. *Doo ... doo ... doo ...* No one picked up. The voice inside was telling me to be positive and dial again, so I did. Naively I was expecting a great conversation. I thought she'd at least kiss me over the phone because it was my birthday. The phone rang and rang.

With great disappointment, I stepped out of the living unit and onto the field. I wandered aimlessly and ended up at the door of the chapel. I stepped inside with my head down, and a chaplain came to greet me. I had stopped by for a few services before. When he found out it was my birthday, he offered to give me one phone call to the outside world. Since the inmates' phone system at the time could only called landlines, I wasn't able to call Allie's cellphone. Without hesitation, the chaplain called her for me and passed me the phone. Someone answered the phone immediately, and I blurted out, "Baby, baby, you finally picked up the phone!"

But it was a male voice that answered. He seemed shocked that I even existed and asked in confusion who was I looking for. In complete embarrassment, I choked out, "So-so-sorry, is there a girl named Allie there? I'm calling long distance."

"Why are you calling this early? She's not available, man," he answered cockily.

"Huh? Oh, so this is the right number? Is she in class or something?" I realized the chaplain had not misdialed.

"What do you want? Leave a message, and maybe I'll pass it on to her." The aggression in his voice mounted.

"What ... what do you mean? Are you with her or something?" I didn't understand.

"Why are you asking so many questions? I told you she's not here!" Then I heard a familiar female giggle in the background. I knew that giggle, and now I knew what had happened. I was boiling with anger, but I managed not to hang up in a rage.

"All right then, I see what's going on. Well, please pass on this message to her. Her boyfriend in prison is looking for her. And you better pass this message to her loud and clear, whoever you are. If not, I'll find someone else to do so. By the way, my name is BOZ! Nice to meet you!" I then slammed the phone down in rage.

The chaplain was a little shocked by my reaction. I apologized to him for my anger and explained what was going on. He said he understood. He'd probably been in this situation a few times.

Later that evening, my mom managed to convince Allie to take my call. The first words out of her mouth were "I told him not to answer my phone for me!"

"Excuse me? Do you know what day it is? It's my *birthday*, Allie! The first thing you should say to me is 'Happy Birthday.' Remember, it was *you* who told me to call you first thing on my birthday, and then this happens? Some strange guy you're cheating with answers the phone. Thanks, Allie. This is just great."

"What do you expect me to do? You have a twelve-year sentence! You want me to sit around and wait twelve years for you, Boz? I have a life. What do you want me to do?"

"Finally we're getting to the truth. This is exactly why I said we should break up when I got convicted. I told you it wouldn't work. I told you it would be like that *Prison Break* episode we watched. You were the one who kissed me on my cheek and told me it would never happen to me. And here it is, *happening*. You know what, that's enough. I understand, I do. It was my mistake. I shouldn't have listened to you, and we should have ended this long ago. And you're right. How can I expect you to wait for me? I'm so stupid …"

"I … I … I still love you …"

"You call this love? I think you're confused, girl. You know what … I'm gonna let you go. You're free. Go back to him. I won't bother you two, but I hope I scared him earlier. Now listen. I promise I won't call you anymore. So you don't have to worry about me no more, okay?"

"No, no! I still wanna hear your voice. I wanna know how you're doing. Just call me whenever. I'll try my best to answer."

"No need. Allie, what's the point? Let's not drag this out any longer. Let's not do this to each other anymore. You have my word. I won't call you until I get out. Please take good care of yourself." A stony silence followed, and it didn't seem there would be much more to say.

"All right, I gotta go. Take care, Allie. Goodbye."

I put down the phone, and my relationship with Allie ended. I was devastated. She was the one thing I could focus my hopes on while I was in prison.

I went into the shower and turned on the cold water. It was a kind of self-flagellation for being so naive. Icy streams poured over my face and down my back until I started to shiver. It felt like I'd been punched in the gut. I knelt down and sobbed in the pool of water that had accumulated on the tile, the cold spray still spattering onto my back. Eventually I found my way back to my cell.

―――

One thing after another, bad news after bad news. I couldn't understand why all these terrible things had to happen to me in rapid succession. It felt like I was married to misery. In losing my last valued possession, I saw no more reason to live. I felt like I had fallen into a tar pit: the more I struggled, the deeper I sank. I was ready to stop fighting and just sink below the surface. Hope was gone.

Weeks passed. I slept most of my spare time away. Nobody cared, not even my cellmate. My eyes were continually swollen from crying. I skipped meals because I just wasn't hungry and I couldn't be bothered going to the trouble of lining up. I started to ache all over from lying around so much, and my muscles wasted away.

I didn't want to see or talk to anyone. I stopped believing that there would ever be a brighter day.

> "Look on my right hand and see, For there is no one who acknowledges me; Refuge has failed me; No one cares for my soul." (Ps. 142:4 NKJV)

CHAPTER 9
SANCTUARY

Cough cough cough ... What's going on? I can't breathe.
  A cloud of pungent smoke billowed up from below my bed, yanking me out of my slumber. With eyes half opened, I peered over my mattress and saw my cellmate lighting up another joint. After a few more puffs he too started hacking. His red digital clock radio read 1:30 a.m.—the same time I'd seen him smoking heroin the night before with a small piece of tinfoil and an empty Bic pen shaft.
  "*Cough, cough!* Buddy, did I wake you up? Sorry, man. I didn't mean to. Hey, you want a puff? Go ahead, it'll make you feel better!" He offered his joint to me.
  "You sound just like my old friends. It brings back ... uhhh ... memories. I'm good, thanks. I quit that stuff a long time ago. You go ahead, finish it up, but can you make it quick? I wanna get back to sleep."
  "All right. You're missing out. I'll be done in no time."
  "Yeah, my friends used to say that too." I put my pillow over my face, trying to block the smoke that lingered under the ceiling in front of me.
  "Ha, ha, really? *Cough!* I bet they are cool people."
  "Well, I'm here because of *them*. So, from my point of view they're not all that cool anymore."
  "Oh ... sorry, man. I didn't know. *Cough, cough, cough!*"
  "Doesn't matter. It is what it is now." I turned toward the window and tried to breathe the fresh cold air coming in through the crack. It wasn't easy to live with a drug-addicted cellmate. Every time he offered me some, I was actually kind of tempted to accept and let the drugs take me somewhere else. In the end, I would always turn him down because, although I was depressed, I wasn't stupid. I knew what it would do to me. Besides, the drugs were extremely expensive and probably transported

here in someone's rectum. So, the combination of my dignity and my need for phone money kept me clean in prison. Everything in prison had a cost. My cellmate had constant debts, and other prisoners came looking for him almost every day. Most of the time I would pretend I was sleeping or tell them I didn't know where he was.

Bam bam bam! The next day, another prisoner was beating on my cellmate. "Where's my money? Where is it?"

"Buddy, you gotta chill! It's coming! It's coming! This is canteen day. You'll get it. I promise!"

"I'd better! I want my money. In full. Got it?!"

"Yes, yes. In full."

It was very stressful always being in the middle of drug use and violence. I did my best to stay away from everything and everyone. All I wanted was some tranquility in my free time, but my cellmate's loan sharks made it impossible.

One afternoon I was lying in my bunk with my head under my pillow so people would leave me alone. "Mr. Poon, you all right in there?" Someone was knocking on my cell door.

I didn't answer.

"Hey buddy, you all right? I'm coming in." The guy pulled opened the door. "Knock-knock, anybody home? Hey, there you are."

I turned over and saw a huge muscular Aboriginal man. He was in his mid to late thirties, with tanned skin and a buzz cut. The smile on his face made him seem friendly enough. Reluctantly I croaked out, "Hey … uh … what's up?"

"I'm Pedro. I'm here to check up on you. I know your roommate is not the easiest guy to deal with. You're not hurt or anything, are you?"

"Uh … no … I'm not hurt …"

"You sure? Don't worry. You can tell me."

"No, really, I'm not hurt. Thanks for asking, though. But you're right. My roommate is a pain with all his shady dealings. He gets into shouting matches and fights right here while I'm sleeping. He's so noisy—even when he's asleep, because he's a super loud snorer to boot." I stretched my arms.

"Hey, I've been here for a *long* time, and I know a few people, if you know what I mean. If he gives you too much trouble, let me know right away, okay?" Pedro's face got serious.

"Uh … okay … I'll remember that." I pondered his motives. Why was this total stranger looking out for me?

"Oh, yeah. You're probably wondering why I'm here. Listen, I'm from the chapel. A bunch of us gather there regularly. We look out for one another, you know? My friend Dave and I noticed you the moment you walked down from A&D. You looked pretty lost. I've seen this place devour too many young kids. I don't want that to happen to you. Don't let your guard down. The chapel is a safe place. Come and meet the guys. I'm sure you'll get along with us much better than you do with your roommate."

"I see. All right, thanks. I'll drop by for sure." I rubbed my eyes. From the look on his face, he seemed genuine. At least he cared enough to come and introduce himself to me.

"Okay then, I'll see you soon! Oh yeah, it's good to get up from that bed too. Sleeping your time away isn't good for you mentally or physically. It's not the best way to do time. Trust me." Pedro turned to walk out the door.

That last comment lingered in my head for the rest of the day. How did he know I was trying to sleep my time away? Was it really that obvious? What did he mean by 'It's not the best way to do time'? Are there other ways to do time? Were there better things to do? I wanted to find out.

The following day, after lining up for a quick lunch in the mess hall, I wandered over to the chapel. The so-called chapel in the previous institution had been just a concrete room with a few plastic chairs. However, this chapel here was actually a fair-sized building of stone construction. The main entrance had two big solid metal doors with a small chapel sign. It was located beside the living units, adjacent to the activity building where the gym and library were. From the front, it seemed to have only one floor. But when I went around and looked at it from the back, I saw a lower level. The sign on the door indicated that a number of treatment programs took place inside.

Walking back and forth in front of the building, I hesitated. All of a sudden, the door opened by itself. "Hey, there you are! Welcome. Come on in." A pointy-nosed white guy held the door for me. He was middle-aged with a few wrinkles on his forehead and crow's feet that showed as he gave me a warm and inviting smile. I could see that from beneath his cap, he was greying. "By the way, I'm Dave. You're Bosco, right? Pedro told me about your conversation. I've been expecting you." People in prison generally called me by my legal name, Bosco, and not the nickname "BOZ" I used on the outside.

With this warm welcome, it would have been rude to turn around, so I walked right inside. The first thing that caught my eyes was a colourful stained-glass mural behind the altar. It was the size of half the building's back wall. I saw a picture of doves and butterflies flying around vine branches. The craftsmanship was very impressive. The sanctuary had a one-and-a-half-storey ceiling and was surrounded by well-tended indoor plants. The floors were finished with dark grey tile, and it had room for 50 to 60 people. Obviously, those in charge were trying to create a contrasting ambience to the one dominating the remainder of the prison, and they were doing a pretty good job. For a brief moment, I forgot I was in jail.

"So how do you like it? This is our sanctuary, as you can see." Dave tilted up his baseball cap.

"Yeah, I see that. This place actually reminds me of my childhood." I was trying to read the poem on the wall.

"Oh, do you have a church background?" he said with some anticipation.

"You could say that. So, you work here?" I turned to him.

"Yeah, that's right. I'm one of the inmate chapel clerks. There're six of us altogether who work for the two chaplains. We have quite a lot going on here with different services seven days a week. Let me show you around."

Starting with the photo collages and moving to the various paintings on the walls and then to the contents of the bookshelves in the resource room, Dave gave me a brief history of everything. To my surprise, he even told me how each plant ended up in the sanctuary. He obviously took pride in every detail. From his encyclopedic knowledge of the chapel, I inferred that he had been involved from the beginning.

"That stained glass up there, who made it?" I pointed to the back wall.

"Ha, I thought you'd never ask. It's a long story. Years ago, when this building was first being built, the chaplaincy wanted to have something colourful inside—something to lift the mood. Back then there was a very skillful artist, an Asian inmate, who volunteered to help make this stained-glass window. It took him quite some time just to finish the design on paper, and then I saw him sweating in the workshop every day for months, cutting, grinding, applying the lead came, and then gradually soldering it all together. You see the butterflies and doves? They represent the Spirit of Peace that God gives us. The vine and the branches symbolize Jesus Christ and His followers. He's like the vine in the middle, and we are like the branches coming out. One little piece of glass at a time, he gradually put the whole thing together.

"On the day he was supposed to complete it, he was up on the ladder trying to install the final piece when the PA system called for an emergency lockdown. It was so rushed that he almost dropped that piece to the ground. Turns out someone had been murdered in his cell. It was a brutal time. Cops were everywhere. They did a huge investigation—one of the biggest I've seen. We were locked down for weeks. I saw them transporting the body out from my cell window. It was a big deal. We didn't get to finish the stained-glass mural until long after that mess was over. You never know what's gonna happen next here." He leaned his elbow on the altar.

"Murder—does that happen a lot?" I was disturbed to hear this story because I was so afraid of dying.

"It doesn't happen every day, but it does happen once in a while. You see, people in here get into fights all the time. Gangs, gambling debts, drug addiction—anything can trigger it. That's why it's so important to choose your friends carefully. In my years here, I've seen too many people go down the toilet right before my eyes. I may not look like a wise man, but I've learned how to live clean and safe in prison." He tilted his cap again. "Well, enough of the heavy stuff. Why don't you make yourself comfortable in a seat over there, and I'll go make you a cup of tea?"

"Yeah ... okay, thanks." I walked towards the seating area.

Perhaps it was the sunlight glimmering through the intricate stained glass, the soothing air blowing down from the ceiling fans, or the natural feel created by all the potted plants—I am not sure what it was, but something in this chapel was making me feel very peaceful inside. This was a very strange and nearly forgotten feeling for me. Ever since I entered the prison world, there was not even one day where I wasn't surrounded by foul language and criminal activity. Sometimes I was hearing the plans and sometimes I was seeing crimes in action. Being in the chapel made me feel separated from all that negativity. With my eyes closed, my mind felt surprisingly at ease. There was such a contrast between this place and my cell. I just wanted to stay there.

"We'll lock you up as long as we want! Your life ends HERE … here … here …" The unseen voices echoed down a tunnel so dark I couldn't even see my hand in front of my face. It was darkness so thick it seemed to have a substance to it.

"You're one of us! No matter where you go, we'll hunt you down! You can never escape! Ha ha ha …" Out of the pitch black, I heard Blade's laughter.

"We can strip-search you and do *whatever* we want to you, convict! No one can hear you," an invisible guard whispered in my ear.

"Ha, loser! I'm screwing your girlfriend every day, and you can't do nothing about it!" I saw a brief image of Allie messing around with another guy.

"Chinaman! I don't like the way you stared at me. Chink, I'll cut you UP … up … up …" An inmate stabbed me from behind.

"Lowlife! You have no hope! Just give UP … up … up …" A kitchen steward pushed me into a black hole.

"No! Stop it! Somebody help me!" I cried out from the top of my lungs as I was falling into an open dark bottomless pit. I was terrified by the notion that no one could hear me and that I would disappear forever into this abyss.

Suddenly a beam of light shone down from an unseen sky. It had the power to stop my descent and held me there in mid-air above the pit. While I dangled there in space, out of it came a comforting, gentle voice, speaking directly to me. "You will not die. This will not kill you. Look up, and you'll see that hope is still alive."

Bang bang bang! There was sudden loud knock at the door, which woke me from this intensely realistic dream. Trying to catch my breath, I looked around to see where exactly I was. The pencil graffiti on the ceiling reminded me that I was on my bed in my cell. Climbing down from the bunk bed, I went to answer the door. "Hey, who's there?" I yelled. The door opened. It was a unit officer. "Poon, a single cell has opened and you're next in line. Do you want to move in?"

"What? Really? Yes. Yes, of course I want to move in!" I couldn't believe what I just heard.

"All right then. Pack up all your stuff. When you're ready, come find me at the office." He walked away.

This hopeful turn of events after the beam of light that had just held me and the gentle voice that had spoken in my dream was too uncanny.

After being at Mission Institution for six months, I had moved from Unit 4 to Unit 1, the drug-free living unit. This was a popular choice for lifers. Everyone who lived here had to do regular and random drug tests. Since I wasn't into doing drugs, I had no problem being tested. Dave had recommended that I try getting into this unit. It was supposed to be the cleanest. For a drug-free person like myself, it was the best I could hope for. However, the day I moved in, I didn't get my single cell immediately. That would come later. Instead I got partnered up with the dirtiest inmate of the entire unit, if not the whole prison. He wasn't dirty in the drug sense. He was dirty in the unkempt sense. The room stunk all the time. Weeks-old laundry and garbage were all over the floor. This was my new challenge—I had moved from choking on drug fumes to choking on biological fumes—but I had no choice. On the bright side, it gave me motivation to stay out of my bed as much as possible during movement time.

There was only a certain number of single cells in every living unit. In most cases they were all taken by the lifers, and in order for someone to get into one, someone else had to move out first. Inmates with shorter sentences normally weren't around long enough to gain eligibility. For about ten months, I'd seen a number of people get called to the duty office for their single cell, and I always looked longingly as they headed for their new-found privacy. Living with my grubby cellmate was a real pain in the neck, or pain-in-the-nose, as the case may be. In addition to his other forms of stench, this guy also had the uncanny ability to stink up the toilet in ways I had not foreseen possible. And just like my drug-addicted roommate, he snored. At least the only thing he smoked was tobacco.

After approximately sixteen weeks with my own personal hobo, my time came for transition to a single room.

"Buddy, what's the deal? You don't like staying here with me?" My cellmate seemed hurt by my urgency to part with his company.

"It's not like that. It's my turn. Of course I'm gonna take it. Wouldn't you?" I was packing my stuff.

"Hey, I have an idea. Why don't you give me your single? I promise I'll hook you up with some really good deals." He tried to persuade me to give him my spot in exchange for sundries and contraband.

"Okay, how about this. I'll take your sentence and you take mine. Then I'll give up my single. Deal?"

"No freaking way, buddy. I'm outta here in three months!" He laughed.

"Well then, no freaking way, buddy. I have eleven more years to go!" I returned to my packing.

Little waterdrops were dripping from the rusty pipes on the hallway ceiling. Gangster rap was pounding out of a cell as I walked by. *Playboy* covers were plastered on a number of doors as I dragged the extent of my earthly belongings in three black industrial garbage bags. The unit officer directed me to my new destination. My heart was pounding. I hadn't enjoyed a space of my own since my departure from RRAC. I figured it had been about ten months of living with a roommate. I had almost forgotten how it felt to have my own privacy. I finally had something to look forward to—some hope, just like in the dream I'd had a few hours earlier.

"Let me help you with that. You need to put some pounds on, man! You probably weigh less than your sack of clothes." Someone lifted two of the bags off my back. As I turned around, I saw Dave's now familiar smile.

"Oh hey! Thanks." My shoulders were relieved.

"Welcome to the North Side. So you're moving next to me. N-1 is your new cell. I'm glad to have you as my new neighbour." He was taking my stuff down the stairs.

"Oh, am I? Good to be your new neighbour, then," I replied.

"All right, there you are. You can go up to the office to get some floor cleaner and bleach to clean the cell. The mop and bucket are at the end of the hall. The last person here was pretty dirty. Well, not as dirty as your cellmate—no comparison—but still. I suggest you really do your room up right, because you'll be here for a while. If you need any help, gimme a shout." He put my bags beside the door.

"Yeah, you're right. Okay, I'm going to spend the next couple hours cleaning it before lock-up. Thanks." I put down my bag and went up to the duty office. When I came back with some bleach, Dave was already mopping the floor for me. He looked up and said, "I got nothing else to do right now anyway. If I don't help you, you might not be able to get it done before lock-up."

"Wow. Thanks!" I was really touched by his hospitality.

Together we were able to bleach the entire room, including the very worn-out bed frame. He even helped me scrape off the hardened boogers the previous guy had wiped on the wall. After the boogers, the manifold cobwebs seemed a minor inconvenience. However, depending on your fears, the nests of baby spiders that the mop had broken open might seem scarier. The spider nest cleanup took the better part of an hour. I can't imagine how the previous guy had tolerated those conditions.

After two hours, we were both drenched in sweat, but the place was approaching a sanitary state, so I squeezed a five-minute shower in before lock-up. Just in time for the count, I rushed back, still drying myself off. Officers came by to check my cell and then locked the door behind me. I was finally alone, which might seem a relief, but as the evening wore on and I lay staring at the ceiling, I was again overcome by loneliness and the remorse that never left me. I missed all my loved ones so dearly. All I could think about was having the freedom to see them again.

———

Tick tock, tick tock, tick tock ... the sound of the clock echoed in the chapel. We were all seated on stackable chairs in a circle, awkwardly staring at one another in silence. It was the kind of thing you see on a reality rehabilitation TV show, but there I was, living it.

Bosco H. C. Poon

Looking from my left to my right, there sat a variety of inmates from different backgrounds and of all different appearances: bony to bulky, tattooed-up to covered in piercings, dwarf to giant, bald to '80s metal hair, young to old. There was a certain appeal in that no matter how different we were, we were unified in our circumstance. But the situation seemed tense. Maybe because it was so early in the morning and everyone was still a little grumpy. No one really spoke. We sat quietly in our chairs for over 20 minutes before the creaking of the door broke the silence.

"Sorry, everybody. We were running a little behind at the board meeting this morning," Pastor Tom said as he pushed open the door from outside.

"Yes, sorry for the wait. We'll get going right away." Father Mako followed behind with two volunteers.

The Restorative Justice Program was run by the two chaplains along with some lay volunteers from the outside. From what I had learned, it was designed to bring healing and support to everyone affected by the criminal justice system, both the victims and offenders, along with their respective loved ones. Going around the circle, we were asked to introduce ourselves and tell the group a little bit of our story. As people began to talk, the stiff and awkward mood relaxed a little, and people gradually warmed up. Before long, guys were opening up to one another in a manner I would have never predicted and in ways that deeply moved me.

"I loved my wife. She was an angel—so beautiful. We had so many good times together. Her cooking was incredible. I worked so hard every day so that we could build a perfect home. I would do anything to protect her. We were immigrants, both come from Iran. We had to fight, you know—to learn a new language and make our way in such a different place. I never meant to ... I ... no ... never ... I ..."

He got choked up mid-sentence. "I couldn't control myself ... they were doing it right there in my bed, *in my own bed!* This stranger was kissing her body. I tried to tell myself that what I was seeing was not real—that I was just hallucinating. But I could not stop hearing the sounds they were making. They were still going at it when I returned with the kitchen knife. I was so angry. They left me no choice. I had to stop them from destroying everything. I had to do what I had to do." He sobbed quietly. We listened, and on some level we all knew that, like him, our own impulsiveness and stupidity had landed us all in the same place, despite our disparate backgrounds. We were all so similar. We were all so different.

A Native Canadian was next. "My granddad was selling it. My dad was selling it. It was the family business. What else could anyone expect me to do? I was surrounded by it ever since I was a kid. You learn by observation. You see and you do, you know? And that's why I did it. Nobody told me it was bad. I tried it, and it made me feel so good. So I thought it must be good. Being on the street was my destiny. It was my playground. I started off selling it at the back alley; later on I had people lining up to do the selling for me. All I had to do was manage them. It was just like that. My family? They are all in jail all over the country. Some in the States, too. We haven't talked to each other for ages."

Risen From Prison

A skinny Caucasian man missing his front two teeth shared next. He hesitated with each sentence, and his speech had the characteristic of someone without a full set of teeth. "I was coming down off my last high and starting to feel so sick. My whole body was in pain. It's not a normal pain coming off heroin ... it's like it comes from deep inside your bones. You can't understand it without going through it. I was sitting on the street; people kept staring at me. They looked at me like I'm a monster. They see the tracks on your arms and they see the look in your face. Downtown, when you're an addict, you're invisible. My time is getting short. I have HIV, and I'm basically dying. I'll probably die here without seeing my daughter. I don't know where she is ..."

Story after story. My eyes were slowly opening to see the other side of everyone's tough exterior. Everyone had circumstances in their lives that had influenced them to make bad decisions. It wasn't all on them. People had faced some terrible challenges—things much more difficult than being an Asian kid from a relatively well-to-do family. I learned that many of the judgments I had made about people based on their appearance were unfair. If I had been born into their circumstances, I may not have done any better, and maybe much worse.

I'd held a private air of superiority since day one. To me, these guys were all scumbags, and somehow, by some terrible turn of fate, I had been cast undeservedly into their unfortunate world. I had kept a distance from all of them and was not interested in getting to know them as people. Participating in this program was an eye-opener and smashed the prejudicial lens through which I had sneered.

When it came to my turn to speak, I hesitated. I didn't want to be just another prisoner, because in my mind, I was still the undiscovered Asian pop star. I wanted to remain superior in some way, but the facts spoke for themselves: I was sitting in a circle of chairs in a federal prison with 11 years of my sentence remaining. I was more like them than I thought.

With the encouragement of the pastors, I gathered up my courage and allowed myself to be vulnerable for the very first time. "Unlike many of you guys, I was lucky enough to be born to a healthy family. I'm an only child, and my family loves me. I was an artist in the Asian pop music scene, and I was planning to travel the world. I loved what I did, and I was really close to being successful. So, my struggles were a little different than the ones you guys have talked about. I never had to worry about food, shelter, family, or addiction—well, not until I ended up in here. Thank you for sharing, guys. It makes me realize how fortunate I was. Maybe even a little spoiled in a way.

"On the outside, I had some great friends. I don't know why I was attracted to the ones who got me in trouble. They dragged me down and talked me into doing things I would never dream of doing. That's how I got involved in a really stupid plan—a kidnapping. I should've just gone to the police when they told me what they were planning. But I didn't. I just went along, and because of that, I lost everything ... and I mean everything. I'm in for twelve years."

Shortly thereafter, Jason, one of the volunteers, took the discussion in a new direction. "That was a very good sharing, everyone. Thank you. Now take a moment. Can you place yourself on the other side and see if you can look at your story from your victims' perspective, if you have one? Put yourself into their shoes if you can. Think about the impact it had on them and their loved ones. Can you see anything?"

This caught me completely off guard. All this time I had only focused on myself. Never once was I actually concerned about the victim, let alone his family. Taking a moment to collect my thoughts, I answered, "Wow ... I never really thought of that. Now that you mention it, I can only imagine how afraid he must have been when they blindfolded him and tied him up. He must have been terrified, and his family must have been so worried. Look at how miserable my parents are right now, and they basically know I'm safe, in a sense. His parents must have gone through something much worse. Man, what have I done?" For the first time I understood that I had been a victimizer, not a victim. Was I taken advantage of by Blade and those guys? Sure, of course I was. But I had contributed to the terrifying experience of this man.

"That's very good insight," Father Mako encouraged me, "and this is the exact reason why we have this program. It's so you learn to understand the impact of crime from both sides. It's a much different goal than the punishment of imprisonment. By helping you guys understand the ripple effects of your actions, you'll be able to learn from your mistakes and make the right choices in the future."

The group session lasted the whole day. We had some breaks to go to the washroom and to eat, but we spent the majority of the time sharing and discussing the effect of our crimes on our victims.

Father Mako brought the session to a conclusion. "It has been a long day, and a lot of emotion has come out. I think it's a good time to wrap up. Tonight, at your convenience, read over the handouts we've given you and think about what we've discussed today. If you have any questions, you're more than welcome to stay behind and talk to any one of us. We'll see you here the same time tomorrow. God bless."

While everyone started stacking up the chairs, I stood in the middle of the room, pondering what I had just now come to understand. I could see the whole sequence of events from a completely different angle. Now I could so clearly remember the man's voice echoing from the basement: *"Help me! Please! Please, let me go! Is anybody up there? Someone, please help!"* Why had I been so blind? Why didn't I help him? Why did I just hide in the computer room and callously do nothing? I was suddenly completely overwhelmed with guilt, and the weight of the accompanying shame made me feel like I might collapse. I felt my strength leaving my body. As I was about to faint, someone tapped my left shoulder and distracted me from my feelings for a moment. I caught myself as Pastor Tom quietly spoke.

"Bosco, would you like to come to my office? We can talk there with some privacy."

"Pastor Tom, I ..." I couldn't manage a reply.

"Come with me. I can see there's a battle going on inside of you. Let's deal with it together. You don't have to do this alone." He led me to his office inside the chapel.

This really touched my heart. All this time I had been trying to fight alone, and it was completely exhausting. As I sat down on his guest chair, Pastor Tom closed the door behind me and gently counselled, "You don't have to worry here. Everything said within this room is confidential. You can be yourself. I know a little about your past, and I could only imagine what you're going through. By the look on your face, you must be suffering a great deal. If you're willing to receive it, I'm willing to help you. For years I've been dealing with inmates. Even though I don't have an answer to everything, I have helped many through the process of healing. Are you hurting inside?"

"Yes, yes, I am ... and the pain is killing me." I sighed.

"I'm sorry; it must be tough, especially in this place. How have you been dealing with this pain?" he asked.

"I don't know. I hide it in my heart, I guess. What else can I do? I'm barely surviving in here."

"Sounds like you haven't dealt with it properly yet. Storing it inside probably isn't going to help you in the long run. Once you've reached the limit of your endurance, you'll break. You see, besides your own perspective and the perspective of others—the one you saw from today—there's one more perspective from which you need to see things. For matters like suffering, we need to approach it from an angle that our physical eyes can't see."

"You mean from the perspective of God, Pastor?" I asked with my eyes closed.

"Yes, we call it the spiritual realm. Even though our eyes might not be able to see it, our spirits can definitely sense that there are other forces fighting against each other inside of us. Good and evil, life and death. Your pain is likely a consequence of the decisions you've made in the past. You know, from your remorse and your desire to go back in time and make different choices. But it's too late. We can't undo our past, and sometimes the regret and shame can completely overtake us. Does that kind of describe what you're feeling?" He crossed his legs on his chair.

"You really hit the nail on the head, Pastor." I was surprised by the way he had so accurately described what I was experiencing. It was eerie, but in a good way—just like when Pedro had shown up right as I had woken from my dream.

"I have to tell you that is absolutely normal, especially for someone in your position. Because of your decisions in the past, you find yourself in here. You see, we can't avoid the consequence of our previous actions. But know this, Bosco, this is *not* the end—not the end at all! Despite the length of your sentence, this chapter of your life will end one day, and how you use the intervening time is completely up to you. Each day, you have the choice to be miserable and bitter or to move on and seek God's purpose for your life." He picked up his cup from the table.

"Purpose? I don't get it. There's no purpose for my life anymore. I've lost *everything*. I've hurt so many people. I can't fix it. God ... He probably hates me more than anyone. That's why He's punishing me so severely."

"Or He loves you so much that He needs to discipline you—to get your attention. A good father would discipline his kids in order to teach them how to live a good life. A bad father would just ignore their misbehaviour and let them fall victim to their stupidity. When we experience pain, we remember the lesson. God is not going to give up on you. He has amazing plans prepared just for you. Look forward, Bosco, not backwards. When you quiet down your heart and cry out to Him, I think you'll experience His presence. Your life has a purpose. It may not be the purpose you'd have chosen on your own. But you are created for an important purpose, His purpose." He looked directly into my eyes.

"Even now? Even after all I've done wrong?"

"Even now. It doesn't matter whether you recognize it or not, but you are created in the very image of God. You're capable of achieving great things despite your circumstances. Trials like the ones you're going through can make you stronger and wiser. Take this opportunity to learn how to become a better man." He was encouraging me.

"Really? I still have a purpose? What about the victim and his family? I keep seeing them in my mind now."

"You can write them a letter. We can help you send it out to them, but there's no guarantee that they will accept it or read it. However, from God's perspective, you only have to do your part and leave the rest to Him. It will be a closure one way or the other, and it will release you, to a certain extent, from your guilt and shame."

"Oh, okay! I think I want to do that. You're right, acceptance of my apology is up to them. But at least I can do my part and say I'm sorry. Thank you, Pastor. I really appreciate your kind words. God has a purpose for me? That's good to know. I still need time to digest all this. As you were talking, I felt a little better inside already. I'd like to talk to you more in the future." I reached out my hand.

"My pleasure. Anytime. Come find me whenever I'm here in the office. We can pray and discuss things more. Remember one thing: have faith." He gave me a firm handshake.

I gained a lot of insight that day. Even though I didn't understand everything, it pointed me in a new direction. That evening after lock-up, I picked up a pen and a piece of paper. In total silence, I closed my eyes to say a prayer and then wrote down these words as a song:

I'm sorry for what I've put you through
All I wanna do is to apologize to you
I'm sorry for the pain you're going through
If I get a chance to take the pain away from you
I would do

Risen From Prison

For everything that I've done
Wasn't thinking of the consequence
Left you alone in the basement
Never think deep of the outcome
Temptation got me good
Doing stuff that I never should
Could put myself into your shoes
Change my whole attitude
You must have been crying struggling even screaming
Even though you're trying deep inside must be hurting
I don't know how you're doing so I've been keep on praying
for you to get over this pain

I'm sorry for what I've put you through
All I wanna do is to apologize to you
I'm sorry for the pain you're going through
If I get a chance to take the pain away from you
I would do

CHAPTER 10
AWAKENING

"Hang in there, man. I know it must be tough. I'll try to come visit you every month or two." Joe gave me a firm hug.

"Thanks for coming, man. I really appreciate it—so good to see some familiar faces."

"How are you doing in here so far? You getting enough to eat?"

I nodded half-heartedly as if to say "more or less."

"I got you some chocolate bars and pop from the vending machines down the hall. I wasn't sure what you like, so I tried to pick a variety." He pointed at the snacks on the small table.

"Thank you. That's great. Don't worry about what I like. Really, I've learned not to be picky. I'm just grateful to see you. Come on. Let's find a place to sit down. I want to know what's going on out there in the real world."

As I opened a brown bag of chocolate M&Ms, Joe began filling me in on what had been going on in his life and among our friends. I lived for these kinds of visits because they sustained me much more than letters or scheduled phone calls could. Previously in the North Fraser Pretrial Centre, I could only have visits with my family behind bulletproof Plexiglas using a telephone, but after my transfer to RRAC and at Mission Institution, I was approved for in-person visits. Not everyone was allowed to visit me though, and not everyone was willing to put in the effort to do so. Beside the arduous approval process through prison management and the hassle of booking a visit time, Mission Institution was at least an hour-and-a-half drive from Vancouver, followed by a 15- to 45-minute wait at the gate. If we were in a lockdown situation, visitors would be turned away entirely and have to start the process all over again. Life was busy in the outside world and not everyone was willing to sacrifice the better part of a day for a few minutes with me—particularly since I had become an out-of-sight, out-of-mind sort of person to the majority of my friends.

"So much is happening out there. I don't even know where to start. Let me think … well, I broke up with my girlfriend." Joe looked a little forlorn and showed a hint of guilt.

"What? For real? How come? You guys have been together for so long—like years? I thought you two would get married!"

"Yeah, that's the thing. I really couldn't see myself marrying her. It's a long story. I never told you before, but I just couldn't picture her as my wife. I tried and tried, but deep inside I knew we just weren't cut out to spend the rest of our lives together. We broke up quite a while ago, before your sentencing, actually. We didn't want to burden you with our problems with all that you were going through. So that's why we didn't tell you. There was so much drama, you know? And, in the end, it was pretty ugly."

"Man, I'm really sorry to hear that. You two should have let me know. I wish I could have been there to help you at the time."

"It's all good. I had to do it. There was no reason to drag it out any longer. But I do wish it could have had a prettier ending."

"How is she?"

"I don't know. She's really angry and doesn't talk to me."

"That sucks, man … I don't know what to say. I'll keep you two in my prayers."

"That's okay. I appreciate the thought, but what can prayer do?"

"Well, I'm sure God can do something. I pray every day now."

Joe sat in a kind of perplexed silence.

"I don't know how to explain it, but I'm starting to trust God, knowing that He is the Almighty."

Joe's facial expression suddenly changed. His hands formed fists and trembled a little as he opened his mouth to reply. "Come on, seriously? Bro, you just got a f*cking twelve-year sentence, and your involvement was only minimal. Twelve years, man! Where is God in that? You don't deserve *that*. Why isn't He helping you get out of here?"

His comment got me thinking. Not having an answer, I kept silent and just pondered it. On some level what he said made sense, and on another I knew that I would never have bothered with God *unless* I was in prison. I was too focused on my own achievements. But surely God could have reached me without all of this chaos in my life, right? Was Joe right? Was I being wronged by God?

Joe interrupted my thoughts. "Anyway, I don't mean to discourage you. I know your parents are working hard with your appeals lawyer. Maybe your sentence will be reduced, right? I'm sure it will work out somehow." Realizing that his strong reaction had hurt my feelings, he was backtracking a little and trying to be gentler.

"Yeah, that's what I'm hoping for. But that also means the lawyer is sucking even more money out of my parents' bank account. I have no idea how their finances are going to handle this."

We talked for another hour and a half before the guards called, "Time's up!" through the speakers. After watching Joe disappear behind the door, I lined up to be searched for contraband before heading back inside. On my way back to my unit, Joe's question "Where is God in that?" kept rolling around in my head. From that day on, it was a question I daily posed to God in my prayers.

"There we go. Now the whole team is here." Dave was waving to Glenn.

"Hey, guys, thanks for waiting." Glenn got into the circle.

"Yeah, yeah, let's do it before they call lock-up." Pedro bowed down his head.

"Okay." I closed my eyes.

With everyone's eyes closed, Dave led the prayer. "Father God, thank You for keeping us safe today in the hostility of this place. Once again we lift up all our loved ones to You. Please take care of them in the outside world. Help us to trust You more day by day. For those of us who have roommates, may You give them peace and protection tonight. As we depart to our units, please grant us rest. We look forward to seeing each other again in the morning. In the name of Jesus, we pray."

The rest of us replied together, "Amen."

Right beside the prison chapel, facing the gym-side doors, there was a tennis court. For months it had been a gathering place for a handful of us from different living units to do evening prayer before lock-up. We would take turns praying for each other's concerns and problems of the day. Slowly we became a core group of friends who truly cared for one another. Still being very fragile, I was helped tremendously by the support group in rebuilding my emotional and mental health.

At this stage of my faith, my knowledge of Christ was minimal, even though I was raised as a Catholic. I had always been just a churchgoer. I didn't really care about faith or religion. Neither did I view my faith as particularly special. I saw all religions as basically the same, and I thought there was good in all of them. To me, trying to do good was all that mattered. In my first attempts to read the Bible after the prison chaplain gave me a copy from the Canadian Bible Society, I fell asleep in minutes. Nothing seemed to click, and I couldn't relate the stories to my own life. The parting of the Red Sea was spectacular, and killing a giant with a stone was awesome, but how would that help me with my prison sentence? Would God give me back my freedom?

"Those are great questions, Bosco! Why don't you join our Alpha program? It's designed to answer questions just like those ones." Dave tilted up his baseball cap.

"Really? So you mean I'm not the only one who has these kinds of questions?" I was a little surprised.

"Of course not. Those are some of the most common questions people have when they first start reading the Bible."

"Really? Okay. That's good to know. And I would get my answers from this program you just mentioned?"

"You'll get some, but of course I can't guarantee you'll get all the answers to all your questions. You see, it's a journey. It's like people going into university: they don't understand everything on day one. They need to take courses in all kinds of different subjects over the span of four years before they can graduate with even a bachelor's degree. If they wanted to become truly expert, they would have to go on and do a master's or PhD. It's the same with your spiritual walk. You'll learn one step at a time. The key is, you have to start walking."

"Okay, that makes sense. I do want to know more. I need answers. All right, please sign me up. When can I start?"

"You're in! I'll arrange a spot for you. We only run it once or twice a year. The next one happens to start next week. Aren't you lucky? Or, should I say, 'Isn't that providential?'"

"Then I guess it's meant to be. I look forward to it."

"I'm sure you do."

The Alpha course created a tremendous amount of curiosity in me. I brought a lot of "whys" to my small group: Why the Bible? Why Jesus? Why is there evil? Why not other gods? Why is life unfair? Why had I received a 12-year sentence? Why are there bad people who don't get caught? Why did my girlfriend cheat on me? Why do bad things happen to decent people? Why wasn't God helping me get out of prison? With every weekly session, the videos, featuring Reverend Nicky Gumbel, and the volunteers who facilitated our discussions helped me understand these things one at a time. Some answers made sense to me, and others didn't. When I wasn't satisfied with an answer, I would go and research it on my own by borrowing materials from the chapel and the library. I dug as deep as I could into books covering different religions and the basics of Christian theology. Something inside was tugging me to find out more about this God in whom I claimed to put my faith. I was also desperate to understand the purpose of my existence.

After six months of research, I still hadn't arrived at all the answers I wanted, but I had gained a lot of knowledge about Christianity and how it differed from other religions. I found that all other religions were merit-based: a reward and punishment system based on how one performs in life. Buddhism called it karma. You do good things, you receive good things. You do bad things, you receive bad things. No matter what other religion I looked at, the ticket to paradise was essentially purchased with good deeds, not unlike any earthly purchase where currencies are earned and spent. My good deeds and bad deeds would be placed on some kind of cosmic scale. If my bad deeds outweighed my good, I'd be doomed to some form of punishment. Otherwise, I'd be off to a blissful eternity. That meant that I would be the author of my salvation through my own efforts. But it occurred to me that this kind of system created a problem; it seemed self-centred. It was all about *my* efforts and *my* achievements to earn *my* own way.

In contrast, I found that Christianity operated in a completely different paradigm. Rather than a merit-based system based on effort and determination, it was a gift-based system founded on love. We do good not because it earns us a trip to heaven. We do good because we have received love freely from God. Then, in turn, we freely pass that love on to others. We don't treat others badly, because we desire their well-being. Salvation is a free gift for everyone to receive through Jesus. More specifically, my good deeds do not earn my salvation, because the problem of my sin remains despite my good deeds—not unlike the notion that poisoned water remains poisonous even if you add some clean water. Since God says that the due punishment for my sin is death and eternal separation from Him, this punishment needs to be carried out. In an act of His mercy on me, He offers to take my place and mete out the punishment for my sin on Himself—that is, on Jesus, the human incarnation of God, who died as an offering for the sin of all people. I can't earn my salvation, because my situation is hopeless. I can only receive it freely. My bad deeds will be forgiven by God's grace if I am sincere and want to change by receiving God's "unearnable" righteousness. As a result, a spiritual transformation will take place.

All other systems were pointing me to hard work based on my own capabilities but *without guarantee of success—because I would never get to preview the all-important balance on the weigh scale before I died.* Jesus was giving me the assurance that I could rely on an almighty God who would walk this journey with me and who would guarantee my eternity in heaven because the success was based on His perfect merit and not mine. It was logical then for me to choose Jesus.

Even though I had considered myself to be a good person, the very fact that I ended up as an accomplice in a kidnapping and a convict told me that I could mess up things in my life very easily. There was no way I was going to gamble my eternity. I needed a God who could work with me in spite of my weaknesses.

This process established my "head knowledge" as to why it was reasonable for me to remain a Christian, but I found that this was not enough to carry me through. Reading all those books helped me understand why I should choose and follow Christ, but I needed to learn how to handle the innumerable emotional challenges of daily life. When I went back to the Bible, I had endless questions. There were many stories I didn't understand, and there were many statements I had lingering doubts about. And I was still so bitter about my girlfriend and hopeless about my future.

I vented to God during one lock-up. I opened my Bible to Matthew 28:20—I even remember the page number I was looking at, 743.

"Jesus," I prayed, "this verse says 'And surely I am with you always, to the very end of the age.' Are You sure You are with me right now? I cannot see You. I cannot touch You. I cannot smell You. I definitely cannot hear You. Are You sure You are with me? Really? Hello, where are You? I don't even know for sure if You are real."

I was overwhelmed with emotion and at the point of tears. With a few stuttering deep breaths I tried to compose myself, and then I continued, "But if You are and if You can hear me, please … please talk to me … because I have nobody else … No one can truly understand me. Would You show me that You are real? Show me that I'm not praying to a dead God."

Bosco H. C. Poon

"You will seek me and find me when you seek me with all your heart."
(Jer. 29:13)

One muggy evening that summer, I went out on the field with Dave after dinner to stretch my legs. The sun began to paint the bottom of the clouds in the west the characteristic orange and magenta you might see in a Roy Henry Vickers' painting. But the prison was far enough inland from the ocean that we didn't always enjoy its cooling effect. It was 30 degrees Celsius, and that year's damp spring along with some marshy land flanking the west fence ensured a healthy population of mosquitos to keep everyone suitably irritated.

If you listened to the chatter of conversations around us, they were constantly punctuated with profanity, as if the F-word and blasphemies were commas and exclamation marks. Since there was forest and marshland nearby, there was also a lot of frogs, which would not have been a problem were it not for the deafening evening din of the boy frogs trying to impress the girl frogs. That night they were so loud that they drowned out our conversation, which in combination with the heat, swearing, and mosquitos was making me pretty testy.

As I looked up to the gradually dimming sky and the rising moon, I should have been amazed by all the beauty in plain sight, but all I could do was focus on how terrible my situation was. Staring at the barbed-wire and chain-link fence, a toxic mixture of anguish, sorrow, and hatred simmered to a boil in my heart. Dave intuited my irritation and suggested we move to the more comfortable wooden bench in the middle of the tennis court where our support team always prayed.

Putting his hand on my shoulder, he took off his cap and said, "Bosco, in the middle of the storm, someone is still in control up there. When nothing is working out around you, all you can do is look up. Jesus cares about you. Let's call upon Him, right here, right now."

Closing our eyes and drowning out the cacophony of frogs and profanity, we entered prayer. At first I couldn't concentrate, and nothing coming out of Dave's mouth resonated with me. Ten minutes passed by before I finally said something in my heart: "Are You there? Are You listening? I surrender. I lost my appeals too. Nothing worked out with my own effort. There's nothing more I can do …" Another five minutes passed by before I realized that all around me it was now totally silent—like the blanket of quiet caused by the falling of heavy snow on a windless evening, except it was the middle of summer. I tried to shift my weight but discovered that I actually couldn't move. Something supernatural was happening.

What's going on? Why can't I move? H-hello? Oh gosh, I can't even open my lips. Where did everyone go? There were still pockets of people cussing on the field a few seconds ago. And what happened to the frogs? All of a sudden everything is so quiet. There must have been hundreds of them. Why would they all clam up at once? Whatever. I don't mind the tranquility. Hey, what's that up there in the sky? It's so bright! Wait a minute. I think it's moving ... Is that a UFO? Am I hallucinating? Hey, I think it's getting closer. Okay, it's definitely getting closer ... whoa, whoa, whoa, looks like it's coming straight at me? What! No way! Is it gonna land here? It's too bright. I can't even look at it!

A cloud of angelic white light descended from the sky and was hovering right in front of me. It was an intense supernatural light but, strangely enough, seemed to have a personality. This light was full of power and authority. It evoked my reverence, and without a moment's hesitation, it approached me and entered my body through my chest. A soothing power instantly filled my heart—strong but as gentle as a mother's caress of her newborn. I felt electrified from the top of my head to the tips of my toes. Still unable to open my mouth, I suddenly felt my body being lifted from the ground. The next thing I knew, I was rising off the ground, through the clouds, and into space. The earth was below me—a vast sphere of intense blues and greens painted over by swirls of white clouds casting shadows on the continents and seas below. I was awestruck. This was a view only astronauts had seen with their own eyes. Except I had no space suit, I was breathing, and I never remembered feeling more physically comfortable.

The heavy emotional weight I was carrying just minutes earlier altogether vanished. I felt physically light, and my mind was at complete peace. A gentle flood of calmness continued to pour over me. Never before had I experienced this kind of tranquility. It felt so good that I thought that perhaps I'd gone to heaven. While I was enjoying the moment, a gentle masculine voice addressed me. I understood that the words did not need to be questioned. They were filled with a confidence and sureness that caused me to *just know* they were true, eternal, and solid as rock. "Do not be afraid. I am your Lord, and I will rescue you."

I then felt someone embrace me from behind, wrapping fatherly arms around me. The feeling was strangely familiar, though I knew I had never been conscious of it before. Though I did not know who it was, I felt as if it was someone I'd known since the beginning of time. Even though I couldn't see His face, I knew with certainty He was someone very close and important to me. After allowing me to rest in His embrace a little longer, He gently and slowly released me. All the while my body continued to tingle from head to toe.

Down I descended like a real-life Google Earth. I saw the Americas and the Pacific, Western Canada, Vancouver and the Fraser Valley, the Fraser River, the city of Mission, the prison, the tennis court, and the bench. The sky that had seemed dark compared to the blinding white light now looked much brighter, and my hands and feet were suddenly able to move. I looked up, and the other inmates appeared again on the back field. The frog chirps returned. Everything was as it had been. I drew in a deep breath, and I turned to my left to see if Dave was still sitting beside me. The second I looked at him I noticed he looked pensive, deep in thought. He tilted his cap up and said, "I don't know if you felt that or not, but I'm sure the Lord was here. I mean like really here, you know what I mean? I could feel His presence so strongly during our prayer. Even all the noise around us disappeared. That was crazy! It was so calm and peaceful. Man, I've never felt anything like that before. It was like He was standing right here in front of us, literally!"

That was an understatement. When I heard this, I was completely dumbfounded. His words confirmed that what I had just experienced was very real. It wasn't a hallucination. Putting my elbows on my knees, I replied in disbelief, "Yeah, know what you mean. For a moment I thought I was trippin'. That was insane. I couldn't move, you know. Literally, I was frozen. When I saw that light, I wanted to call everyone over to see it. But I couldn't even utter a word, like I was muted or something. I still can't believe what just happened—"

"Wait, what? What light? What are you talking about?" Dave was perplexed.

"Huh? I thought you saw the same thing? The light. Come on! You didn't see the ball of super-bright white light? You couldn't have missed it. It came out of the sky, landed in front of me, and then went right into my body! You're telling me you didn't see it?"

"Whoa, really? Was that what happened? Darn it! My eyes were closed! I didn't see any of it. All I felt was the presence of God. I knew that He was here, for sure! Wow, what else did you see? Did you hear anything?" He looked very serious.

I spent the next ten minutes describing every detail of the experience. Dave listened with rapt attention. Towards the end, I added, "This must sound crazy. Even I find it very hard to believe, and I was there. But I haven't touched any drugs. We ate the same food from the kitchen. It can't be food poisoning, right? That was so real. I'll never forget that voice."

"My oh my ... I've never heard anything like this, at least not in this place. This is unreal! You just had a very special interaction with God. Jesus appeared to you and spoke to you in person. He even dialed down all the distractions so that you could hear Him clearly. Wow, you must be someone very special! I believe He has some amazing plans for you, beyond your wildest dreams. Brother, I have no doubt that He's going to use you mightily." He stood up from the wooden bench, put his hands in his pockets, and continued, "Now that you've encountered God, your life will never be the same. You may not recognize it yet, but you are chosen. You probably have been sleeping for too long—spiritually speaking, that is. Jesus has come to waken you. It's time to wake up to fulfill His purpose in your life. I'm excited to see how He's going to use you for the Kingdom. It's my honour to witness what just happened tonight. That was so very special."

I didn't even get a chance to take it all in before the PA system crackled as the announcement came: "Lock-up, lock-up time! All inmates return to your units for count!" We walked back to the unit together. After the guards came to do count and locked my cell door, I looked at the Bible sitting on my small desk. I was immediately reminded of how I had vented to God just weeks earlier. While still wrestling with the many questions of what'd just happened, I whispered, "So I guess You're telling me that You are real? You just showed up. That was quite something—really spectacular. I've never experienced anything like that. And the peace was so good. I miss it already." I strolled to my bed and sat down.

Staring at the grey ceiling from my bed, I kept thinking of the white light. I couldn't wrap my head around it. Dave's words also lingered on. Not everything he had said made sense to me, and I didn't have a clue what he meant by saying God would use me mightily. Even though it was too much for me to digest all at once, my heart was at ease, knowing that this whole experience had proven that Mission Institution was not the end. My perspective started to change.

From that day on, I was not the same person. It was like something had awoken within me. It marked the beginning of a new journey.

CHAPTER 11
ONE LAST TIME

"Poon to visit. Poon to visit!" The PA system was calling inmates to the visitation area after the Saturday morning lock-up.

"Bosco, you hear that? They're calling you to visit." Dave knocked on my door.

"Hey, yeah, I heard it. Thanks, Dave. I'm just fixing my hair. Going up right now." I placed my small black comb beside the sink and walked out of my cell.

"Have a good one. Say 'Hi' to your mom and dad for me. I'll see you back here later on." Dave gave me a fist bump.

"All right, thanks, Dave. I will. See you after."

A long set of stairs led up to the top of one of the higher buildings adjacent to the living area. This was where visitations occurred. I was so excited for visitors that I always got palpitations, and by the time I would reach the top of the stairs my heart would be pounding with anticipation.

My parents had developed the habit making weekly pilgrimages to Mission to see me on Saturday afternoons, so even though the announcement didn't say who was visiting, I was sure it was them. I lined up at the big metal gates while a guard communicated my whereabouts on his walkie-talkie. Sometimes the guards would let us proceed after the full body search. Sometimes they would make us wait. The longest I had ever waited was about an hour and a half. This time it wasn't too bad. They let me in after five minutes.

I passed by the second door and saw my parents at one of the small tables, eagerly peering down the hall. As was now my tradition, I ran up and threw my arms around them.

"Hi, Mom! Hi, Dad! It's so good to see you."

"Ayayay, son, how come you look so skinny? Are you losing weight? Aren't you getting enough to eat? Here … here … take these. We picked up some pop and chips and chocolates for you at the vending machines out at the entrance. Eat, eat! If it's not enough, we can go get some more." My mom forced a bag of Old Dutch dill pickle chips and a can of Coke into my hands. Like many Asian moms, force-feeding and being overprotective were her "love language."

"Okay, okay, Mom, thank you. This is good enough. I'll eat. But let's sit down first."

We usually spent the first 30 minutes catching up from the last visit. They would tell me their daily routine and update me with any news about my grandpa, my bandmates, and my relatives overseas. So, as usual, I just listened intently while munching my way through two bags of chips. When they were done reporting the news of the week, I put down the chips and took a sip of Coke. "Mom, Dad. I have something really important to tell you too. Something really crazy happened this past week!"

"What do you mean crazy? Did somebody try to hurt you?" My mom scanned me from head to toe, looking for injuries.

"No. No. Nothing bad happened."

"Easy, Mom, you're jumping to conclusions. Just let him finish his story," my dad said as tapped my mom gently on her shoulder.

"Ahem, okay. I know this is gonna sound strange. But I want you to know that what I'm about to tell you really happened. This was not my imagination, and it was not a dream."

"Okay, what is it? Tell us." My mom was now ready to listen.

"So, during one of the evening prayers, I heard God's voice, like literally. Not just a feeling. I actually heard God's voice. Initially, I was so shocked. He appeared before me in a great white light, and He entered into my body. Then, I heard His voice. Masculine, but very gentle and loving, you know? It was unbelievable! It just happened. One moment we were just praying, and the next moment, there He was talking to me."

Crickets. All I heard was crickets. My mom and dad sat there in stunned silence. Their faces revealed their thoughts. *Is our boy using drugs? Maybe he has a mental illness. Has he joined a cult?*

"No, seriously, I'm not kidding. It was so crazy! I was pulled up in the air. And then my body was electrified but in a positive way, by His great power. Then I heard a voice saying to me, 'Don't be afraid, I am your Lord, and I will rescue you.' After that my whole being was filled with this incredible peace—a peace like I have never experienced. I didn't know what it meant at first, and then Dave explained to me that I had met God. I was like wow, really? He said—"

Before I could finish the sentence, my mom cut me off by putting her right hand on my forehead, checking my temperature. She used her left hand to check it again. Within ten seconds, she burst into tears, sobbing, "Oh God, oh God, this is the end.

No, no, no! We lost in court, and now we are losing you as well. No! No ... why, why?! What did we do wrong?"

"Oh no. What have we done to deserve this? This is too much. Son ..." My dad looked at me with a mix of disappointment and despair.

"Wait ... what? Oh, no, no, no! It's not what you think. Come on, I'm not going crazy. Look at me. I'm totally fine! Look, I'm healthy!" I was frantically trying to explain.

"No, you are not! You are sick, son!" My mom's sobbing now turned to wailing.

"What do you mean I'm sick?"

"Yes, you are! You must have had a mental breakdown. You are seeing things and hearing things. This is not normal. You are delusional. We've got to get you in to see a psychiatrist." My dad stared at me with compassion but deepening distress.

I could not believe the predicament I was now in. I had this incredible news to share with my parents, and I had inadvertently sent them into a tailspin, thinking I'd developed schizophrenia or something. I looked them both in the eyes. "Come on. Mom ... Dad ... trust me. I'm totally fine. I'm not going crazy. I know you might see it that way, but it's not true. I thought I was hallucinating too at first, but then Dave said he had felt God's presence very strongly during our prayer too, so I knew that something real had happened."

"Well, who knows? Maybe this Dave guy is mentally unstable too. I mean, who is he anyway? We don't know him. How do you know that he is a trustworthy person? Maybe he is some kind of crackpot."

"Because he helped me out so many times in here without expectation of anything in return. He's a good guy. He made some mistakes in the past, just like I have. That's how he ended up in here. But God has changed him completely. Anyway, I didn't want to turn this visit into a debate about my sanity. I'm fine, Mom. Please believe me. Why are you still crying?"

"Because you are sick!" My mom was now managing to sob a little more discreetly, with her face cupped in her hands.

"I'm not sick. I'm fine. How many times do I need to tell you? Ask me about anything. You'll see that I am not losing it."

"Son, you need help. We'll try to find out what we can do to help you. Maybe we can ask the lawyer to find you a doctor or something. There's got to be something we can do." My dad frowned and gently shook his head, staring dejectedly at the floor.

"Wow, this is not what I expected at all. This is bad, really bad. This was supposed to be exciting news. I hoped you would be happy for me. I've really found God, and here you are trying to diagnose me as insane. This is terrible. Dad, you don't have to go back to that lawyer. Your retirement fund is gone, and somehow I still got double Blade's sentence. So why on earth would you trust him? I'm totally fine. I'm not going crazy, and I'm not delusional."

"But we want to help you—"

"I know, I know. But God is helping me. Don't you believe in God? Can't you just trust Him? I'm learning to trust Him more and more. Besides, there's a doctor here I can visit. If I'm sick, I can go see him, okay? You don't have to pay for anything."

They sat there silently.

"Mom, would you please stop crying? The only thing driving me crazy is your tears."

More silence.

For the rest of that visit, all three of us sat there in silence. I didn't know what more to say. The whole experience was very unpleasant. Now my beloved parents thought I was descending into some kind of madness, when in fact this was the most positive thing that had ever happened to me.

Why am I going through all these trials? Why does everything in my life have to turn out so terribly? Things are going from bad to worse. Honestly, what's next?

"Be gracious to me, O Lord, for I am in distress; my eye is wasted from grief; my soul and my body also." (Ps. 31:9 ESV)

It was 12:40 p.m. on January 16, 2008. I was standing in the meal line, waiting to get my lunch. Suddenly I felt someone tap me on my left shoulder. As I turned around, I saw Big Circle Lee. He stood at about five foot four—so he was only "big" in the metaphorical sense. Big Circle Lee was a diminutive Chinese man who spoke broken English. He was one of the local leaders of the infamous Big Circle Gang (大圈幫). Normally, he loved to joke around, but today his face revealed that something was troubling him deeply. "Hey, is everything all right?" I asked.

His eyes were red and puffy from hours of crying. He was still teary. He leaned toward me and quietly spoke into my left ear. "My mom ... is dying. She's in California." My heart sank as I heard the terrible news. I tried to figure out the right words to comfort him, but I just couldn't. My mind went absolutely blank, and I completely zoned out until the kitchen steward yelled from behind me, "NEXT!" I quickly did a 180, grabbed my meal, and told him, "Your mom definitely needs some prayer. Come meet me in the chapel in 15 minutes, and we'll pray together."

"Oh ... okay, I'll be there. Thanks," he replied with some obvious trepidation. But he had no other alternatives.

As one of the very few chapel workers and inmate peer counsellors in Mission Institution, Dave was allowed into the chapel during movement time without the supervision of the chaplains or guards. I shared the tragic news with him, and he was willing to come to the chapel with me for support since no chaplain was around that day. After asking the prison guard to unlock the chapel door, we waited patiently for Lee's arrival. Meanwhile, I closed my eyes and asked the Lord for guidance.

Since I didn't have a whole lot of experience in this kind of situation, I really needed to depend on God.

It was about 10 minutes before I heard a loud "click" from the door. I knew it must be Lee, so I opened my eyes slowly and welcomed him with a warm smile, which he returned half-heartedly. He then turned to me and said, "Can we talk privately?" From the expression on his face, I understood that he would like to speak in Cantonese, which is also my mother tongue. I nodded and led him to the back meeting room, leaving Dave in the main area.

While I was pulling out two chairs and setting them opposite one another, Lee broke down behind me. The sound of his weeping filled the four corners of the room. It was full of pain and anguish. I helped him into one of the chairs and spoke to him gently. "It's okay, it's all right. Let it out. I'm here for you."

Still sobbing, he muttered in Cantonese, "This is too painful. F*ck! It's tearing me apart. I miss my mom. She's dying. What can I do? I'm stuck in here, helpless." He took out a napkin from his pocket, blew his nose, and continued, "I haven't felt this way in a long, long time. I haven't cried for more than 25 years. The last was when I was about 15 years old. Ever since then I promised to myself that no matter what happened, I would never cry! And I have always been able to keep that promise." He sighed heavily and pulled up his T-shirt to show me his chest and arms. "You see these scars, Bosco? They're from the bullets that hit me during a territory fight the night before I ended up in this place. Those bullets hurt—a lot. But I didn't shed a tear. Now look at me. I'm crying like a baby."

This bold statement caught my attention. I focused my eyes on the scars and counted them one by one—five in total. It must have hurt immensely when those five sizzling bullets cut through his muscles like that. While I quietly contemplated this, Lee's tears continued to wet the floor.

"Aaaaah … I'm crying like a little child! Why? What's happening to me?" He let out a deep wail from the bottom of his heart. Silently I asked the Holy Spirit to guide my words.

I looked up at him and said, "That just shows me how much your mom means to you. Your breakdown is because you love her. I'm sure you love her because she loves you too. There is absolutely nothing wrong with loving your mom like this. There is nothing wrong with crying for your sick mother."

Stunned by my comment, his eyes grew big as he exclaimed with a flash of insight, "Yes, you're right! I do love her! I never thought that she would die. I always thought that she would be around for me no matter what. I just can't accept the reality that I won't see her anymore. I should have never played the games I did, and I wouldn't have ended up stuck in here. I thought I was so big, I could get anything I wanted and no one could stop me! I got power. I got money. I got women. I thought I was on top of the world. I thought I could control everything. But I was totally wrong. Look at me now. I can't be there for my mom on her deathbed. I will never be able to see her again!"

"There's really no point in beating yourself up about your past. Everyone makes mistakes. Everyone. What matters is that you have learned from it and use what you've learned to do better, right? Although the world might not forgive you for what you've done, I am sure your mom forgives you, just as our merciful God does. And please don't conclude that this is the end. The Word of God tells us all who belong to Christ will spend eternity together in heaven with God. So basically, the end of this life on earth is actually the beginning of the new life in heaven if you put your trust in Jesus Christ," I explained to him calmly.

"That I know, but ... you see, for 70 years my mom has believed in Buddha and the Chinese goddess Guan-Yin. She has dedicated her life to Guan-Yin. As a matter fact, my brothers and sisters in California have already hired a high-ranking Buddhist monk to perform a ceremony to prepare her soul."

"Prepare her soul for what?"

"Don't you know? In Chinese traditional religion, the Buddhist priest has the power to lead souls to the underworld safely using a special ceremony and chanting. So the idea is that she won't get lost or stuck in this world and become a lost ghost."

"Hold on, hold on! This sounds a lot like witchcraft to me. Before you continue on with that stuff, answer this one question: Do you want your mom to go to the underworld or heaven?"

"To heaven, of course!"

"Then she needs Jesus, because He is the only way to salvation. No special ceremony or chanting can save her."

"Man, then there's no hope. There's no way she could believe Jesus. I know her."

"How do you know? Have you ever tried? Do you believe in Jesus?"

"Yes, I do believe."

"Then don't compromise, brother. Make a stand for the Lord. Tell your mom about Jesus, the only way to heaven."

"It's too late. She's dying. The doctor said she will be gone by tonight." Streams of tears poured from his eyes and ran down his face.

I was saddened by his despair. I laid my right hand onto his shoulder. "Jesus is God Almighty. Nothing is impossible for Him. Let's ask Him to make the impossible possible.

"Let's pray. Dear Heavenly Father, we come to You through Your son Jesus Christ, our Lord and Saviour. Lord, Mr. Lee's mom is dying in California, and she doesn't know You. We know she needs You in this crucial moment. Can You please make a way for Mr. Lee to proclaim his faith in You to his mom, as her beloved son? We kindly ask You to knock on the door of her heart one last time. Please save her soul, Father, so that Mr. Lee can be reunited with her in the kingdom of heaven."

After my prayer, Mr. Lee cried out, "God, if possible, take five years from my life and add it to my mom's life! I promise if You do that, I'll do my very best to lead her to faith in you!"

All of a sudden, I felt a strong energy enter into my body. My mouth then opened spontaneously, and I said, "What if she can only live for three more years?"

"Good enough; I will still do it!" he replied without hesitation.

"Then what about five more months?"

"No problem; I will still do it!"

"What about three weeks?"

"Man, you're pushing it. All right, I will do it!"

"Now, think carefully. What if she only has five more days to live? What will you do then?"

Lee became silent, not knowing what to say. Still moved by the Holy Spirit, I continued, "Do you really love your mom?"

"Of course, I do! Look at me; if I don't love her, I wouldn't be f*cking crying like this!"

"Then don't hesitate! You should still do it. Don't you give up on her, just like Jesus never gave up on you."

"Okay, okay, if I can get ahold of her right now, I'm going to tell her about my faith in Jesus!"

As he finished this sentence, a knock came on the door. It was Father Mako, our Catholic chaplain … at the very moment we needed him. In total shock, I was jumping in the air, giving praise to God. Miraculously, our prayer had been answered in seconds. As I was trying to explain the situation to Father Mako, he told me that Dave had already told him we were in the chapel and that we needed to help Lee call his mom. Watching them enter the chaplain's office, a Bible verse came to my mind: "Before they call I will answer" (Isa. 65:24). This whole experience proved to me that it was all true: God knew exactly what Lee needed.

Twenty minutes later, Big Circle Lee came out from the chaplain's office making a beeline for me. "I did it! I told my mom about Jesus."

"Good; how'd it go?"

"I've gotta tell you it was real close. After my sister picked up the phone, she told me that my timing was perfect because mom was leaving. She passed the phone to Mom. The first thing she said to me was 'Son, take care of yourself. I have to leave now. The soul reapers Ox-head and Horse-face are here to take me. I shouldn't keep them waiting.' Then I yelled to her, 'Mom, believe in Jesus; He can take you to heaven! I believe in Jesus, so if you want to see me again, then please also believe in Him. He sends angels, not animal heads, to lead us to heaven. Mom, trust me; I love you!'

"She then replied in a very weak voice, 'Why did you speak so loudly, son?! You've scared the Ox-head and Horse-face away. They're gone!' I then spent a couple more minutes explaining to her about Jesus. Man, I was so worried about her that I just went off. You know what I mean? Trying to convince her that Jesus is the only true God. Now that I'm thinking about what she said about the soul reapers it gives me goosebumps. What was that? It sounds way too creepy." Lee shivered.

"Wow, amazing! I can't believe what I just heard. It's that real! Wow—but hey, it's all good. Look what you've done! You pushed those soul reapers away with the mighty name of Jesus. I'm sure that there's hope for your mom. Just keep praying for her; a miracle will happen."

"Really? You think so?"

"Of course; miracles happen all the time. I've seen many in front of my eyes. You just experienced one, didn't you? Didn't God just give you a call to your mom at the perfect moment? Our God is an awesome God, man."

"Yes, you're right. Okay, I trust you. I believe you."

"No, no. Please don't trust me. Trust Jesus. He's the way."

"Of course. Of course. You know what I mean. Hey, thanks for everything." Lee gave me a firm handshake with a big smile.

"You're very welcome. That's what a brother in Christ is for." I shook his hand and walked him back to the living unit.

For the next couple days, Big Circle Lee was elated by the news that his mom's heart condition was getting better and she was becoming more stable. Even though she wasn't able to talk, the doctor said the fact that she was still alive was a miracle in itself. I had taken the time to pray with Lee and had shown him numerous Bible verses to comfort him. I had lifted up his mom in prayer during our chapel services and in my personal prayer times. I had repeated the same prayer over and over: "Lord Jesus, please knock on Lee's mom's door one last time. Since she's not able to speak, only You can hear from her now. Please show her the way to heaven."

Frankly, I didn't know what would happen to her. For a 76-year-old Buddhist to turn to Christ on her deathbed seemed impossible. Logically speaking, it wasn't going to happen. Though Jesus definitely heard my prayers, it was ultimately her choice to accept Him or not. I kept my concerns from Lee and lifted the matter up to God, quietly hoping that things would turn out okay.

On January 22, 2008, Lee came to me early in the morning with a warm smile. "Hey Bosco. She's finally gone."

"What? You mean your mom?"

"Yeah, she passed away last night. I actually kind of knew it, 'cause her picture on my desk fell down around 10 p.m. My heart told me that she was gone. And I got the confirmation from my family just now. However, I'm glad that she is finally with the Lord."

"Whoa, really? What happened? How come you're so sure?"

"It's hard to believe, eh? That's what I thought when my youngest sister first told me. But after all my brothers and sisters told me the same story, I know it's true."

"Wait, aren't all your brothers and sisters Buddhist?"

"Yeah, and that's what makes the story more believable."

"Okay ... so what happened?"

Lee took a drag on his cigarette and exhaled as he explained, "Yesterday, the doctor said that my mom was unlikely to make it through the day. So all my brothers and sisters and their families gathered around her hospital bed along with my dad. Not too long after, she suddenly sat up under her own strength, put her hands together, and said, 'I believe You, Jesus. I believe You. Please take me to heaven, the paradise You've prepared for me.' Everyone in the room was completely shocked. They were terrified by what they'd seen and heard. No one could believe that my very sick mom, whose faith in Buddhism was so strong, was able to sit up in her bed without any help and start praying to Jesus. They didn't know how to react, and they also found it very frustrating. It was well into suppertime, so they all left together for dinner, except for my youngest sister. Not too long after, my mom smiled at her and said, 'My baby girl, I'm leaving now. He is here. Help me to say goodbye to everyone. I love you.' And those were her last words."

I got a chill all over my body. I was so touched by what I'd heard. I was so happy that I started laughing and crying at the same time. After wiping my face with my hands, I looked up to the clear sunny sky, thanking the Lord. I then turned to Lee. "So, are you all right? How are you feeling?"

"I'm ... I'm happy, knowing where she is now. I look forward for the day I can see her and hug her again up there. Thank You, Lord, and you too, brother. I couldn't have done this without you. Thank you." He gave me a hug.

"It is my pleasure."

We walked a couple of laps on the field, spent a couple of minutes in prayer, and then headed back to our work.

At the end of the day after lock-up, I took out my spiritual journal. It had become a habit for me to record all the major events and prayers of each day in it. As I was starting to write, I flipped back one page to review all the prayers of the week. I stopped on the day that we first prayed for Lee's mom in the chapel. Pointing at the dates, I started counting: 16th to 17th was one day, 18th, 19th, 20th, 21st ... it was then that I realized that she had lived for five more days after our prayer, exactly what the Holy Spirit said to Lee through me in the meeting room. My mouth fell open in amazement. God had shown me that He had everything figured out, even the exact number of the days we would live. There was absolutely nothing to worry about. Still trying to wrap my head around this experience, I thanked God for answering my prayer—to knock on Lee's mom's door, one last time, before she passed away.

CHAPTER 12
UNEXPECTED DEPARTURE

"Man, why are you looking so down? Something bothering you?" Matt extended his lighter to my cigarette as I leaned forward.

"Boy, it's a long story. I don't even know where to begin." I gave it a few puffs to get the smoke started and then took a long draw, hearing the familiar quiet crackle of smouldering tobacco.

"Come on, you can tell me. I won't judge. What's going on?"

"Well, you see, I'm not sure if I'll be around too much longer. Maybe it's time for you to find a new hairstylist."

"What do you mean? You leaving? You sick or something?" Matt's eyes grew big.

"Yeah, it's a deadly disease. It's called a lawsuit. I've been in and out of the courtroom for two and a half years, and it's killing me."

"Whoa, for real? What for?"

"Man, it's something real stupid. My high-school gang kidnapped a guy and used my parents' house in Coquitlam to hold him ransom. It was such a stupid plan. I should never have gotten involved. It ruined my music career, my parents' finances, and everything good in my life. And now I'm cutting hair in my parents' basement, waiting for the outcome of my trial."

"No freaking way! Kidnapping is serious, man. My boys don't do this kind of deal. The risks are too big. We play smart. We only want money. When people's lives are at stake, we steer clear. That's way too hot to handle. But that sucks to hear, bro. Man, how many years are you facing?"

"Ten to twelve—"

"What the heck? Seriously? No freaking way! That's some serious time, man!"

"Tell me about it. As you said, because a human life was at risk, they don't take it lightly. It is some damn serious stuff. Well, it's too late to really get into the details. What's done is done. The long battle is coming to an end. I should get the verdict in the next month or so. If you don't hear from me, it means they've sent me to prison." I squeezed my cigarette between my thumb and index finger and took another long drag, then exhaled a thick grey plume.

"Man, it must be tough. Hang in there, bro. The result may not be as bad as you think. Keep your chin up. I promise I'll keep you in my prayers." The last word echoed in my head.

So ended a flashback of a conversation I'd had with one of my hair clients, Matt, just before my imprisonment. It somehow appeared in a dream during an afternoon nap. After reliving my exchange with Matt, I saw him slowly disappear into the fog. I turned my head left and right, trying to see where he went. The fog kept growing, until I was lost in the mist myself. As my panic rose, a sound of metal-on-metal woke me.

Clink, clink, skrrreeek, clink, skrrreeek, clink ...

"Hey, hey, Bosco! You there?"

Stretching my back, I yawned and then got up from my bed. With my eyes half opened, I saw a straightened metal coat hanger tapping my window bars from the next cell. It was Dave, trying to get my attention. I opened my window a bit more and replied, "Hey hey, how's it going?"

"What you up to, man?"

"Nothing much. Just woke up from a nap. You?"

"I've been gathering information. Here's the latest update. So apparently this lockdown is because someone OD'd in his cell. Rumour is that he swallowed a balloon filled with crack on his way back from the court. To his surprise, they made him wait an hour or two longer in the holding cell while his buddy was waiting for the delivery back at his cell. By the time he got back to his own cell, I guess the balloon started leaking before he could puke it out. And he got himself into a bad situation."

"Whoa, whoa, whoa, that's messed up! How big was that pack? I mean, is he still alive?"

"Big enough that he died. But that's not the most messed-up part. When he got back to his cell, he was already getting super sick, but his buddy, who was waiting for the package, tried to force him to puke it out. Of course, he couldn't. So his buddy got so frustrated and grabbed something sharp and tried to cut open the guy's belly to get the drugs."

"Whaaat? Whoa, that's crazy!"

"Yeah, very nasty. I saw they were bagging a body out from the unit below last night. I guess that must be him. They probably are going to do a big investigation and lay charges on the other guy. Who knows how long this lockdown is going to last."

"I can't believe that. Wow, that's so morbid. But hey, how do you find out all these things? You got a phone in your cell or something?"

"Ha, when you live here long enough, you learn how to get info."

"I guess … But you said it's just a rumour though, right? So it's not 100 percent?"

"Well, there's no way we can find out the exact truth until we get unlocked. That's how we receive news in here, by people passing on messages. Sometimes it's correct, sometimes it isn't. Depends on the source."

"Yeah, I understand. Well, it's the second day in. To be honest, I don't mind the tranquility and safety of my cell. I can do Bible study and write letters and songs."

"Yeah, me too. I was catching up on my Crossroads Bible study course. I should be able to finish this one by tomorrow. Then I can mail it out to my instructor."

"Good stuff. All right, I'll let you get back to your studying then. Thanks for the update. I'm starting to get hungry. Dinner should be served soon—half an hour or so?"

"Yeah, room service. That's one of the things I like about lockdown too—we don't have to line up in the mess hall. But the downside is that the food's normally cold by the time it arrives."

"True. Well, I'm just grateful to have food going into my stomach instead of a pack of crack."

"Ha, ha. Yeah, good point."

"Okay, I'll talk to you later then. I'm gonna do some stretching. My back is sore."

"All right, bye for now. I'll let you know if I find out more."

"Sounds good. Keep me posted."

I never liked lockdown when I was double bunking with a cellmate. Being trapped with someone 24-7 for days was really torture, especially if the other person got diarrhea or snored like a bear. It created a lot of tension. But now that I had the whole cell to myself, it actually wasn't too bad. While many others would just sleep their time away, thinking there was nothing to do in the cell, I used my time to write letters to my loved ones and get deep into God's Word. In the past 21 months, I had written many letters describing my ongoing encounters with God in prison as testimonial to my parents, music partners, friends, and relatives overseas.

The only two things that I didn't like about lockdown were 1) we did not get to shower and 2) we did not get to call our families. Before the lockdown ended, I would use the water from the sink and the little light-blue face cloth to give myself a sponge bath every night before bed. This particular lockdown lasted for a whole week.

As expected, after we were released from our cells I saw two long lineups: one for the phone and one for the shower. Having to pick one, I chose the phone, since my parents hadn't heard from me in so long and I knew they'd be worried. After standing in line for over an hour, it was finally my turn.

I inserted my inmate phone card and carefully punched in all the numbers, and the phone started ringing.

"Hello, hello?"

"Hey, Mom, it's me! We've been in lockdown. That's why I couldn't phone you."

"Son! Do you know the news? Do you know?!" My mom started to cry.

"What's going on, Mom? You okay? Why are you crying? What news?" I was worried.

"It's about your friend, A.C. He was just here the other day." She was sobbing uncontrollably.

"A.C.? So? He always comes over to our place. What's the big deal?"

My dad took the phone from her and spoke in a trembling voice, "Son, don't you know? Didn't you read the news? A.C. is gone. He's gone!"

"Gone where? To Hong Kong? I know, he told me last time I saw him that he was going for a record deal meeting there. Dad, I was in a lockdown. I didn't get to read the news. What's going on?"

"He is dead, son. He died outside a nightclub. One of the ones you used to perform in."

"Wha—what? What are you talking about? What!" I was shocked.

"Yes, A.C. is dead! He got stabbed. We saw him just a few days ago." My dad's voice was tremulous, and he was breathing heavily into the phone.

"What! No, no—what? Hold on, I must be hearing this wrong. We are talking about Aaron Chan, right? Dad, are you sure?" I couldn't believe my ears.

"A.C. got stabbed to death outside a Vancouver nightclub. Your friends said it was the one you used to perform at with Syndicate a few years back. It happened right outside the door. He was trying to stop a fight and then got stabbed. He died in the ambulance. It's all over the news."

"What the—You serious? No way! Oh sh*t ..." I just couldn't believe I was hearing about another unexpected death in such a short time span, but this time it was way more personal.

"I know it's hard to believe. His family is preparing for the funeral. Bonny and Yuen are helping. It's been a terrible shock for everyone."

"No kidding! My, my, my ... why, Dad? This doesn't make sense. He just came to visit me a few weeks ago with Yuen. This is impossible." I covered my eyes with my hand, trying to collect myself. I took a few deep breaths and continued, "Oh, man, sorry I went off there. This is just so shocking. Anyway, Dad, please give my condolences to his family when you see them, especially to his sister, Minerva. I've known her ever since high school. I'm sure you can connect with her at the funeral. I can't believe this is happening. Let Bonny and Yuen know that I got the bad news and that I will keep everyone in prayer."

"Okay, okay. So, you are out from the lockdown now, right? Can we come visit you on Saturday?"

"Yes, I'm out now. Please do, yes, come visit me. I need to know more. I should be okay unless something crazy happens again. Someone just died here as well. That's why we were locked down."

"Okay, we'll make an appointment tomorrow. We can talk more when we see you. I've got to go take care of your mom now. She's been really rattled by this."

"All right, Dad, go, go, go. I'll see you soon. Take care of Mom, please."

"Okay, we'll see you soon. Bye, son."

"Bye, Dad."

As I hung up, I was flooded with overwhelming sadness. I had a hard time grasping what I'd just heard. I looked around in the common area for a newspaper but couldn't find any. While I paused to think about where else I could look for one, Dave happened by. He noticed that I looked upset. "Hey, buddy, what's wrong?"

"I'm looking for a newspaper. I really need one!"

"A newspaper? I don't know where it went. Glenn might have them to check the sports scores. Why? What's so pressing?"

"A.C., my music partner, got stabbed to death outside a nightclub downtown. My parents just told me over the phone. I wanna read about what happened."

"What the—really? That's so terrible. Okay, okay, let me go find one for you! Do you know what day this happened on?"

"I don't know, man. I forgot to ask. Must be sometime within the past few days. It happened during the lockdown."

"All right, I'll see what I can find." Dave raced off to the second floor. Meanwhile, I walked to the other side of the unit to find Big Circle Lee.

"Brother Lee, have you been listening to the Chinese radio station in the past few days?"

"Yeah, yeah, of course. I listen every day. Why?"

"Did you hear news about a guy, a musician named Aaron Chan, getting stabbed to death outside a club in Vancouver?"

"Let me think ... oh yeah, yeah, now that you mention it. It was all over the news. A young musician, quite famous locally, they said. Outside a club ... over a fight or something. You know him or something? What's wrong? You don't look too well."

"So it's true. Man! That's my music partner—my protege. I taught him how to rap. I can't believe it. He's dead."

"What? Really? You knew him? That was your music partner? Whoa, I'm sorry to hear that."

"Bosco! Bosco, I found the newspaper and the article! Is this the one?" Dave ran over with the newspaper in his hand.

Grabbing it from him, I looked straight at the headline: "Musician's murder 'unfair, cruel,' VANCOUVER—Tearful friends gathered at a makeshift memorial yesterday for an aspiring young music producer and singer stabbed to death outside the Atlantis nightclub in downtown Vancouver early Sunday."[1] In the small photo underneath the headline, I saw some people bringing flowers in front of a banner with a few pictures of A.C. It was really him. Staring at the page, I was speechless.

"Bosco, is that him?" Dave asked.

"Yeah, Dave. Yeah, that's him."

"I'm sorry, bro. I'm really sorry."

---

[1] Jack Keating, "Musician's murder 'unfair, cruel,'" *The Province (Vancouver)*, Aug. 26, 2008.

"Thanks for the newspaper. I'll just go back to my cell and …" I was holding back my tears.

"Yeah, yeah, you need some alone time. Go ahead. We won't disturb you. I'll be praying, okay?"

"Thank you. I appreciate that. I'll see you guys tomorrow." I slowly shuffled back to my cell with my head down. After I closed the door behind me, I broke down.

That evening I couldn't sleep at all. I dug out all the letters and photos my music team had sent me. Tears kept pouring down my face as all the memories of A.C. flooded back. I recalled the first time Yuen introduced him to me as our newest artist. The times we sat side by side while I tutored him in how to rap. The times we went to the mall. The movies we watched. The countless nights we spent planning events. The demo songs we produced at the recording booth we'd built together. The photo shoots. The farewell at the courthouse and the last time he visited me in this prison … the last visit. *Oh yeah,* I thought. Something had happened during our last visit that arrested my train of thought. I recalled the intense conversation we'd had—A.C., me, and Yuen.

"Hey bro, we're working hard to make the dream come true! I just finished performing at Fairchild TV. It was one of our biggest projects so far this year. Remember last year when we did our launch concert at the Atlantis? It's been a year already, and things are gradually coming together! Man, I wish you were there with us for all these gigs, Boz. We miss you so much. Now we're preparing for a meeting in Hong Kong for a potential record deal. We're leaving at the end of August." A.C. opened a can of soda.

"Yeah, B, that's why we came to see you before we go. Abraham is busy today, so he couldn't make it. Bonny has school. Both of them say 'Hi.' By the way, I picked up some candy for you." Yuen opened up a bag of Skittles and passed it to me.

"Yeah, I heard from my parents. They give me an update every time they see me. I saw photos in newspapers and magazines. Good work, you guys!" I took a purple Skittle and put it in my mouth.

"Oh, oh, yeah, before I forget. The song we wrote for you, 'Home.' Have you heard it yet? We've performed it at several venues. People love it! We sent you a copy in the mail. Did you get a chance to listen?" Yuen put a bunch of Skittles into his mouth.

"Yes! The chaplain helped me get permission to listen to it, but it has to be the property of the chaplaincy. So basically I have to borrow it from the chapel when I want to listen. Man, it's really good. I was so touched. I broke down pretty bad 'cause the whole thing caught me off guard. Thank you, guys. It means so much to me. I heard all the personal shout-outs to me in the lyrics."

"And B, we meant it. We're waiting for you to come back. Don't you give up in here." A.C. gave me a pat on my shoulder.

"Yeah, man, our musical kingdom will be built when you get out. Don't worry. We're climbing to the top, and we'll be holding a spot for you, B. That's our promise!" Yuen spoke with such confidence.

"Thank you, guys … I feel the love. It's great. You guys are doing good and making me proud." I gave both of them a fist bump. After that I took a sip of the pop they'd brought me, cleared my throat, and continued, "Oh, hey, wanna change the topic a bit and share something with you if that's okay—like, some insights about life. You see, I've been doing quite a bit of research and getting really interested in the Bible while I've been here. My perspective is starting to change. I see life from a different angle now. It's been, well, kind of like an enlightenment. You know what I mean? You remember how much time we spent planning our success? Planning to make our music dreams come true at all costs? Well, I'm seeing now that there's more to life and that personal success is not everything. We can use our energy and talents to help better this world. It's a greater form of success so to speak—for humanity instead of just for the individual. You know what I'm talking about?"

Both A.C. and Yuen paused for a moment. Then A.C. said, "Yeah … yeah, B, I feel you. I read your letters about God and everything. I understand you are very serious about your faith now. That's good for you, bro. And yeah, success can help people, totally! I agree with you."

"Yeah, you feel me? I mean, we can do something with our music for a greater purpose. I know I used to say how to get gigs in the clubs and sexy models for the performance because sex sells. But now I see things differently. Actually, now I can see things more clearly. The image and message we portray is important because it influences our world. Alcohol, drugs, and casual sex are destroying people, and we shouldn't support or promote these things. There are young people looking up to you guys now. Be good role models. You know what I mean?"

A.C. and Yuen looked at each other awkwardly. Scratching his head, Yuen then said, "All right, all right, that's good. Our music can influence the world. And that's what we are doing, B. We're heading to Hong Kong, and the prospects for a record deal are very good."

"That's great. Let the record company know that your music and your influence can serve to make this world a better place. This is a great opportunity. Use your gifts for God. This broken world needs talented people like you two."

A.C. got a little agitated, since we were not really on the same wavelength. "Okay, okay, you want to save the world, Boz; we understand. We're not quite at that stage yet, you know? We're not Jay-Z or Kanye West. We can't do much. Wait 'til we get up there. Then we can help better this world, K? I know you've changed because you've been locked up. I know it's quiet in here. But it's a different world out there. We have to strive to survive, man. We got no time to think about saving the world. We gotta save ourselves first."

Bosco H. C. Poon

"No, no, you don't understand. Every day we can do something to better this world. We don't have to wait. Look at me, for example. I can't do much now, being locked up, can I? But you guys are different. I never knew what I had until it was gone. Freedom is one of the greatest gifts, and you guys have it. Use it wisely. Life is fragile. It is full of unexpected events. We don't even know for sure that we will be alive tomorrow. You have freedom, so go do something good. Go make a difference today! You don't have to save yourself; God has already done that. Believe in God. Do something good for God and for this world. You don't have to wait! How do we know we have tomorrow?"

The last sentence of my statement snapped me out of my flashback. I now recalled everything I said to A.C. in our last visit. It was almost like God was using me to give him a message that day. Who could have predicted that he would be dead within weeks? I got goosebumps all over me just by thinking about it. We don't know when our lives will end. Only God knows the number of our days. That's why it's so important to care about what we can do today. From what I'd heard from Dad, A.C. was trying to make peace and stop a fight. *A.C., were you taking my advice and trying to make a difference? Bro, if you stopped a fight, maybe you saved someone else's life at the expense of your own. That would make me proud, very proud indeed! Now may you rest in peace in paradise. I'll see you again when my time on this earth is over.*

Taking the CD from its plastic case, I gingerly put it into my small silver Sony portable boom box. I turned it on, hesitated a little, and then pressed the play button. As the background music started, I closed my eyes. When I heard A.C., I began weeping. There was no way for me to contain my emotion. I missed him so much, especially listening to the song that he'd written with Yuen and Abraham for me. I kept pressing the rewind button to hear him speaking to me.

Have times that seem impossible
to deal with all of life's damn obstacles.
And it gets frustrating, hard to swallow
trapped in a maze of unbelievable sorrow.
It's always harder to stand back up once you fallen.
Roller-coaster emotions get you spinning
Polluted with confusion and now you're gasping.
Try to find a way out. Your time's been stolen.
Sometimes all you wanna do is get home
and escape from the pain of the unknown.
Wanna get back what you used to own
live life to the full and not be alone.
Yo B, we got your back. Yeah we promise that.
Think of this as an opportunity to get back.

*Learning ways to cope with the past.
Be a better man we miss you.
We all waiting for the day you come back.*[2]

I played this song on repeat the entire night. In response to the death of A.C., I made a promise to do my best to become a better man, no matter how hard I had to fight. Every day of my life, I would try to make a difference. No more would I remain in my self-pity. I would strive to create a brighter day for the people around me by showing them the love of God. I would learn to live every day as if it was my last.

> "LORD, remind me how brief my time on earth will be. Remind me that my days are numbered—how fleeting my life is." (Ps. 39:4 NLT)

---

[2] Am3ition, "Home" (Vancouver: Phonic Architects, 2008).

CHAPTER 13
THE TRUTH

"Lup Lup, did you bring enough warm clothing?" my grandpa said, addressing me by my nickname over the phone. "The weather report says it's snowing in Toronto. It must be freezing cold there. You must take good care of yourself." My mom's side of the family called me "Lup Lup" (粒粒), meaning "tiny" in Cantonese. When I was born, I was among the tiniest of the babies in the hospital, and after that, the name stuck.

"Oh, of course, Grandpa. Yes, it's snowing pretty hard here, and yes, it's below zero, but don't worry, I'm old enough to take care of myself. I'm a grown-up now, not Lup Lup anymore. But that goes for you too, Grandpa. You aren't getting any younger, so please take good care of yourself and be careful and watch your step when you go up and down the stairs. Okay?"

"What? What did you say? It's really hard for me to hear you even with my hearing aid turned up. I guess my ears are getting worse. Old age ... old age."

"I said you are not getting any younger, so please take care and be extra careful when you're going up and down the stairs!" I covered my mouth and spoke as loudly as I could into the old-fashioned handset of the prison telephone, hoping he could hear me.

"Oh, oh. All right, all right, you sound like your grandma. Anyway, I'd better let you get back to your homework. Work hard. Get through your coursework as quickly as you can so you can come back home, okay? I can't hear you very well, so let's not waste any more long-distance charges. I'm going to hand the phone back to your mom now."

"Okay, Grandpa. I love you!"

"Hey, it's me." My mom took over the phone.

"Mom, this is hard for me. I don't know if I should keep lying to Grandpa," I said with a sigh. Most of my loved ones knew that I was in prison—except for one person, my grandpa. My grandma in Hong Kong was really concerned about my grandpa's heart condition. For this reason, she forbade us to tell him that I was *not* off in Toronto for university and I was actually in jail. Out of respect to her, I complied.

"Son, we have to keep going with this. Let me go to another room. Okay, come on. This is not the first time we've talked about this. You know how frail his health is. We don't want to cause him any extra stress. His heart won't be able to handle it. You know that," she whispered.

"Yeah, but Mom, were you listening to the conversation? He just asked me if it's snowing in Toronto while I'm staring at the rain in Mission. He asked me if it's below freezing, but since it's raining, I can't even tell a half-truth. Every time he tells me to study hard and graduate soon, I look at the bars behind me, and I don't know what to say."

"I know it's hard for you. But we've got to do this. There's no other way."

"What do you mean, 'There's no other way'? There's got to be a better way to do this. It's been two years already. I have a twelve-year sentence. Are we just going to keep lying to him until he dies?"

"Enough! Your grandma is very clear that she does not want to let your grandpa know about this situation. We don't want to go against her wishes, so we're going to keep it the way it is, okay?"

"Mom—"

"I'd better hang up now. I don't want Grandpa to overhear any of this. We'll talk more on Saturday when we visit you, all right? Take care, son." With that, my mom hung up on me with uncharacteristic curtness.

Two years had passed by since I'd been handcuffed at the back door of the Supreme Court. I had seen many of my relatives and friends during this time, with the notable exception of my grandpa. And now, we had lied to him so many times that my parents didn't see a way to change course.

I always had a close bond with my mom's parents. When I was little, my parents both worked long hours to support my family. It was never easy getting by in Hong Kong, one of the most expensive cities in the world. From kindergarten onward, I had been left in the care of my grandparents, living at their place during weekdays and only going home on the weekends. I continued to live with them five days a week right up until my emigration to Canada.

This made my grandparents my primary caregivers during childhood and the ones from whom I had learned the most. It was my grandpa who taught me how to use chopsticks and my grandma who showed me how to write Chinese characters with brush and ink. They had firmly rooted me in my Chinese heritage. I shared a lot of special memories with them, and many of these moments are captured in the family photo albums still sitting on the bookshelf of my home today. I loved them with the same love I had for my parents.

Risen From Prison

In Asian culture, family honour and pride are very important. For example, among the elderly, it is normal and acceptable to boast about the achievements of grandchildren, and accordingly it was one of my goals to give my grandparents something to boast about. That was one reason success in the music industry was so important to me. With every one of my accomplishments, no matter if it was riding a bike for the first time or getting an award at school, they would come to me separately and say, "Good job, Lup Lup! You're so smart." That encouragement began to fuel my achievements.

In the years when I was pursuing my music career, while everybody else saw it as fruitless effort, my parents and grandparents never doubted me. They believed in me wholeheartedly, no matter what others said. While encouraging me to pursue my dreams, my grandpa shared his wisdom with me when I considered abandoning music. "Grandson, there is nothing wrong with shooting for the moon. I know what everybody says, but you've got to pursue what you love. Many great men in the world have never gone to university, but they were still excellent at what they did. So, be excellent at what you do, and you will see the fruit of your efforts. You work very hard. Good job, smart Lup Lup. Just keep doing your part, and life will naturally lead you to the next stage. If it doesn't work out, you can do something else. It's not a big deal, but it would still be good to have a backup plan. Find something you enjoy to provide you a living—something like hairstyling, you know? Everyone needs a haircut, no matter how bad the economy gets. Think about it."

That encouragement kept me going for years despite the hardships and humiliation I faced. Grandpa's suggestion was the primary reason I went to hairstyling college. Trying to keep the music going while studying hairstyling, I would put on my headphones and write down my lyrics while going for a smoke break during lunch hour. That became my routine, even when I was working at a hair salon after graduation. Whenever I had time between clients, I would go outside for a smoke, hum out melodies, and write down lyrics. Seeing my uncompromising effort, people eventually stopped telling me my dreams were unrealistic. Yet, from time to time, I would feel insecure about my future. There were days I really doubted myself when after many submissions no record label had responded to my demos. When distracted by this uncertainty, it was the encouragement of my grandparents that brought me back into focus. It wasn't the money or material wealth I was after. It was the pride rooted in my Asian upbringing. I just wanted to hear my grandparents say, "Good job, smart Lup Lup" to me.

That dream was completely shattered with my incarceration. When the weight of the law took everything from me, the encouragement of my grandparents was also lost because we had to maintain a facade that I was off in Toronto attending university. Further, having a criminal grandson could only bring shame to my grandpa and on the family. There would be nothing for them to brag about anymore. My grandmother's insistence that Grandpa should be kept in the dark was proof of that. While I did not agree that we should lie to him, her concern for his health was legitimate, so I never argued. I wanted to fix everything so badly, but what could I do from my jail cell?

"How long do you want to live in these lies?"

"I don't want to live in them at all, but do I have a choice?"

"Come on. That's just an excuse."

"What! What are you talking about? What choice do I have? I'm locked up. I'm a total failure."

"That's your justification for lying?"

"Shut up! What do you want from me?" In my dream, I was split into two people and arguing with myself. One of me was in a white suit, and the other in a navy blue prison uniform.

"I want you to tell me the truth. How long are you going to lie?"

"I already told you. I don't want to lie."

"Then why are you still lying?"

"Gosh! Are you talking about my grandpa? I was told not to tell him the truth. This isn't my decision. I can't handle this pressure. I already brought enough shame to the family. I don't want to bring about someone's death on top of all that."

"So when is it going to end? Are you just going to keep lying to him? When four years are finished and you're supposed to have a bachelor's degree, are you going to have a fake certificate made so you can show him? Are you going to tell him you aren't coming home because you started another degree or got a job? More lies to cover up all the others? You've been down this road before. Take your ex-girlfriends. How many times did you have to lie to them over and over to cover up the first in a string of lies? And your parents—look how much suffering has come from lying about your gang activities. Have any of your lies led to a good ending so far?"

Blue Boz had no reply to White Boz.

"Let me ask you something. What would happen if your grandpa dies during your imprisonment? Are you going to let him die believing your lies? Do you think you would regret not telling him the truth while you still had the chance?"

"I ... don't ... have a choice. My whole family is against it."

"Even though you are locked up, that doesn't take away your ability to choose to do what is right. You have the freedom to choose. You always have."

"I ... do? Really? Even if I choose to tell Grandpa the truth, what would happen if he gets a heart attack right after hearing it? I can't bear that responsibility. My grandma would never forgive me."

"I can assure you that your grandpa won't get a heart attack because you tell him the truth." The man in a white suit, no longer obviously me, started to shine with intense white light. I recognized it clearly as the same kind of light I'd seen at the tennis court. The voice continued, "The truth sets people free. Never be afraid to tell the truth. It has the power to overcome the bondage of lies. As a man of integrity, your grandpa would appreciate your honesty. It's time for you to do the right thing. The burden of deception is too heavy for you and your family. Be brave and set them free. You can do it. I'll be here with you." After he finished the sentence, the white light expanded until it consumed everything in the dream. It was so bright that I was awoken by it. Opening my eyes, I saw the sunlight shining upon my face through the window of my cell.

Was that just a dream? It felt so real. It was that voice again. The message was very direct and spoke straight to my heart. Yes, my whole life, I'd been using the concept of "the white lie" to allow myself to keep on lying. It was too exhausting to keep building lies upon lies. I was too tired to keep up the facade. For once I really wanted to be completely truthful. I didn't want to live with regrets anymore. Taking in a deep breath, I looked over to the Bible sitting on my desk. *God, if You say so, I'll speak the truth. I entrust my grandpa's life to Your hands. Please see me through this.* Carefully picking up a pen, I sat up on my bed. As the sunlight shone upon my notepad, I began to write a letter to my grandpa in traditional Chinese characters:

My dearest Grandpa,
How are you? Are you taking good care of yourself? I haven't seen you in person for about two years now and I want you to know that I miss you so much. There are so many things I want to tell you that I don't even know where to start. Maybe I should begin with this. I want to say "thank you" for pouring your love and care into me—something you have done faithfully since I was a baby. I remember everything you've taught me. We shared many good times together. Do you still remember how you patiently took me to the park day after day while teaching me to ride a bike? First it was a three-wheeler, then a bigger bike with training wheels. I was so afraid of falling, so you would hold the handlebars steady for me. And on the day that I could finally ride the two-wheeler without training wheels, we were so happy, shouting together. Do you remember those times?

I spent my childhood with you and Grandma until I moved to Canada. I had so much difficulty adapting to the new culture in the beginning. I had to relearn everything and struggled with homesickness all the time. In high school, I felt as though I lost my identity. I used to be spoiled by you, Grandma, and my parents. I was loved by many people in primary school. You and Grandma introduced me to all your friends at the community centre. Everyone in our apartment complex knew me. But in this new country, nobody knew or cared who I was. I was lonely and directionless.

In the midst of all this, I discovered my passion to become a performing artist in the Chinese music industry. Despite the fact that many called it a "pipe dream," I'd made a commitment to strive for it. Thanks to your encouragement, I never gave up. I went to hairstyling college because of your advice to have a backup plan. You know that, right? Working at the salon while still trying to find a way in music: it was tough, real tough. I had to swim upstream. So many people told me to give up. I don't even know where the energy to keep going came from. But you were right. Life did find a way to direct me to the next stage. After years of hard work, I got connected to some major record labels in Taiwan. I thought I was going to make it big, and with some good reason—our band got picked up by EMI Music Taiwan. We were going to sign a contract. But something happened right before that. Something I have not told you yet.

Grandpa, I haven't told you the truth, probably because I was too scared. Even now, I'm scared I'll never hear you say "Good job, smart Lup Lup" again. There was something I did that I am very ashamed of. You see, I have had a bad habit of telling white lies to cover things up and to get what I want. In this case, I didn't want to affect your health. But recently I have come to realize that you deserve to know the truth. No one likes being lied to. Despite the many people telling me to keep this matter from you, I am now, once again, going to have to swim upstream. So please, sit back and prepare your heart for what I am about to tell you.

Do you remember when I told you I had decided to go to college, so I turned down the record contract? That was a lie, and it didn't even really make sense, did it? I mean, I had worked so hard for the music dream, and when it finally came true, why would I turn it down? Do you remember when I used to wear a suit and told you I was going to class? This was also a lie. Colleges in Canada don't require a uniform, let alone a suit. The truth is, I was going to court because I had been charged with a serious crime. Back in 2004, after we moved out to Richmond, I lent the old house in Coquitlam to a few friends. To make a long story short, they used the house to hide a victim of kidnapping and extortion. I got dragged into the whole mess because I lent out the house. In the end, we were all caught by the police. Mom and Dad bailed me out and hired a lawyer for my trial. The court case was a long one: two and a half years. Those were the times when you saw me wearing a suit.

Mom and Dad were so concerned about the possibility of a negative effect on your health that we all decided to keep the tragic news from you. Every day, they had to scan through the newspaper and remove any articles about me before putting it on the coffee table for you. I felt so disgusted every time I lied to you while putting on a smile to make like everything was okay. There were many days when I was going to tell you the truth, but I didn't have the courage and instead just headed outside for a smoke. It was a long battle.

On November 14, 2006, that morning you thought I was going to Toronto to further my studies, I was actually going to the courthouse to *receive my sentencing. I was convicted and sent to prison. At the door, you said I was looking smart and you were very proud of me. I looked at you and thought in my head, "I'm lying to you. I'm heading to prison, not school. And you shouldn't be proud of me because I'm very ashamed of myself." For the past two years, every time you asked me how I was doing in Toronto, I had to keep lying to you. When it was raining outside the prison, I told you it's snowing in Toronto. It wasn't right, and I cannot keep doing it anymore. I am so sorry for lying to you. You are my dear grandpa. I respect you so much, and I care for your health a lot. I didn't want to lie, and I had no intention to hurt you. I just didn't want to affect your health. Would you please forgive me? I have made many mistakes in my life, and I am starting to learn from them and become a better man.*

Right now I am in a federal prison in Mission, serving my time. Even though I have lost everything, in here I have gained something much more valuable. In my difficult time behind bars, I have experienced God in a very deep way. Through Him, I have understood the purpose of my existence. All my life I had placed my value and identity in the wrong place, and by that means I've been hurt over and over. Never was I able to appreciate the blessings around me. I remember being so focused on chasing my music dream that I would neglect everything else. I wouldn't even take a second to look at the flowers. But now when I see a small tree outside the prison fence, all I want to do is throw my arms around its trunk. In the outside world I was restless. Worries kept me from falling asleep all the time. In here, even though I am physically locked up, after placing my trust in Christ, I have peace. I have never been as calm as I am today. I'm sure this sounds hard to believe, right? How is this even possible? I would love to tell you more and share the many stories of my journey with you soon.

I know this is a lot to take in. I'm sure it's very shocking to you, and you must have many questions for me. If you want to come visit me, my parents will help you fill out the application forms and walk you through the procedures. I also want you to know this is not the end of my journey. If anything, this is just the beginning. Now I have God on my side, so don't you worry about me. I am in good hands.

Before I end this letter, I would like to do a prayer together with you, would that be okay? If so, please repeat the following with me:

"Father in heaven, we come to You through Your Son, Jesus Christ. We want to lift up all our burdens, worries, and concerns to You. We understand that we are not perfect. We make mistakes. That's why we need a Saviour. Please come into our hearts, forgive our sins, and make us whole. Thank You for Your unfailing love displayed beautifully on the cross. Please guide our every step, lead our every way, and protect us every day.

Bosco H. C. Poon

May Your Spirit be with us as we place our trust in You. In Your holy name, we pray. Amen."

May this prayer bring you peace in your heart. Please don't let my situation worry you. I am doing well. If you have any doubts about this, please come visit me. You will see it with your own eyes. I hope my honesty shows my respect and care for you. I pray that you will start to experience God's presence also. Once you have a relationship with Him, you will never be the same. I am a living testimony of it. I love you, Grandpa. All right, I'd better stop here. Oh, one last thing, don't forget to watch your step when going up and down the stairs. Take good care of yourself, please. I am looking forward to seeing you in person soon. I miss your hugs.

Love,

Lup Lup

———

"Lup Lup!"

"Grandpa!"

"Lup Lup! My, oh my! I can finally see you." Grandpa ran to me in the visiting area. We hugged each other very tightly. Tears poured from both of our eyes.

"It's been so long. I'm sorry—"

"That's okay. That's okay. You don't need to say any more. Come, let me take a good look at you. My, my, you have gotten skinny. But you're still looking very smart."

"Ha. You're looking good too, Grandpa. You look healthy. Thank God. You know everybody thought that you wouldn't be able to handle the bad news."

"Come on, I'm your grandpa! I raised your mom and uncles with these two hands. I'm tougher than that."

"Yeah, that's what I said." I gave my mom a look, trying to tease her.

"All right, all right. Let's just grab a seat before the officer tells us to do so over the speakers." My mom smiled. "I got you dill pickle chips as usual."

"Thanks, Mom. And thank you for bringing Grandpa here."

"It wasn't easy to go against your grandma on this, but after reading your letter, I knew it was the right thing to do. Dad and I showed Grandpa your letter together in the living room. He gave us a tongue-lashing for not telling him the truth sooner and asked us to apply to come see you right away. You're right. He is stronger than we thought. I'm proud of your courage, son."

"The credit doesn't go to me. I had a dream where God revealed to me that my habit of lying has been bringing more harm than good, both to me and to those around me—just look at the pain I've brought on the family by ending up in here. Seeing that more clearly, I didn't have any choice but to change."

"God talked to you in your dream?"

"Yeah, He shows me stuff all the time. Sometimes it's hard to take, but the truth is good for me."

My mom pondered what I'd said.

"Lup Lup, didn't you say you have a lot to share with me? Tell me some of the stories. I am curious."

"Of course, Grandpa. We only have two and a half hours. Where should I begin?"

"Anywhere is fine. I am just happy to see you again."

"Yeah, me too."

I filled my grandpa in with more details of my trial, my time in prison, and my new-found faith. He asked me a lot of questions, and I did my best to answer them. We continued to chat until the officer called to tell us time was up. It was one of the best visits I'd had. The burdens of my family lightened substantially after that as we learned to speak more openly to one another. It was a wonderful new beginning with them, and telling the truth was the right way to repay them for their care for me.

> **"Jesus said, 'If you hold to my teaching, you are really my disciples. Then you will know the truth, and the truth will set you free.'"**
> **(John 8:31–32)**

CHAPTER 14
SERVANTHOOD

"Rise and shine, gentlemen! Time for a morning bath." With a toilet brush in my right hand and a spray bottle of bleach in my left, I began washing the urinals and toilets of the men's washroom in the chapel. After getting fed up with the negativity of the kitchen, I applied to work for the church and got hired as the chapel worker. Like most jobs I had to start on the bottom rung. This meant that I was on janitorial duty, cleaning the toilets and mopping the floor. I grew up listening to Mom's story of how she worked her way up in real estate and hotel management. She too had started with washing the toilets every morning. Instead of being grumpy about it, she used to talk to the toilets while she was cleaning them as if they were people. I adopted her spirit and did the same thing.

Bang! Father Mako rushed through the entrance, sending the door swinging on its hinges and hitting the adjacent wall. "Guys, listen! There's a knife missing from the kitchen. From the records, it was last sent to the chapel with the meal cart for the dinner gathering last night. It hasn't been returned since. Did anyone see it? If we don't find it right away, there will be an emergency lockdown."

"What? Impossible! We returned the cart back to the kitchen as usual before count time. You sure they didn't overlook it?" Dave scratched his head through his baseball cap.

"Yeah, we brought it back as usual," Glenn said in agreement.

"According to the report, they've done a thorough search of the whole cart and couldn't find the knife. So it should still be here in the chapel unless someone took it, which is why there'll be a lockdown if we don't recover it." Father Mako unlocked his office door and headed over to the phone.

"Did anyone make sure the knife was put back on the cart? To be honest, I never looked. Maybe someone *did* take it." Pedro looked at Dave.

"Well, I don't recall seeing it, but I wasn't looking for it specifically," Dave replied.

"Me neither," said Glenn.

"Okay, guys, can you search through the chapel now? I'm going to call upstairs and see if I can buy us some time." Father Mako picked up the phone and punched in the numbers.

"All right, everyone, let's get to work!" Dave tilted his cap.

All of us went separately to the four corners of the chapel and searched. We lifted up every single chair, bookshelf, and even the flowerpots, but we found nothing but dust bunnies and insect carcasses.

"Nothing here, man!" Pedro shouted.

"I went through everything. I couldn't find anything either. It's not here," Dave replied.

"Me too ... nothing. Someone might have taken it back to his cell. It's not here. I guess we'd better prepare ourselves for a lockdown." Glenn sighed.

The whole time I didn't say a word. I searched through both washrooms but couldn't find anything either. Instead of joining the conversation, I prayed to God in my heart for guidance. In the middle of my prayer, the three big garbage cans caught my attention. Just then, a thought came to me: *What if the knife got thrown away with the leftover food?* Without thinking twice, I rushed to the garbage bags and started digging out the trash.

"What are you doing there? Forget it. It's not in there. That's just trash!" Dave yelled to me.

"I'll clean up the mess afterwards. I just have to check." I tried hard not to breathe through my nose while replying to Dave.

Digging out everything from the first garbage can, I didn't find anything. So I moved on to the second one.

"You found anything?"

"No, not yet."

"Because it's not there. Father Mako, I think we're ready to call for the lockdown."

"Just one more minute! Maybe it'll be here."

I didn't know what got into me. Something inside was telling me that the knife was in the garbage cans. After searching through the second one without any luck, I moved on to the third. Piece by piece, I dug out and examined every item of trash. When I got to the bottom of the third garbage can, I felt something hard on my fingertips. Carefully taking it out, I found the missing knife.

"I found it! I found it!" Yelling at the top of my lungs, I ran to the washroom to give it a good rinse before I handed it to Father Mako.

"Good job, Bosco! Thank you. I'll take it back to the kitchen right away." Father Mako took the knife from my hand immediately and walked out of the chapel.

"Wow, that was impressive. How did you know it was in the garbage can?" Dave asked, his voice full of curiosity.

"I didn't know for sure. All I did was say a prayer in my heart and ask God for guidance. Then the garbage cans came to my attention. So I took it as a sign from Him and went for it. Lo and behold, it was there. We must have dumped it with the leftover food while cleaning up last night."

"Ha, it must have been God then. A clean freak like you rummaging through garbage cans—how else could we explain *that*? What an awesome testimony. You're truly becoming His servant. Now let's give you a hand cleaning up."

"It's quite messy. I'll go get the mop." Glenn smiled.

"And I'll go get a pot of coffee ready. It'll be ready to serve when you guys are done." Pedro patted my shoulder.

Knock-knock!

"Bosco, you there?" Dave was knocking on my door.

"Hey, what's going on?"

"I need to tell you something."

"Everything all right? You sound serious." I closed the door.

"Okay, some weird things are happening to a friend of mine. I've known him for years. His name is Sean. You might have bumped into him here and there. But I never officially introduced you two."

"Sean—you mean that young British guy?"

"Yeah, that's him. Anyway, long story short, he's on some heavy psychiatric medications. The doctors have been giving him a lot of drugs because he's constantly hurting himself. He does all sorts of crazy things just to see himself covered in blood."

"What? Really? He seemed pretty normal to me."

"On a good day when he's out of his cell, yes. Here's the thing: I've walked him through many difficult times over the years. He used to come to the chapel but has stopped for quite a while now. I visit him from time to time. I just made a trip to see him and found that he was all bandaged up around his face—"

"Whoa, is he all right?"

"Apparently he banged his head against the mirror last night until his face was all cut up. It's pretty bad."

"My goodness. Why did he do that?"

"He said he hated what he saw in the reflection, so he smashed his head into it. He also heard a voice taunting him and telling him to do it. You see, that's the part that's got me worried. He tends to follow that voice in his head. The psychologist and psychiatrist use some complicated terminology to describe it as a disease and use drugs to sedate him. But whenever the drugs wear off, he gets right back up and starts following the instructions of that voice again. The real problem is the voice. I personally believe that is the voice of the devil, not just a mental disease you can treat with medications. This is a spiritual matter, not just a physical one. If I'm correct, then it explains why the psychologist and psychiatrist haven't been able to help him all these years. The drugs are only acting as a Band-Aid."

"The voice of the devil? You mean the *devil-devil*?" This really caught my attention.

"Yes, I mean real demons, fallen angels: God's sworn enemies. The Bible talks about them plenty, as you've read. They are mentioned throughout Scripture. Jesus cast out many demons, and so did His disciples. The end of the Gospel of Mark even says that one of the signs of Jesus's followers is that they will cast out demons in His name. This is nothing new. All cultures describe the phenomenon of demonic possession."

"Now that you mention it, I had a similar experience once. When I first started my sentence at North Fraser, I heard a demonic voice telling me there was no hope. It was dark. The sound reminded me of Darth Vader, only creepier. The voice made me feel totally hopeless. At one point, I was actually choking too. I actually couldn't breathe for a moment, and I knew it wasn't my imagination. It was real."

"Wow, you experienced that? How did you get out?"

"As I was struggling, I saw that someone had written 'GOD help me' on the wall. I repeated that in my heart, and then that dark force slowly disappeared."

"Bingo! You see, it was spiritual warfare. You got out because you asked God to help you. That's the cure. You see what I mean now?"

"Yeah, now that you put it this way, I can see it. I wondered for a long time what that was. I didn't have a clue then, but in the context of the Bible, now it makes sense. If Sean was experiencing something similar, only stronger and more tenacious, I can't imagine what he must be going through. I mean, smashing his head into the mirror? That's some serious stuff."

"For sure. That's what I want to talk to you about. Now that I know you had some similar experiences I believe we're discussing this for a reason. Listen, I want to bring you along to visit Sean. I see God's light in you. It's important to provide you more training because you've been chosen to do His work. But this time it's not just a visit. We're going to follow the teaching of the Bible and cast out some demons."

"Cast out demons? You mean like an exorcism?"

"Yes. But not like the way you see in movies with props and gore. We're just going to go in with the Spirit of God, plain and simple. We'll use the authority of Jesus's name to call them out. There's a record in the Bible about a boy possessed by an evil spirit that would throw him violently on the ground and cause him to seize—even throw him into fire and water. Jesus cast out that evil spirit, and the boy was instantly healed. Doesn't that sound like something we could do for Sean by the power of God?"

"Yeah, it does when you put it that way." I was in deep thought.

"So you'll go with me?"

"Well, I've been experiencing a lot of unusual things. I saw God's light, I heard His voice, and I've seen some miraculous things, like the salvation of Lee's mom. I'm open to whatever God wants me to experience. Why not?"

"Good stuff. That's a great attitude. You don't need to bring anything special. Just follow me. I'll bring the Bible. Oh, there's one more thing to take note of. When we pray over Sean, just lay out your hand like this towards him. Repeat after me when I say 'Devil, in the name of Jesus Christ, you come out.' Remember to say it together with me. The key is to have faith in the power of our Saviour through His Holy Spirit. Okay?"

"All right, I'll turn my faith up and follow your lead."

As we walked to the other side of the unit to see Sean, I felt like a special agent on a classified assignment, like in the *Mission Impossible* movies, except I was in ratty blue jail clothes instead of a cool black outfit from Hugo Boss.

We passed by the unit office, where the guards were chatting over snacks. I was acting as casually as I could. Dave, on the other hand, cracked a joke to them. That was his normal, I guess. "You guys just sitting around and doing nothing again?" He was playing with them.

"Shut up and get out of here, Dave!" one of the guards shot back in a jocular tone. Dave had been there for a long time, and he had earned the respect of everyone, including the guards. It showed in the way he treated them and how they treated him.

The moment we arrived at Sean's cell, Dave gave me a nod, then knocked on his door. "Sean, it's me, Dave. Can I come in?"

"Dave? Sure, come on in."

"Hey, buddy. How you feelin'?"

"All right, I guess. I was trying to sleep but couldn't." Sean was on his bed.

"Okay. Hey, I brought a good friend to see you. He's a very nice guy and works with me at the chapel. This is Bosco."

"Hey, Sean, I'm Bosco. Nice to meet you." I smiled at him.

"Oh hey, Bosco. Nice to meet you too. Uh, actually I've seen you around. Sorry, I'm not in the best of shape right now." Sean tried to sit up on his bed while brushing his curly hair back with his hands. His face was one-third covered by gauze. There were bruises and cuts all over his knuckles. His muscular physique showed that he had been going to the gym, but his voice sounded weak. Looking around his cell, I noticed that the window was covered up with a blanket. The mirror above his sink was gone, of course. There was an atmosphere of darkness in his room. What I saw in front of me was a handsome young man tormented by some horrendous thing. With compassion, I said, "It's okay. It's all good. You don't have to get up. Just relax and rest."

"Sean, I really wanted you to meet Bosco. He has a caring spirit. I told him a little bit about you and what you were going through. I hope you don't mind. I just thought he could be a positive support for you. It's always good to have some close friends around us, especially in this place, right?" Dave explained as he closed the door behind us.

"Okay. Is he like you? Is he a good Christian who goes to church?"

"Yes! He is like me. He attends all the services at church."

"Okay, I trust you, so I can trust him too. Good people go to church." Sean smiled back at me after Dave's affirmation.

"Besides introducing you two, I also want to see if we can offer you some support in what you are going through. To be honest, seeing you hurting yourself over and over is painful for me. I want to see you get well."

"I know. I wanna get well too. The voice in my head comes and goes. The pills just put me to sleep. When I'm sleepy, it doesn't matter what the voice says; I have no energy to do anything stupid anyway. But when I wake up, that's the problem. I listen to the voice and hurt myself when I have energy. The worst is when I look in the mirror. I just want to kill myself because I don't like what I see. I hate it!" Sean was getting frustrated.

"The pills these doctors have been giving you, do they help you?" Dave said as he sat down beside him on his bed.

"No, not really. They help put me to sleep for sure. But I don't get any better, so the doc has just increased the dose over the years. But I don't like sleeping all day. I feel so useless. So I stopped taking them for a while, and then I hurt myself again. This is a curse, man. It's just a curse."

"Hey, hey. Don't give up hope. There's a solution to every problem. God has an answer to everything. He can help you." Dave put down his Bible on the desk beside him and put his hand over Sean's shoulder.

Sean looked at the Bible, then looked into Dave's eyes, and said, "No man, this is a curse. This Bible, I tore one in half before. I'm cursed!"

"What do you mean? What happened?"

"It goes way back, when I was a teenager. I got into boxing. In the garage of my dad's place I put up a punching bag and trained there. Back then I used to get into all kinds of arguments with Dad. He was a Christian man who went to church. He was always telling me 'Bible this and Bible that.' I had a different set of values than him. We never seemed to see eye to eye. There was one evening I got fed up with him while training. We got into a huge fight … like huge. I then snatched the Bible from his hand and ripped it in half. I yelled at him, 'I want nothing to do with your God! Today, I submit myself to Satan!' I tore the Bible into pieces right in front of him. Not too long after, I left home and started off on my own journey. Eventually, through a series of bad choices, I ended up here."

Both Dave and I were shocked by the story, but now we understood how Sean had become the centre of a spiritual battle. Submitting himself to the king of the devils, even if he had only said it for shock value, had opened Sean up to Satan's intrusion in his life. The consequences of this could be massive and, of course, eternal. I didn't know what to say. Fortunately, Dave was there. Not wanting to make

Sean feel as if he was being judged, Dave replied with encouragement, "Oh, okay. Well, that's some heavy stuff. We all make stupid decisions as teenagers. I know I did too, but God is merciful, and there's no sin He cannot forgive when we confess it. You know?"

"You don't understand, Dave. I pledged my life to Satan, and he won't let me go. I'm cursed for life."

"No, that's not true. There's always hope. Christ defeated Satan on the cross. He came to save us from Satan. We're here to help you fight this battle. Let me ask you something—do you want to get well? Do you want the voice in your head to leave you?"

"Of course I want to get well. I hate that voice. It's always tormenting me."

"Okay, okay. Then can we pray over you, using the authority of Jesus to call that demon out? This is nothing new. Jesus did this often while He was on earth. His disciples did the same thing too. Can we do that for you?"

"Well, okay, whatever that means. As long as you can make that voice disappear, go ahead. Do what you need to do."

"All right, I'll have Bosco come here next to me. You can just relax and close your eyes. Just calm your heart as we pray for you. Okay?"

"Okay." Sean closed his eyes as I moved forward and extended my hand towards his heart. Dave laid his hand over his forehead and started to pray. "Father, we come to You through Your Son, Jesus Christ. We ask for Your favour boldly on behalf of Sean. Lord, You know what Sean is going through and the chains the enemy has placed on him. May You break those chains and set him free from the curse of Satan. Please cleanse him from the inside out by Your righteousness. We believe Your power is far greater than the enemy's. No weapon against us shall prosper, because You alone are God Almighty. Sean, can you repeat after me?"

"All right."

"Lord Jesus, I let go of my past and submit myself to You."

"Lord Jesus, I let go of my past ... and submit ..."

"Submit myself to You."

"Sub ... mit ..."

"Myself to You. Yes, just say it after me."

"Sub ... mit ..."

"You can do it, Sean."

"Sub ... mit ... No, I can't ... He won't let me ..."

"Who won't let you?"

"The shadow ... the dark shadow that lives inside me won't let me say those words. He's stopping me from saying that."

"Okay, we'll cast it out. Bosco you ready? Say it with me. Remember what I told you?"

"All right, let's do it!" I replied.

"In the Mighty Name of Jesus Christ, devil, you come out!" Dave and I said it together. We waited for a second before Dave asked, "Sean, is the shadow still there?"

"Yes, it's still here."

"All right, we'll do it again. In the Name of Jesus, demon, you must obey our Lord. Now come out!"

"That's right, by the power of our Lord, demon, you must come out!" I prayed over Sean, and as I observed he started to shiver a little.

"Sean, where's the shadow now?" Dave asked.

"I saw a person in white light standing in front of me. I wanted to go to him, but the shadow is holding me back. He won't let me go."

"That's Jesus; I can sense Him here. Sean, you have to speak to the shadow and tell him that he has to release you. The old curse is already broken by the blood of our Saviour," I said, holding his hand.

"I can't. He said I'm his because I made an oath to him."

"Don't listen to him. He's lying. His power is no match for our God's. Sean, submit yourself to Jesus, and that demon will flee. Can you do that? Do you want to submit to Christ now?" Dave asked intently.

"Yes!" Sean ground his teeth.

"Okay, devil, you heard Sean. In the name of Jesus, Sean renounces his connection with you! He is set free by the sacrifice of Jesus. The price has been paid. You have to let him go! That oath no longer has power over Sean because of the saving blood of Jesus."

After this last prayer, Sean's whole body shook for a bit, then calmed down. His face was slowly becoming more relaxed.

"Hey buddy, how are you?" Dave asked.

"I'm all right. Weird—I feel a lot lighter. That shadow seems gone. I can't feel it anymore. Is it really gone? Am I going to get better now?" Sean slowly opened his eyes and looked at us.

"It should be gone. If so, you are going to be better. However, you are extremely vulnerable right now. You must guard your heart and not let the enemy come back in. The Bible talks about that specifically. We'll continue to pray for you. Come to our chapel services whenever you can. We'll ask the pastor to pray over you as well. The more spiritual support you can receive, the better it will be for you." Dave took off his baseball cap.

"Okay, I'll try that. I'll start coming back to church again."

"Good, good. All right, we better get going and let you rest. You probably will sleep like a baby tonight." Dave patted my shoulder, giving me the sign that it was time to leave.

"Thank you, guys. I really appreciate what you've done for me."

"No problem, brother. It was a pleasure to meet you. May God's peace be with you." I gave him a firm handshake.

"Have faith in God, all right? You'll be fine." Dave gave him a hug. Afterward, we left Sean's cell and headed back to ours for lock-up.

It was quite an experience to learn how to cast out demons. I had read about it in the Bible, but I didn't really think that this was something still happening in the modern era. But if the God of the Bible hadn't changed, I guess the devil's contempt for Him hadn't either. I learned a lot through this experience and gained insight into the reality of spiritual warfare.

"Poon! Turn around and bend down, now!" A guard was strip-searching me in the anteroom between the two sets of heavy metal doors in the segregation unit. After the search was complete and I was putting my clothes back on, the guard asked, "Poon, what are you here for?"

"I'm here to provide peer counselling for my fellow inmates here in the hole, to give them emotional and spiritual support," I replied while putting my shoes back on.

"Peer counselling? How come I don't recognize you?"

"It's only my second time here. I just finished the course to become an inmate peer counsellor two months ago. My friend and I take turns coming down every other week. The last time I was here was a month ago. Maybe you weren't here that day."

"You aren't lying to me, are you? Cause I can find out real quick if you're playing games."

"No, sir. I'm not lying. As you said, you can find out very quickly if I'm lying. I work at the chapel, and I'm living in Unit 1. You can verify my identity from them. I brought some small spiritual booklets for the guys, just so they can use their time reading something beneficial to their souls. If you allow it, I'll hand them out."

"Hmm … nothing hiding inside these booklets, right?"

"No, sir."

"Looks legit. I'll check on your file in a bit. Sign your name here. No drugs on you, right?"

"No, of course not. You just strip-searched me, didn't you? I'm just here to provide counselling as part of my job."

"Okay, go ahead. I'll keep an eye on you. I'll be a few steps behind the whole time, so don't do anything stupid." The guard gave a hand sign to the other guards behind the window to unlock the door.

Segregation is a heavily guarded twenty-four-hour lock-up unit (with a very short movement break for shower or phone each day) for inmates who violate the rules in prison. It's literally the prison within the prison. People were put there for all sorts of infractions: fighting, drug debts, putting others in danger, etc. Other times, it was used for protection from other inmates, as was the case for rats and skinners (prison slang for "pedophiles"). Walking through the hallway towards the last cell at the very end, I was reminded how I first began my sentence with full-day lock-up time and I shrunk into a skinny little waif. When I stopped in front of the metal door of the first cell, I took a deep breath and knocked on the door. "Hello? Hello, I'm the inmate peer counsellor. You interested in talking with me today?"

"What? What do you want?" The inmate was giving me a really bad attitude, probably thinking I was a guard.

"I'm the inmate peer counsellor. I'm an inmate myself. I'm here to check up on you and provide some support. Do you mind if I talk with you for a bit?" I politely explained myself.

"Oh, okay."

With the inmate's permission, I knelt down and opened the meal tray slot to begin a conversation. I looked inside through the rectangular tray hole and saw that he was getting up from his bed. "Hello, how are you? My name is Bosco. I work in the chapel."

"Hey buddy, what do you want from me?"

"I'm just here to show you some support, especially spiritual support. I know it must be tough to be in here. I just want to let you know a bunch of guys at the chapel are praying for you."

"Praying for me? You don't even know me. How can you pray for me? What do you want from me?"

"Nothing. I don't want anything from you. We pray for the guys in the hole in general because we know how lonely it can be down here. Now that you know there are people who care about you, we hope your spirits are lifted while you're in here."

"Care? What do you get from this? How much do they pay you?"

"Nothing, really. Beside some insults and humiliation. In order to get in here, I have to apply at the unit office and answer a bunch of questions similar to the ones you've just asked. Then the guards strip-search me, and, as you know, showing your private parts to a stranger is pretty humiliating. Then I have to answer a bunch more questions before I finally have a conversation with you."

"Exactly! That's what I mean. Why do you go through all those troubles for nothing? I don't believe you. Who sent you here?"

"Good question. Who sent me here? God sent me here, because someone did something similar for me before. I, like you, was very skeptical at first. That person invited me to church and showed me a lot of support in this place. My time is short. I only get a few minutes for each cell. Do you want some prayer before I move on?"

"Nah ... I'm good."

"Okay, that's fine. I have a little booklet here, called *Our Daily Bread*. There's a very small read for each day with some inspiration and encouragement. You can take a look when you have time. I'm gonna pass it to you, okay?"

"Yeah, you can just toss it on the floor."

"Okay. All right, buddy, I gotta go now. Take care. I won't be back for another month. If you get out of here to the general population before my return, you're welcome to come find me at the chapel. I work there every day. Oh right, I didn't get your name."

"Scott."

"All right, Scott, hopefully I'll see you again. Remember to keep your chin up. God bless." I smiled at him and stood up to walk to the next cell. The guard closed the meal tray slot as I left. The "clank" echoed down the hallway and accompanied my footsteps until I arrived at the next door.

I repeated the same procedure fifteen more times. Some people were very receptive and asked for prayer right away. Others rejected me and even told me to "F-off." I didn't have enough time to finish all the cells, because some guys talked for more than just a few minutes. After about 40 minutes, the guard called me from behind and told me my time was up. I slid the last booklet into the cell of the inmate I was speaking with and quickly made my way back.

On my way out, I was strip-searched again. Scott was right. Who would want to go through all these troubles for nothing?

It reminded me how Jesus was humiliated by prison guards and how the people He came to save also persecuted Him. If it wasn't for the love of God, I would never go through that kind of humiliation just to get abused by both the guards and inmates. Putting my pride and comforts aside, I was learning how to be a servant.

> "Yet it shall not be so among you; but whoever desires to become great among you, let him be your servant. And whoever desires to be first among you, let him be your slave—just as the Son of Man did not come to be served, but to serve, and to give His life a ransom for many." (Matt. 20:26–28 NKJV)

CHAPTER 15
FORGIVENESS

In a multicultural society like Canada, prisons are full of people from different parts of the world. I learned about these other cultures by attending the gatherings of different ethnic groups during my time in prison. Every time I smelled a delicious aroma of curry as I walked through the chapel door, I knew the East Indian group was having their home-cooking night.

"Bosco, come join us! We have plenty of food. Come eat!" Ted invited me to the table in his strong Punjabi accent.

"Wow, thank you. That's very kind of you guys. But I have to work." I smiled while heading to the janitorial room to grab the mop and broom.

"Come on, don't be shy. You can work after you eat. Come, come!" Ted insisted.

"Ha, all right. If you insist." I walked towards them.

"Yeah man, help yourself. We made yellow, green, and red curry. This is beef and this is chicken. Oh, and this is our all-time favourite: samosas. You'll love them." Chris was showing me the dishes on the folding plastic table they'd borrowed from the chapel meeting room.

"Hmm, what's a samosa? It looks like a pastry." I grabbed one to try.

"It's a traditional dish. The inside is filled with potatoes, onion, and spices, and it's deep fried to perfection. It's the bomb, man."

"Mmm hmm, this *is* good: lots of flavours. I taste the cumin, and it reminds me of the curry puffs I used to have in Hong Kong. There were a lot of East Indians there too. But the one I'm familiar with was a flat triangle instead of pyramid shape, way smaller, and it had curried beef inside instead of potatoes. You know what I'm talking about?"

"Flat triangle? We don't make them like that. Maybe that's from another part of Asia. The ones we've grown up with are packed with potatoes. My family never uses beef in our samosas. Today you got a real taste of India." Ted put another one on my paper plate.

"Really? Wow, there's so much to learn. I always thought the flat triangle curry puffs were authentic Indian food. That's what I was told back then at least. And this curry tastes different than the ones I've had in the Indian restaurants in Hong Kong. Is this how you usually make it?"

"Yes, this is our family recipe. It's pretty close to what my mom used to make, but we're missing a few ingredients because we're in prison. So it's not quite perfect. But I'd say it's pretty close. The ones you get in the Indian restaurants here have been Westernized. Maybe the ones you ate before had been Hong-Kong-erized."

"Now that you mention it, you're probably right. Just like the Flying Wok in the food court at the mall tastes nothing like the food in real Chinese restaurants, let alone my mom's home cooking."

"Yeah, that's the concept. Wait, if that's the case, then does the same go for the fried rice we get in the mess hall? Does it taste like real Chinese food at all?" Ted looked at me.

"Ha, not even close to anything from *my* hometown. Each grain of rice in real fried rice has to be dry on the outside but soft inside, with a perfect blend of fresh ingredients. This can only be achieved using specific techniques and by cooking it in a big wok over a huge burner. The one from the prison kitchen is nothing more than some sauce poured over cooked rice with frozen vegetables. Oh man, how I miss my mom's home cooking," I said, longing for home and my mom's care.

"What? So we've been eating Chinese food that isn't real Chinese food and you've been eating Indian food that isn't real Indian food? That's messed up, man! We've all been fooled." Chris looked at the other guys at the table and started speaking in Punjabi to them.

My knowledge of different cuisines gradually increased as I hung out with inmates from different countries and cultural backgrounds. This also broadened my understanding of how different cultures use the same ingredients in totally different ways. Using just flour and water, Asians make noodles, Italians make pasta, Middle Easterners make flatbread, and East Indians make roti. Isn't that how God works too: different races made by the same Creator? As I got to know different inmates on a more personal level, I got to see how we actually shared things in common. As prisoners, we had committed different crimes and ended up at the same place. All of our hearts had the same deep yearning for something that could set our souls free. We all wanted forgiveness and a second chance.

Risen From Prison

I want revenge! Hire me a hit man and set him loose on Blade! I wanna see him suffer. Cut off that finger he used to point at me from the witness stand. Cut out that tongue he used to mock me. I want him wiped off the face of this earth. He has to pay for dragging me into this sh*thole! He has to pay!

"Whoa, whoa, whoa, what was that all about?" I woke up suddenly from a dream, my whole body shaking and soaked in sweat. "My goodness. Where does all that anger come from? I thought I'd long ago forgotten about Blade. I sure don't like remembering that stupid, smug look on his face. Why on earth has he popped up in my dream? Man, even thinking about him makes me feel so angry!" I was speaking to myself.

Getting up from my bed in frustration, I went to the sink to splash some cold water on my face. From time to time, I would feel extremely bitter when I pondered my situation. Especially after I received the news that I have lost my appeal to reduce the length of my sentence. The hopelessness of being trapped in that tiny cell drove me crazy. This reality fuelled my anger toward Blade. The anger that was obviously hiding in my subconscious mind would bubble up in its fullness from time to time. On a good day, I wouldn't even think of Blade. On a bad day, like the one I was having that day, it would pour out a kind of venom I didn't even know existed. With this kind of vitriol inside me, I was afraid I would do something stupid if I didn't get it under control. The outburst of anger I'd just experienced in my dream told me that the root cause had clearly not been dealt with. I had a spiritual parasite.

"Bosco, I see that you're spending a lot of time in the chapel helping the people around here." Pastor Tom was counselling me in his office. "But how about you? How are *you* holding up? You don't have to pretend in front of me. I won't judge. And what we discuss will stay in this room."

"Thanks for asking. I guess I'm doing okay. I'm learning new things every day. I'm trying my best to survive in this place, but I do have my moments, you know. After all, this *is* prison. Working in the chapel keeps me occupied." I sat back on the wooden chair.

"I understand. It's not easy to live in a place like this, and you *do* have a longer sentence than many others. It must be hard on you. But you're on the right track. Your behaviour has shown your desire to change—to become a better man. It's a rarity in this place." Pastor Tom grabbed his cup of coffee and continued, "However, I have observed one thing that concerns me. You're always smiling, which is great. But behind that smile, I sense a hint of bitterness. Now, I don't want you to ignore that bitterness. There are probably a lot of emotions inside you that you haven't had a chance to properly deal with yet. Without doing so, little time bombs can form inside you that may one day explode. You know where I'm coming from?"

"Yeah, you're right. There are many emotions I don't know how to deal with, so I just hide them inside. It's better than blurting them all out, you know?" I looked outside the window.

"That's exactly what I thought. Listen, you don't have to blurt them out to just anyone, but it is important to get healing and be made well inside, so that you can pass that healing to others. Is there anything I can do to help you—besides getting you out of prison right now, of course?" We both smiled. "That will eventually happen on its own if you stay on the right path. Is there anything you want to tell me? I can be a listening ear for you."

"Well, there are a lot of negative aspects to prison life that I encounter everywhere I turn. People's never-ending foul language and all the other filthy stuff that comes out their mouths. Violence and bullying are everyday occurrences. And the criminal mentality—it's always about money or sex. I really can't stand it. On top of all this, I'm often haunted by bad memories from the past, even in my dreams. I guess I'm angry about many things. I'm angry at the person who's responsible for putting me here. I'm angry at my girlfriend for cheating on me. I'm angry about losing my music career. I'm angry at myself for disappointing my family. The worst part is, there's nothing I can do about any of these things."

"I see. From what you just said, I can tell there are a few layers to the problem. We'll need some time to process each layer. We probably won't be able to deal with all of them at once. What we can do today is to pick one of the more important layers and see what we can do about it." Pastor Tom took a sip of his coffee and put the cup down. "Let's see. It seems to me that anger is the primary problem in a number of these issues. Now know this: you are not alone. Anger is one of the most common problems people have. To break it down, there are actually two types of anger. One pushes us to do the wrong things, and the other pushes us to do the right things. The anger that causes you to feel contempt and vengefulness toward others is not the good type of anger. You want to get rid of that. What you want to keep, however, is the anger that makes you take actions to help those who are weaker than you. The right type of anger cannot bear injustice and, therefore, makes you do something to better this world. God has that kind of anger in Him."

"Okay, so how do I get rid of the bad kind of anger? I tried many things, like meditation and stuff. I become calmer after doing it, but eventually the anger and frustration just come back. What should I do?"

"You need to understand the root of your anger. Like, where does it come from? What is it telling you? Anger is really a signal, an alarm our bodies give us to indicate something needs to be done. Once that need is fulfilled, that signal will turn off. It's like a car engine's light. When it turns on, it means it's time to check the engine. Once the engine is repaired, the light will turn off. Does it make sense?" He looked at me to make sure I was following him. I nodded, so he continued, "When you're angry at someone, as you described earlier, you hold a grudge and are not willing to forgive the person. Without forgiveness, your anger won't subside. The signal light won't turn off."

"A signal? Forgiveness? Ha. How can I forgive the person that got me into this hellhole and made me lose everything? Because of that pathetic moron I literally lost everything!"

"See, your anger is spilling out right now. Bosco, this is the thing that is sucking out your life and killing you slowly. You've got to deal with it before it takes control of you. Many people do things out of anger and regret it later in their lives. Forgiving someone doesn't mean you have to pretend the person didn't hurt you, but it does mean that the person has no more power to hurt you today. You see how the person who got you into prison is still hurting you today? Why give him that power? By forgiving him, you will take away his power to make you angry, and he won't be able to hurt you anymore. We can't go back in time and change the past, but we can do something today to change the future. By you holding on to what that person did to you, you're letting that pain affect your future. You have to let it go."

"Pastor, I don't know how. He made me lose everything. How can I ever forgive him? It'd be progress if I just got to a stage where I didn't want him dead."

"Revenge is not the way to go. God says, 'Vengeance is mine.' God is the ultimate judge. He alone knows the hearts of all humankind. He knows who deserves what. Leave room for Him to repay. But for your sake, you have to forgive. Think about it. Don't you want your victim to forgive you? The Bible tells us if we don't forgive others, God will not forgive us. God wants us to pass on the same mercy to others that we have received from Him. That's why I said you need healing inside, so you can pass on healing to others. It's important for you to do that, since you try so hard to help here."

"I ... I ... I don't know how to do it. I don't think I can do it."

Pastor Tom put his hand on my shoulder. "With God all things are possible. By His strength, you can forgive. You have come so far. It's just one more step. Your world would become so much better. Why don't we pray together to ask our God to help you?"

> "Love your enemies, do good to those who hate you, bless those who curse you, pray for those who abuse you." (Luke 6:27–28 ESV)

Forgive Blade? How could I ever do that? This is very hard for me. What should I do? I haven't read today's devotional yet. Maybe I should read it to get my mind off this.

I went back to my cell after the counselling session. I picked up the devotional on my desk and flipped through pages to find the day's message. I was shocked the moment I read the title: "Forgive Your Enemy." *Is this a joke?* I kept on reading the Scripture of the day from Luke 6:27–36, which pointed out that if we only love those who love us, it's no credit to us, because even sinners love those who love them. But if we can love our enemies and do good to them, then our reward will be great and we will be children of the Most High. For God is kind to the ungrateful and wicked. "Be merciful, just as your Father is merciful," it read. My eyes stopped at the word "merciful." I didn't quite understand the full meaning of it, so I took out my dictionary and checked its definition.

Bosco H. C. Poon

Mercy means compassion or forgiveness shown toward someone whom it is within one's power to punish or harm. What? It's the word "forgiveness" again. How is this possible? Is God really trying to tell me to forgive Blade?

I read it over and over. I struggled with it so much, I threw the devotional down on the desk. *Do I have to do this? Mercy. God has mercy on me. That I know. By His mercy my sins are forgiven. Be merciful, just as my Father is merciful. Do I have to forgive if I myself want forgiveness?*

After struggling with my thoughts for the whole evening, I knelt down on the icy concrete floor of my cell. With the lights off, I prayed out loud: "God, Father, is this really what You want me to do? To forgive the very person that brought all these troubles on me? I mean, what do I owe him? I treated him with respect. I saw him as my best friend. And look how he repaid me. He always asked me for money. He took the last bit of my allowance to go to a casino on my birthday, only to lose it all and returning empty-handed. And then I was the one who had to pay for a McDonald's cheeseburger to share with him, using the last few coins in my wallet. That's how he celebrated my birthday. He's pathetic. He dragged me into prison. He ruined my life, my family, and my music career! And he only got half of my sentence. Does that seem fair to You?! And You want me to forgive him? Really?"

I punched my bed to release my anger. "Agh, agh, agh! But … what can I do to him now? His sentence is finished. He's back out to the free world while I'm still locked up in here. It's not as if hiring someone to kill him would release me from prison now. I've had enough of him. I don't want to give him any more power to hurt me. Love my enemy? That's tough. Do good to those who curse me and abuse me? I guess giving up the idea of vengeance on Blade is to do good to him. But to have mercy on him? To forgive him?"

Tears began pouring from my eyes. I felt a rising torrent in my heart. My whole body shook, and I squeezed my fists to the point that my nails were digging into my palms. I cried out bitterly, "Jesus, help me! If it is Your will, help me to forgive Blade! Help me to forgive my enemy. I don't know how to do it myself. Please help me!" I pressed my forehead to the edge of my bed and shook my fists towards the walls. "I have to let this anger go. I release my anger towards him. I no longer give him the power to hurt me anymore. This has to go! Lord, You said even bad people love those who love them. So we have to go beyond them to even love my enemies. God, this is so hard, so hard."

I paused a little to regain my strength and opened my mouth again. "But despite my feelings, please look after Blade. Look after his well-being, and please draw him to Your salvation. He needs it. Deal with him on my behalf please. I … I … I forgive him, just as You have forgiven me. I forgive him. I forgive him!" I lay flat on the floor while tears kept falling from my eyes. Having my eyes closed, I kept repeating three words: "I forgive him."

I fell asleep shortly after that heart-wrenching prayer. The next morning, even though I woke up with my puffy eyes, I felt something was different. The weight on my shoulders was surprisingly absent. The heavy burdens created by hatred seemed to have left my body. My anger toward Blade was completely gone. It was just as Pastor Tom had said—the engine light had turned off. Forgiveness had set me free. It was so painful, but it was so worth it. Ever since that day, I have learned the true meaning of mercy, which allowed me to appreciate Jesus's love so much more. In my spiritual journal, I had a list of people whom I always prayed for. Carefully picking up my pen, I added Blade to the list.

It was a snowy day, one of the biggest snowfalls during my entire stay in the Mission Institution. Sitting in the unit the whole day on account of the inclement weather made me kind of stiff. Looking out the window and seeing that the snow was now over a foot deep, I decided I wanted to go outside and play. As I put on my dark green jail jacket and red baseball cap, Dave opened my door. "Hey, there you are. Oh, I see that you're getting ready to go out in the snow. Guess what? Me too! Wanna go together?"

"Perfect. Let's go. I need some fresh air."

Snow fell peacefully, creating a quiet hush and releasing a sense of childlike freedom I had long ago forgotten. The flakes reflected the orange light of the prison streetlamps against the dark-blue backdrop of the darkening sky. The snow was now up to mid-shin, but the groundskeepers had cleared paths between the buildings so we could walk freely. A handful of other inmates were enjoying the outdoors on the field, but the rest of them just stayed in their cells.

Walking towards the tennis court, our usual walking routine at night, Dave and I started to engage into conversation. After five minutes or so, I saw there was a layer of snowflakes on Dave's cap. Assuming that mine was likewise covered, I took my hat off and gave it a shake. The moment I put my cap back on, the V&C officer yelled over the PA system, "Poon to visit, Poon to visit!"

I looked at Dave and asked, "You hear that? Did they just call me to visit?"

"Sounds like it. Are you expecting anyone today?"

"Not that I know of, especially in weather like this. Who wants to come all the way here to visit me in a snowstorm? Besides, I went up to V&C at lunchtime and I didn't see my name on the visitor list. Maybe they made a mistake?"

"Just go up and check regardless. I'll wait for you here. If you don't come back in ten, then I know you're in a visit. I'll then just keep walking by myself."

"All right, sounds good. See you in a bit." I left the tennis court and walked up the long stairs towards the visiting area.

"Poon, there you are. Your visitor is waiting for you. Let me do a quick search on you before letting you in. Now turn around." The prison guard started to search me from top to bottom. After he was done, he spoke into the walkie-talkie, "Okay, Poon is good. Let him in."

Following a loud buzz from the metal door, I pushed through and headed inside the visiting area. As I looked around, I didn't see as many people as usual. Only two tables were occupied, and it was Joe who was sitting at one of them. Filled with elation, I walked up to him and gave him a firm hug. "Bro, it's so good to see you! What brought you here tonight? It's snowing like crazy out there. I thought they'd made a mistake by calling me up."

"Bro, it's good to see you too. Man, it wasn't an easy drive tonight. I had to pay extra attention. Cars were spinning out all over the place. But you were right; it's kind of like a mistake that I'm here now. Well, maybe more of a miracle."

"What do you mean?" We sat down before we continued the conversation.

"Well, I didn't call to book an appointment to visit you 24 hours ahead. In fact, I didn't call at all. I just knew I had to come see you today. Something inside told me so. That's why, despite the crazy snow, I still came, fully expecting that I probably would get turned away at the gates. But I just had to give it a try. And the crazier part was that the guards at the front gates didn't see my name on the list but still let me in. Maybe because of the snowstorm they felt bad about turning me away. So I'm here."

"What?! Wow! I have never heard of the prison guards letting anyone in without their name on a list. They even turned my family away one time because someone in the prison had mistakenly put them on the list for the following day. They are very strict. This is crazy."

"Tell me about it. That's just proof that it's meant to be. I knew it." Joe looked down to the table.

"Bro, is everything all right? Why is it so important that you see me today? What happened?" I was full of curiosity and a little worried.

"Tell me something, honestly. Is ... is God real?" Joe was looking at me with real intensity.

"What ... what? Am I hearing this wrong? You're asking me if God is real? Am I correct?" I was shocked to hear this coming from Joe of all people.

"Yes, that's what I asked. Is God real?"

"Oh man, I can't believe this. Of course, He is! If not, why have I kept telling you about Him for the past year and a half? But you've never responded to it in a positive way. I know how hard it is for your engineer's mind to believe something that's seemingly illogical. Why are you asking such a deep question today? Did you change your mind?"

"Well ... I don't know if I've changed my mind yet. But something did happen to me—something I couldn't explain logically. Many things happened actually. I guess we can start with the DVD you recommended to me—"

"*The Case for a Creator* by Lee Strobel? You watched it? Nice. Isn't it cool to see how science can actually point us to God?"

"It's interesting. Yeah, there were many points I'd never thought of before. It showed me perspectives I hadn't considered and certainly ones that I hadn't learned in school. That got me rethinking my view of science a little. But that wasn't all. It was the stuff I've experienced lately that really threw me for a loop. I just couldn't wrap my head around it. Remember the many times you prayed for me, for my safety and stuff? I never took it seriously. I always thought you were just speaking to the air whenever you prayed for me. I never believed your prayers actually *did* anything. But I respected you, so I kept my doubts to myself."

Joe cleared his throat, then continued, "Until recently I got into a few car accidents, but miraculously both me and even my car came out totally unscathed. Just last night, I drank a little too much. I wasn't in a good mood, and I was driving pretty fast down the highway. The road was slippery, and when I came to the exit, I took a turn with too much speed, and my car started to spin. There was no way I could stop it, and just as I was about to hit the concrete barrier and was thinking 'Whoa, this is gonna hurt so bad,' it seemed as if something pressed down on the top of my car and stopped it. Like, it completely stopped. With the speed it was going and the rate I was spinning, it was impossible for my car to stop like that."

He continued, "I thought about the events over and over, but I couldn't explain them logically, no matter how hard I tried. And this wasn't the first time. A similar thing happened to me just a few months ago. I haven't been very happy, so I've been going to a lot of parties to get wasted and drink my sorrows away. Getting hammered was the only thing I looked forward to each day when I left work. Bro, you have no idea. I didn't feel like I had a reason to live. The only escape was to be high." Joe took a deep breath and continued, "Anyway, when I had to drive home after partying, sometimes I was so tired it was difficult for me to focus on the road. On a few different occasions, I lost control of my car, and right before it was gonna hit a partition or go into a ditch, something stopped it. Every single time, bro. It was so weird. I mean, if it happened only once, I could dismiss it as chance. But more than once? The more I thought about it, the more the things you'd been telling me came to mind. That's why I have to see you. I need some answers."

I got chills as I listened to Joe. On the one hand, I was sad that he was dealing with all of this pain and sorrow even though he was free on the outside. I knew the pain of trying to escape with alcohol and drugs because I'd been there. On the other hand, I was ecstatic that he'd experienced some miracles and was eager to find out more. "Wow, a lot has been happening in your life. I understand how you feel about the ugliness of this world. I also understand why you tried to escape by partying and getting high. I understand, bro, for real. And as for the close calls, I mean, just hearing what you've described, I totally believe those were miracles. After all, we did pray together many times for your safety, and on top of that, I always keep you in my prayers. There can be no doubt that God hears our prayers. I think you're right; it must be God trying to get your attention."

"Really? You think so? Then why didn't He show up in front of me like He did for you so that I can just believe more easily?"

"Bro, I think He did. Didn't you say you felt something stopped your car every time you were gonna hit the wall or whatever? That was Him."

"That's what I wanna ask you. How do you know it was really Him? I mean, how can you tell? What if these were just uncanny circumstances? How can I really be sure?" Joe was getting a little frustrated.

"Great question. The very fact that you are struggling with it shows me that it *was* God. Believing in God *has* to involve faith. Faith is to believe in something our physical eyes cannot see. Take travelling on an airplane, for example. You have faith that the plane is going to take off and stay in the air even though the plane isn't flying when you get onboard. It is by faith that you board *that particular plane*, not by your experience with *that particular plane*. There are indeed planes in the world with faulty engines, and you take it on faith that your plane is not one of them. Faith started growing in you the moment you chose to believe that God might have been the One who saved you from dying in those close calls. Atheist Joe would never have even entertained the idea those near misses were anything but pure luck, because he had no faith. Now you are questioning if God is real because you have moved beyond the stage of a purely materialistic perspective. Can't you see? You're starting to have faith. Bro, I'm so happy for you. I can't believe this is finally happening."

Joe kept silent, digesting what he had heard.

"You see, I don't believe in God because I have scientific proof. I believe in Him because there are too many things in my life I cannot explain with logic alone. These things keep pointing me to Him. I had to let go of the need to fully understand everything I claim to believe so I could make room for Him. Do you remember when you scolded me for believing in God even though I got a 12-year sentence? I went back to my cell that evening and reflected on what you'd said. Your perspective was 'God can't exist, because your 12-year sentence is unfair.' My perspective was 'I have peace of mind despite receiving an unfair 12-year sentence.' How could I have peace in spite of such a huge sentence? We're talking about 12 years, man, not 12 months. My peace is a fact that cannot be explained with logic. Besides, I cannot blame God for my long sentence. After all, it was my fault that I got involved in that crime. God didn't force me. I did it myself out of my own stupidity by trusting the wrong people. So, my punishment is my own fault."

"Man, I don't know what to say. You're strong. You have a strong heart and a strong spirit. I doubt I would have the same reaction if I were in your shoes."

"I'm not strong—totally not. You have no idea how weak I feel sometimes. If I relied on my own strength, I would probably have gone crazy already. I'm weak, so weak. But it is just as the Bible says, God's power is made perfect in weakness. So when I'm weak, then I'm strong. It's by God's power that I can face all the challenges with a positive attitude. By God's grace you are looking at another miracle. Even though physically I'm incarcerated, spiritually I've been set free by Jesus Christ. Can you explain that with logic? I don't think you can; I tried, but I couldn't. If God can do that for me, surely He can do the same for you, especially since you're living in the free world."

Joe's eyes grew a little, as if something had really hit home.

"If you still have doubts, I can point you to another miracle you've just experienced. As a matter of fact, you yourself just called it a miracle. How did you get in here without previously booking an appointment with the prison system? It's impossible to get in here without going through the system properly. You know that, right? It's a prison. Bro, you're surrounded by miracles." I smiled at him.

Joe took another deep breath, looked at me, and said, "Maybe, maybe you're right. I don't know how to make sense out of all this. I'm not certain if God exists, but as you said, I'm questioning. Faith is something I've never had. A long time ago I lost faith in what *I could see*, people, never mind having faith in *what I could not see*, God. Humans always stab you in the back, you know? You can't trust anyone out there. Well, I'm not talking about you, bro. Being in here has kind of changed you. The people out there are so poisonous. They're like animals: always devouring one another."

"In here isn't much better. People in here still devour each other. But it's by forgiving the people who hurt us that we truly can be free. Hating others is painful and stressful. Those people we are angry with don't feel a thing—well, unless we go and physically harm them. But you get what I mean. They don't feel a thing when we're thinking about how much we hate them. We're the only ones who suffer because of our anger. But when we forgive them, we are literally setting *ourselves* free."

"Oh man, I don't know if I can do that. I've been hurt by so many people. I have so many bad memories."

"By your own strength, of course you can't. That's why you need God's strength. That's why we pray for His strength. I've just gone through all this myself, having to forgive the person who got me involved in the kidnapping and then took the stand against me in court. It was tough, real tough, but God helped me do it. The moment I forgave him, a huge weight left my shoulders. I felt so much lighter instantly."

"How do I do that? It's not as if I can just call you up to pray for me whenever I please. Plus, how do I know if He's gonna answer me? I don't even believe in Him yet. I'm just questioning right now."

"I'm glad you asked. Before you go today, we're going to pray, just like before. But when you're on your own out there, you can try praying on your own just like I've been praying with you. When you face a challenge, just tell Him what you need in your prayers. Never mind the 'if-He-will-answer-or-not.' Just pray. Think about it this way: if you pray and God doesn't answer you, the most you lose is a minute of your time. But if He would indeed answer you, then you gain so much more. Also, you'd gain the certainty that He is real. What have you got to lose?"

"Okay ... I can try that, I guess. It sounds pretty logical to me. Thanks, bro. I think you've given some reasonable answers tonight."

"My pleasure! It's so good to see you, especially on a snowy evening like this. It was a wonderful surprise."

"Yeah man, it was a wonderful surprise for me too. It was pretty impulsive, but I'm sure glad I came. Only now I gotta drive back in this snowstorm. Oh boy." Joe finally cracked a smile.

"Have faith. It's all good. I'm sure if God provided you a way to get in here and see me, He will provide you a way home as well."

"Ha, I guess you're right. Enough about me. How about you? How have you been?"

"Same old, same old," I said. "My life in here won't have as much variety as yours. But I'm learning a lot of things that I can't learn out there. I'm growing every day. Now I look at this place as a spiritual boot camp. So, I'm good. All right, time is almost up. Why don't we pray before you go?"

"Sounds good. I'll follow your lead." Joe closed his eyes and bowed his head.

We prayed together as we had on the other visits. This time I especially asked God to help Joe to forgive those who had hurt him and to grant him another opportunity to experience hope in this world.

These were just the first of many answered prayers Joe would experience later on in his journey. He would come back to see me every other month and would share with me how God had worked in his life. Eventually, he got involved in a church and some small groups. Step by step, Joe was slowly becoming a new person once again filled with hope. This was yet another miracle I witnessed during my imprisonment.

CHAPTER 16
A HINT OF FREEDOM

"Poon, you know the drill. Fill the urine container up to the line. When you're done, put the container on this table. I'll be waiting outside. Knock on the door when you're finished, okay?" The unit officer was giving me the usual instructions for my routine monthly drug test. After that, he locked me in the washroom and let me take care of business.

Because I lived in the drug-free unit, participation in drug screens was mandatory to remain there. Despite the efforts to contain it—constant monitoring, room checks, and pat downs—drug use was rampant in the prison. I have no idea how the drugs got in, but however they did, it must have been creative. For my family to come visit me, they had to go through two to three layers of body checking before they were allowed to enter the visiting area. Visitors were not allowed into prison until they passed this extensive search for contraband. If they were caught with anything forbidden or if any prison alarms happened to go off, they would be turned away at once … or perhaps be themselves apprehended if the contraband was illegal. I never did fully understand how contraband made it past such high security. In any case, the sieve must have had a few holes in it, because the drug lords seemed to keep the place well-stocked.

After I was done, I'd carefully screw the lid back on, trying not to make a mess. After that, I'd place the container on the table and knock on the door, and then the officer would let me out. Normally I would be called to the duty office within an hour or two to get the results. This time was the same: "Here are your results, Poon. You're good to go." On the test results sheet, it listed out my name, the date, the time, and the officer's name. Then below were all the results: CTRL—valid. Marijuana (THC)—NEG. Opiates (OPI)—NEG. Amphetamine (AMP)—NEG. Cocaine

(COC)—NEG. Methamphetamine (MAMP)—NEG. As I walked back to my cell, I heard my name through the PA system: "Poon, Poon to your IPO office."

Sometimes I got called to the IPO (institutional parole officer) offices from other units. Most of the time it was because the IPO needed a translator for a Chinese inmate. There were times where I felt extremely uncomfortable because the inmate and the parole officer were having a heated conversation and I was trying to translate for both sides in an emotionally neutral fashion. Sometimes I had to use the crisis communication techniques I'd been taught in my peer counselling course. A good example of this had occurred on the previous week.

"Sai Poon, tell this man that I want my parole now! They've had me locked up in this place way too long. Tell them to stop playing games with me!" Mr. Wu slammed his hand on the table, nearly yelling in Cantonese. Sai "細" in Cantonese means "little," but unlike "Lup Lup" had been with Grandpa, this was not being used as a term of endearment.

Hearing his aggressive tone and seeing Mr. Wu's body language, the parole officer, Robert, sat up and put one hand on the phone to call reinforcements in case things turned ugly. "Mr. Poon, what did he just say?"

"He said he wants his parole now because he's been locked up for too long." I tried to rephrase Mr. Wu's crass verbiage into something more refined in English.

"Okay, tell him that he has to be patient and wait for the hearing date from the parole board."

After I translated the reply to Mr. Wu, he got even angrier. "This is BS! Again? More waiting? I've been through this same process for over four freaking years! I'm already four years over my parole eligibility date. You're playing games with me! What do you want me to tell my family, 'Just wait another ten years'? Screw you!"

"Mr. Poon, what did he just say? It didn't sound good. Let me know if anything doesn't sound right, okay?" Robert looked at me with one hand still on the phone.

Discerning the situation, I knew if I simply translated plainly what Wu said, he could easily end up in segregation and get a report on his file that would hurt his parole application. I tried to convey what I thought was going on in Wu's heart, giving him the benefit of the doubt. "Mr. Wu just said that the waiting is really painful. He has been through the same process over and over for four years, and his parole eligibility date is already four years past. He thinks there must be something wrong. If not, why would there be so many delays? He would like you to tell him plainly what has gone wrong so he can work on it and doesn't just have to keep waiting. He wants to be released because his family has been waiting for him in China for over ten years. How much longer should he tell them to wait?"

After hearing my translation, Robert looked down to the paperwork on the table, then released his hand from the phone. "Okay listen, we're doing all that we can to get Mr. Wu parole. The problem is *him*. If he had admitted what he did was wrong and had shown some remorse, the parole board would have let him go ages ago. His poor attitude during the parole hearings is what is holding him back. Look at how aggressive he comes off. Without your translation, I'd have thought he wanted to kill me. Why should the parole board let someone like that go free?"

I was shocked with this explanation and asked Robert in English, "Really? Has anyone ever explained this to Wu? I think a logical explanation like that would help change his attitude. His aggressiveness is nothing more than his frustration with the delays, and it's probably partly the language barrier as well. Can you imagine living in a place like this without being able to understand what anyone is saying to you? It'd be pretty terrifying, don't you think? And besides, Chinese people do speak loudly sometimes. Perhaps his tone has been misinterpreted. It's a cultural thing."

"Yeah, I know what you mean. That makes sense." Robert looked more relaxed and eased back into his chair. "I'm not sure if anyone has ever fully explained this all to him in Chinese. This is what we have been trying to tell him through translators over the years. But normally inmates see us as their enemy. Between their presuppositions and the things that are lost in translation, who knows what has actually gotten through? Maybe you can talk him through this."

"Okay, this is what I'm gonna do. I'll take him out for a walk and try to explain everything you've just said to him. I'll counsel him and pray with him, and hopefully he will learn from his past and strive to become a better man for his family. If he changes his attitude, we can hope that the parole board will change their minds and let him go."

"Wow, that'd be great. Our job is to make sure society remains safe. If Mr. Wu doesn't come off as a threat to the community, since he's already way past his date, there's a significant chance that he will get out soon. But he still needs to understand that his hearing date is anywhere from three to six months away."

"Sai Poon, what did you guys talk about? Tell me what you said! Is he just gonna lock me up again?" Wu was impatient, not understanding what we were saying in English.

I turned to Wu with a smile and explained in Cantonese, "No, he's not going to lock you up. As a matter of fact, I've got some good news for you. He's trying to help you to get parole, but there are some steps you'll have to take. Why don't we leave this office and take a walk at the tennis court beside the chapel? I'll explain everything to you."

Wu calmed down immediately. He was at a loss for words. He nodded his head and followed me to the tennis court. Initially, he argued with me about the intentions of the prison staff and didn't believe that his parole officer was actually willing to help him. I spoke with him for over two hours, explaining their perspectives to him, and I tried to tie in the gospel. I explained to him the importance of seeking peace, which the Bible talks about. Digesting it slowly, he gradually acknowledged that what I was saying had some validity. I prayed with him at the end to accept his past, admit his wrongdoing, and commit to changing for the better. Something changed inside of him that day. I believed that with understanding and the proper guidance, Mr. Wu would be able to endure the rest of his time in prison peacefully until the day of his release.

> "Blessed are the peacemakers, for they will be called children of God." (Matt. 5:9)

While I would see the various parole officers in different units on behalf of other people on a regular basis, I didn't get to see my own very often. There were a few reasons. First of all, I didn't get myself into trouble, and all my reports were good, so there was nothing to discuss. Second, my parole eligibility date was so far off that there was no particular need to discuss it. In short, there was no reason for my parole officer to see me except for the mandatory semi-annual assessments.

Why on earth does my parole officer want to see me? I hope it's nothing bad. With a sense of concern, I knocked on the door of my parole officer.

"Come on in, Mr. Poon! Close the door behind you and have a seat."

"Hi, Ms. Anderson. It's good to see you." I sat down cautiously, still wondering why I was here.

"I was looking at your file. Your reports caught my attention. You've been in the prison system for over two and a half years. Is that correct?"

"That is correct."

"Since your incarceration, you haven't had any major incidents, and you seem to have a good way with both the staff and your peers. You have great work reports with excellent comments from your employers. You're voluntarily taking multiple programs, you're actively involved in peer counselling, and you've even enrolled in some university courses. You have strong family support with regular visits. All in all, I see that you have been keeping yourself very busy, in a good way." She looked at me with a friendly smile.

"Yes, that's what I'm trying to do."

"Well, this is superb. Today, I have some good news for you. There is a pilot work-release opportunity, initiated by the Citizen's Advisory Committee, the Silverdale Wetlands Conservation Project, and the District of Mission. They are potentially looking for five offenders to work on building trails in the Silverdale Creek Wetlands and Conservation area about fifteen kilometres west of here. The duration is five weeks, Monday to Friday. We've looked through the entire system, and you are one of the very few candidates from this institution who we think are capable. We need to find someone that we can trust, and we need to be sure that we are not posing a risk to public safety. And naturally, we have to be sure that you won't try to escape. This is a very rare opportunity for a medium-security prison. I don't believe a work-release program has ever been granted here before, at least not within my time working here. Are you interested in participating? It will most likely improve your scores and help you get to a minimum security afterward."

I couldn't believe my ears. "Sorry ... I ... just want to confirm what you just said. You mean, I have been selected for a pilot work-release program? You mean I go *outside* of prison to work?"

"Yes, that's right, but under close supervision from two officers, of course. You would go out with them in the morning and return in the afternoon for five weeks. Are you interested, Mr. Poon?"

Without any hesitation, I replied immediately, not wanting to waste another second, "Yes! Yes, I'm interested!"

"Good. Here's what I need you to do. Fill out this application form and give it to the duty office. We'll need a signature from them. I'll prepare the rest of the paperwork. You'll be notified in advance of the program's start date, which is in a month. Good luck, Mr. Poon."

I walked out from my IPO office completely shocked. I could not believe what I'd just heard. I looked at the application form in my hand. The title said "Work Release Application." *This is real.* As I was filling out the form, I couldn't stop asking myself, *Am I getting closer to freedom?* My excitement preoccupied me for the rest of the evening. I couldn't wrap my head around the idea that I was going to step on the soil of the outside world once again, and this before my parole eligibility date.

"Okay, something happened to one of the other inmates. So I guess he's not going to be joining us, and it's just you four today." Officer John and Officer Owen issued us instructions after making the strip search. They had to make sure we weren't carrying anything out, and we had to go through the same procedure on the way back in. "Okay, everyone! Get to the van one by one. Don't do anything stupid. We'll be watching all of you closely. Now let's get going, chop-chop!"

It was the first day of our work release. Many curious inmates were gawking at us through the gates as we boarded a dark-blue eight-seater correctional vehicle. Through the fence, some were yelling at us out of jealousy, "Lucky guys! Why do they get to go and not us? That's not fair!" It was a big deal for Mission Institution because these kinds of programs did not come along very often. Work-release programs were generally for inmates in minimum-security prisons to prepare them for reintegration. I was nowhere close to that point in my sentence. To me, this chance was a miracle given by God.

I had not sat in a vehicle for over two years. Last time I was in one was the day I got transferred from RRAC. The memory of that day flashed back in my head as I buckled up my seat belt. I couldn't believe two years had already passed.

After the officers finished handing in all the paperwork, a guard checked the bottom of the van with a mirror while another looked on with his hand on his gun. Were they checking for a prisoner clinging to the undercarriage of the van? I'm not sure, but in any case, eventually they got into the van and started the engine. It was amazing how I appreciated all aspects of the ride. *Wow—I have forgotten what the vibration of a vehicle feels like. Did I ever take driving for granted!*

As we moved forward past the gates, my heart started racing. We went through the parking lot, where I saw many cars of different colours. *Oh, so here's where my parents park their car when they come visit me.* My head was pressed up against the window like a toddler on his first field trip. I wanted to take in as much as I could. As we passed from the prison and through the front gates, I anxiously anticipated my first step onto the soil of the free world.

Just outside the prison perimeter, there were some individual houses on an adjacent property. They were built in the same style and looked like some sort of government housing. "That right there, boys, is Ferndale Institution. If you guys behave, you may go there for minimum after this work release," Officer John explained.

"Not me! I'm getting out in three months no matter what. I just gotta get this done and I'm outta here," Francis replied from behind me with a flippant attitude.

"Well, that's you. But I wanna go down there. I still have a year to go. Everybody says minimum is way better. You can cook your own food! I can't wait, man. The crap served from our kitchen really sucks. Fake eggs. Fake milk. I want the real stuff," Pete, sitting next to me, chimed in.

The van kept going downhill for another 15 minutes. Along the way I saw houses, cars, people, dogs, and big trees. I had no idea where I was, but it didn't matter to me. It was just amazing to be able to *see* all this again.

After a few big turns, Officer Owen stopped the van and parked beside some huge trees outside the entrance of the Silverdale Creek Wetlands. The officers let us get out. As I placed my foot on the gravel road, I took in a deep breath and filled my lungs with the air of freedom. It was indeed different than the air in prison, even though the oxygen in the air should have been the same. It must have been the trees or the damp soil by the winding creek. I couldn't smell any tension out here and felt instantly relaxed. My whole being was refreshed by the beauty of God's creation. This moment was very special to me. I did a 360 to look around and take as many mental pictures as I could.

Standing beside the entrance was a balding and somewhat rotund man in his late forties or early fifties. As we got closer, he greeted us. "Hello everyone, welcome to Silverdale Creek Wetlands. I'm George. It's good to have you guys join us for this project."

Officer John went to shake his hand. "I'm Officer John, and this is my partner, Officer Owen. Here are the four guys from Mission Institution."

"Very good. I'll be here today to show you around, provide the necessary equipment for your work. After that I'll be here once or twice a week depending on my schedule. Once you get the hang of it, you guys will be fine working here on your own." George took out some shovels from the back of his truck. "All right, here are some tools you guys can borrow. You're more than welcome to bring your own in the future if you prefer. Just make sure you return what's mine at the end. You can always come down to my warehouse and get more tools as needed. But today we'll take it easy and keep it simple. Officer John, this is my card. It has my number on it."

Following a brief history lesson from George, each of us grabbed a shovel and followed him into the park. Carrying my shovel on my left shoulder, my senses were inundated as George talked about the park. Every single one of us—including the officers—was in a good mood. Both sides of the gravel road were flanked by beautiful trees so tall and thick they obscured our view of the sky. Birds were singing everywhere. Bees buzzed through the wild roses and berry blossoms. The scenery took me out of the prison mindset completely.

Five minutes into the park, we came out of the forest into an open area with branches of a creek, one on the left and one on the right. Just past this point, the gravel road stopped, and only a muddy road continued thereafter, with a mountain of gravel beside it. Our task was to move this mammoth pile of gravel, and I could not have been happier.

"Guys, this is where your work begins. This reserve is quite big. But what we're allowed to work on for the park is very limited. In order for visitors to be able to explore more easily, we need to put down some gravel trails and afterward build a bridge over the creek. The basics of the trails have already been excavated and levelled. You'll see when we walk a bit farther in. The gravel truck will come again tomorrow. This pile here should keep you busy for the day. Let's take a tour inside before we start."

George led us deeper into the park where there were some lookout areas along the river. Wild plants were everywhere, and some would need clearing before hikers could get a clear view of the wetland. All of a sudden, Don, another inmate with us, shouted, "Man, there are blackberries here!" He ran over to pick a few and threw them into his mouth.

George chuckled. "Yes, we have quite a few blackberry plants here. But we have to pull them out each year. They are invasive species and harmful to the native plants of the park. When you guys are finished with the gravel trails, we'll need your help to clear these berry plants too. You have to wear heavy duty gloves though. Those thorns are sharp. Oh and I wouldn't pick the berries at the bottom. That's where the bears and foxes like to pee."

"What!? I just ate some—" Don hurried to spit the berries out of his mouth. Everybody laughed at him.

Officer Owen picked a few berries from the top plant and said, "From now on I know where to pick my berries from."

With George leading, we continued to walk toward the very end of the muddy road. Along the way there were birdhouses built on long wooden poles out in the middle of the water. Ten more minutes into our walk, my prison-issue running shoes were covered in mud. I picked up a small rock to scrape them off. I had to do that a few more times before we stopped at the last lookout of the river, where tiny frogs were jumping in and out of the water. George then said, "There are other species of frogs and toads in this watershed. Some are pretty big, like the Western toad, which can be as big as about half of my hand. Their tadpoles are really big too. You can spot them in the water very easily. Now, this is the end of the road. But what we want to do is to build a wooden bridge across the river and connect the rest of the trails together. If you guys can finish the gravel trails before our term ends, maybe you can help us with the bridge too. We'll see how things go."

We paused at the lookout, in awe of the natural beauty we had ignored in our previous lives. This place was like a little paradise to me. For an urban kid like me, raised in the concrete of Hong Kong and then Richmond, and for someone who was extremely sensitive to mosquito bites, there was absolutely no way as a teenager I would have called this muddy wetland a paradise. But after being locked in a cell for so long, my perspective had completely changed.

We went back to the big pile of gravel and started working. One shovelful at a time, the seven of us worked hard all day. In the beginning, while everyone still had energy, the progress was brisk. We developed a sequence where one laid down his load while another followed right behind to put down his. We formed a little trail-making assembly line. But gradually our energy declined. After three hours of non-stop shovelling, we'd slowed to a crawl but kept going nonetheless. When I finally asked about time, it was already past noon, and Officer John called for a lunch break.

Instead of walking all the way back to the entrance, because we were all tired Officer Owen went back and drove the van to us at the lookout area next to the gravel pile and the creek. That particular spot became our "basecamp," as it were, for the rest of our work release program.

While the officers were getting our lunch from the back of the van, the rest of us gathered big rocks and logs for everyone to sit on. The kitchen had packed our lunch in a container along with one water jug and one juice container. Not surprisingly, the juice was not real but a crystal mix. While the rest chowed down their sandwiches, I looked up to the sky and said grace in my heart, thanking God for the beautiful day and the food in my hands. As I began to bite into my baloney sandwich, some water splashing in the river caught some our attention.

"What was that? Did you guys see it?" Don asked.

"What? Salmon? Who cares?" Officer Owen kept eating his sandwich. Within a minute, the water splashed again.

"Look, there it is again! I think it's a beaver. I saw a tail." Don went over to the edge of the lookout to take a closer look.

"Well, well, well, I think you're right. That explains a lot. The level of this river has risen quite a bit for the past few weeks. If it's caused by a beaver dam, that explains it. We have to take it down, unfortunately for the beavers. Let me go investigate farther downstream. Wait for me here, guys." George went away with the last bite of his sandwich in his mouth.

"Can I go too?" Don, full of excitement, looked to the officers for permission.

"All right, I'll go with them." Officer Owen gave Officer John a nod, then headed off with Don and George.

Ten minutes later, they came back with the news. Don shouted from a distance, "Guys, there's a beaver dam! It's blocking the water."

"Just as I thought. The beaver has been building a dam. From a distance it doesn't look too big. But if we leave it as it is, they will make it bigger and bigger. That's how they operate, and by then it'll be really tough to remove it. We have to take it down now before we get flooding up here and all this whole place turns into a pond. I'll need your help, guys. Is that all right?" George asked with a serious look on his face. We all looked at each other and nodded our heads. George then continued, "Let me go to the warehouse to get us some waders and boots. I'll be back in twenty."

While waiting for his return, we went downstream to inspect the beaver dam. At first glance, the water looked free of activity. But when we kept quiet and waited patiently, we could see the beaver's tail occasionally appear on the surface. Branches would suddenly float on the water and then disappear underneath. Obviously, the beavers were actively working. We stayed at that spot until the sound of a truck engine broke the silence.

George came back with multiple sets of brown chest waders and rubber boots. Carefully picking up a size M, I tried it on. It was a little too big for me, but there was no size S, so I had to live with it. After gearing up, we all headed down to the water under George's direction, except for Don. He didn't bother with the waders and just jumped straight into the water in his underwear. His screaming from the shock of the cold water scared the beaver, and it fled with a big smack of its tail.

Walking towards the dam, we started to remove the branches one by one. As we took out the top layer, water started flowing back downstream. The sudden flow of water helped loosen up the middle layer of branches. However, the bottom layer was packed solid, so I grabbed hold of a big branch that seemed to anchor the whole dam in place and rocked it back and forth under water with my right foot, but it still wouldn't budge. Taking a deep breath in, I got hold of it with both hands and pulled it back while shoving the other end forward using my foot with all the strength I could muster. Finally, I got it free, but my left thumb got a small cut from a branch and started bleeding. Luckily, it was not very deep, so I rinsed it off under water. One by one, we all continued pulling the branches out and tossing them downstream, and in short order, the remains of the dam washed away under the pressure of the current. Within minutes, the water level dropped to its natural level, and somewhere or other a group of unhappy beavers inevitably started planning their comeback.

"Good job, everyone! We did it!" George shouted with delight.

"Yeah, this feels good!" Francis flung a branch into the air.

"All right, all right, let's not get too excited, guys. Good job, everyone." Officer Owen walked back up onto land. Don didn't want to leave just yet and kept swimming along the river in a circle.

"I want to go upriver and see if the beavers are still around. Bosco, you wanna come with me?" Officer John looked at me.

"Oh … yeah, sure." I grabbed a branch I'd pulled out earlier and used it as a staff to balance myself as we waded upstream side by side. We were in chest waders, and the water level was above our waists. Little fish and frogs startled from the shadows darted downstream between our legs. Fortunately for us, it was a time of year when there weren't many mosquitos. The riverbank was covered with all kinds of wild plants. Not being much of a nature boy, I felt like I was in the middle of some kind of National Geographic documentary.

We soon came across a widening in the river where the current slowed and water lilies grew along the edge. A group of crows was spooked from the trees as we heard a branch snap. Looking up into one of the trees we saw an indistinct black ball of fur. I didn't clue in until Officer John yelled, "Whoa, it's a bear!"

"What!? For real? What do we do now?" I was shocked.

"Just stay put and hold on to your stick." He seemed a little panicked too.

"All right, but do you think we can fight it off if it charges?"

"Probably not, but just hold on to it. Better to have something than nothing."

"Hey, it looks like it might be leaving, 'cause I can only see its back."

"Yeah, you're right. And it also doesn't look all that big. Maybe it isn't full grown, but that can mean the mom may be around too."

"What!? That isn't good."

"Wait … look, he's taking off. Maybe we disturbed his nap, and he just wants to go back to sleep."

With that, the bear waddled off into the dark woods and disappeared. No mama bear appeared, so gradually we felt safe again.

"Okay, we're all good now, thank God."

"Oh yeah, amen to that. I thought we might be in trouble there for a moment."

"Tell me about it. Let's go. We should hit the entrance right up ahead."

"That was crazy."

"Yeah, man. Let's just head back."

While we continued our way up the river towards the park entrance, I kept looking in the direction where the bear had disappeared. After another ten minutes wading and walking, we arrived to a set of stairs leading back to the entrance where we first arrived. I was still diligently clutching my staff. We soon reached the lookout where everybody was waiting. We told them about our bear encounter, and they were happy we'd arrived back in one piece. Don, true to his eccentricity, was still in his underwear, drying himself in the sun as if no one was watching.

Having taken care of the beaver dam, the day was nearly done, and so we returned all the tools and gear to George. After storing them away, he knocked off and headed home. We soon followed after him in the van and headed back to Mission Institution. Looking out the window, I savoured all the memories I'd made that day. In some ways it felt like a lot to take in. In prison, nothing exciting happened for days on end. It had been a really priceless day. I had forgotten how much fun people on the outside world got to have. My heart was full of gratitude—I'd tasted freedom again. Thanking God over and over, I made a promise to Him before I went to bed that evening that I would never take freedom for granted ever again.

CHAPTER 17
TIME TO MOVE ON

Outside of going to church, my spiritual growth came from the daily study of the Bible. In the beginning when I first tried to read it back at the RRAC, I always ended up falling asleep. I never understood the purpose of reading an ancient book, the stories of which seemed so irrelevant to the modern era. Every time I picked it up, I barely made it past a page before I started nodding off, only later to wake up with the book splayed open facedown across my chest and drool accumulating in the corner of my mouth. It wasn't until after I finished the Alpha course at Mission Institution that I got a better understanding of how God revealed Himself through His Word. It was only then that I made a commitment to study it diligently. Because it is a spiritual book, I would not be able to understand it fully without the help of the Holy Spirit. So every time before I started to read the Bible, I would ask God to open up my spiritual eyes so I could understand His message for me that day.

My first Bible in prison was given to me by the chaplain in RRAC. It was the New International Version (NIV), published by the Canadian Bible Society and it was this Bible that I first read cover to cover. However, when I got into deeper study later on, I needed to borrow different Bible translations and concordances from the chapel. The more I studied, the more questions I had. Week after week, I would wait patiently outside Pastor Tom's and Father Mako's offices for a chance to ask questions. Pastor Tom, who used to instruct at a Bible college, saw my enthusiasm and decided to teach me college level courses along with a few co-workers, including Dave and Glenn. I didn't miss a single class and throughout every session diligently wrote what I was learning on a white notepad. My appetite for God's Word grew and grew, and so Pastor Tom, who saw my peculiar enthusiasm, helped me obtain permission to enrol as a correspondence student at Summit Pacific College.

Bosco H. C. Poon

One evening while I was studying the story of Samson, his seven braids (or locks as it says in some translations) caught my attention. I remembered when I was with my hip-hop group Syndicate, I wore my hair in cornrows and braids. The reality was that I had always wanted dreadlocks but never followed through in getting them because of the cost and maintenance. Pondering the lengthy sentence ahead of me, I regretted that I had not seized opportunities to do the many things I'd wanted to while I still had freedom—in this case, as trivial as it sounds, getting dreadlocks. Gently putting down the Bible on my bed, I looked around my cell. *Well, I don't think I will have dreadlocks anytime soon.* With a sense of sadness, I closed my eyes and said a prayer: "Lord, only You know when I'll get out. There are many things that I wanted to do but didn't do when I had the chance. Foolish me. Now I have so many regrets. I don't know what my future holds. I just want to serve You with all I have. Today I want to make a covenant with You, like Samson and his Nazarite vow. When You let me out of prison, I'll go get dreadlocks, and they will be my symbol of being Your servant. As long as I'm on the stage for You, I'll keep my dreads, no matter how hard they are to maintain. Maybe I'll cut the ends when they get too long, but I'll still keep them. May You give me strength to accomplish Your mission for me on this earth."

After the prayer, I looked up to the ceiling and wondered if I'd ever perform on the stage again. I sank back into a daydream, remembering the audiences we'd performed for. *Oh, how I miss performing.* Just thinking of the stage put a smile on my face. I took out my spiritual journal and looked at the date. *Only three years have passed by and still such a long way to go. It's time to come back to reality for now.* Picking the Bible back up from my bed, I continued reading the rest of Samson's story.

"How did your work release go, son?" Mom was opening a bag of dill pickle chips for me in the visiting area as always.

"Very fun! I got to see the world again. My goodness. It was so good! I got to take down a beaver dam and walk in the river. Oh, and I saw a black bear! It was pretty close to us too."

"What? A black bear?" Dad's eyes grew big.

"Yeah, I was walking up the river with an officer, and suddenly there was a black bear jumping down from a tree. But thank God it just wandered off into the woods and never approached us. Maybe God wanted to show me some of His creation to welcome me back to the world." I smiled, opening a can of pop.

"Oh, okay. I'm glad you had so much fun. You got quite a tan. You must have been under the sun for a long time." Mom looked at me with a hint of worry.

"Yeah, we were out in the sun every day for the past week. It was a work release, after all, so we *did* have to work. We were building gravel trails in the park, and so there was a lot of shovelling involved. It was quite tough working in the hot sun like that—it was all physical labour. I slept like a baby every night after working outside all day. My whole body was sore, and I'm still sore even now. But I thank God for the opportunity to breathe the fresh air of the outside world once again. I'm really grateful."

Mom kept looking at me and started to tear up, "Son, you have grown a lot. I ... I feel like I don't even know you anymore, but I mean that in a good way. You used to be very spoiled and complained about everything. Your pride used to make you look down on others. You only liked beautiful and expensive things. But look at you now. You are going out to shovel gravel, and you are grateful for it." Mom paused for a moment, grabbed a tissue, and continued, "And you tie everything back to God. You just saw a black bear, and you should have been worried for your life, but all you could think of is that God was showing you His creation. I mean, who thinks like that?"

She blew her nose and then finished her sentence. "Son, I've been watching you for the past three years. When you first told me you heard God I thought you'd gone crazy. I mean, seriously, I had never heard anything like that before. And whenever you told me about God during our visits, I was quite turned off. I wasn't sure about your intention, and you were acting as if you were trying to teach me something. But as time passed by, I saw something different in you. You didn't complain as much anymore, and you stopped swearing. The letters that you sent us were full of encouragement and Scriptures. You see the good in everything and always smile. How can anyone locked up in prison smile all the time? You try to comfort us every time we come to see you. Shouldn't it be the other way around? I'm really amazed by the changes I see in you."

Mom placed her hand on the side of my head and caressed my cheek. "This is not the son I used to know. It's obvious that you've become a different person. I was with you every moment since you were a little baby. I was with you every step of the way, and I knew you inside out. You were very stubborn and selfish at times. I hate to admit this, but, in many ways, it was probably my own fault. I didn't know how to teach you well. I spoiled you instead of making you the way you ought to be. But look at you now. You've changed, and without any help from me at all. I barely recognize you, but the wonderful thing is that way you've turned out is actually the way I always wanted you to be: someone who is mature, full of understanding, and who deliberately lifts other people up. I have no other explanation except God taught you Himself. I can't take any credit for this. I guess I can finally believe you now. I believe you've seen and heard from God because you have become a completely different person. You yourself—you are my proof that God is real." Mom sobbed and wrapped her arms around me.

I was shocked by my mom's words. Before I could even respond, my dad began to speak. "I agree. I see it very much like your mom does. I thought you'd gone crazy when you told us you heard the audible voice of God. I'd never heard any priest tell me anything like that before. And you know my whole extended family are devoted Catholics. Your grandma was the first laywoman at the church of our village in Hong Kong in the early 1950s. I grew up serving in church. And when you came to tell me about God, I thought, 'What on earth do you think you can teach *me* about God? What do you know?' But you've proven me wrong. You introduced me to a God who speaks to you just like a person does. I did not even know this was possible. I was very skeptical at first and thought you had gotten involved in a cult. But you took your Bible here and went through it with us every time we visited you, and this encouraged me to study my Bible for myself, which I had never really done before. You kept challenging us to get into a deeper relationship with Jesus. I didn't know how to do that, so I went on Youtube and searched for Chinese sermons to watch. The more I learned, the more I wanted to know. Because of your encouragement to seek out different Chinese Christian communities, your mom and I went to a number of different churches. It really opened up our eyes. Son, it's very humbling for me to admit that you've shown us just how far we were from God. Like your mom, I have no other explanation for the change in you other than the work of God."

After listening to my mom and dad's kind words, I replied, "Thank you for telling me this. To be honest with you, I was quite upset and discouraged when you dismissed my experience with Jesus as crazy. But I also understood how hard it would be for anyone to take my story seriously. So in a way, I kind of expected the response you gave me. Even so, when I saw your reaction, I didn't quite know how to take it. It was hard to be treated as if I was going insane when I knew that I was perfectly fine and in fact much better than I had ever been. But as I said, I understood. There were far too many miracles happening around me for me to have any doubt of God's existence. When I placed my identity in God and not the approval of people, I found the strength to keep moving forward. That's how I could remain grateful even when I was shovelling gravel—because I've learned the secret to being content in any and every situation, like what Paul said in the Bible.

"After going through so much, I'm not the ... well ... spoiled kid anymore. As a matter fact, I believe that I've been put in this cage and had everything stripped from me in order to gain true value and purpose in life. It has forced me to seek God when everything I'd built with my own hands had collapsed. I thank God for this journey, even though I've really struggled every single second of it, but I would never have come to know God the way I have without His tough love. And you're right, I *have* changed. Ever since that encounter with God—I mean, how could I not? All I want now is for others to know how good our God is and get to heaven one day. I've been praying for everyone I've ever encountered in my life. There is a long list of people's names in my spiritual journal that I constantly pray for. Even Blade is on it."

"Blade? The guy responsible for this nightmare?" My dad seemed almost irritated.

"Yes, even Blade. I know. I feel the same anger about what he did as you do. How can I ever forgive such a horrible person? I couldn't, but God has allowed me to, and only by His strength have I been able to do it. Remember, the Bible says, 'Love your enemy'? This is a very hard thing to do. I don't think anyone can do it without God's help."

"See, this is what I'm talking about," Mom said. "It's the things you're able to do now that show me how real God is. Forgiving Blade and praying for him? Son, I don't know how you can do that. I know that's what the Bible teaches us, but actually doing it is a different thing entirely. It angers me just to hear his name. How many times did I tell you not to hang around him? I knew he was bad news the first time I laid eyes on him." She held both my hands tightly.

"Mom, it angered me too. I hated him—I loathed everything about him. I had even thought about hiring someone to kill him. That's how much I hated him. But Jesus showed me that my hatred toward him was actually killing *me,* not *him*. He is out there living as a free man now. No matter how much I hate him, he won't feel a thing, and it won't shorten my sentence. Ultimately, it's me who suffers from my anger. That's why when I forgive him and stop imagining myself strangling him to death, it's actually me who stops choking. As long as I don't forgive him, he's actually still hurting me, and I need to take away his power to hurt me. What he did to me caused me plenty enough suffering, and it needs to stop there. And besides, it's not all his fault anyway. I played my part in all the stupidity as well. Plus, the Bible says if we love those who love us, what is the credit to us? Even the wicked love those who love them. But to love our enemies and pray for *them*, just as Jesus loved those who crucified Him, *that* is the real credit to our character. It was really hard for me to do it, but once I did it, I felt so relieved. I'm not under the curse of that hatred anymore."

I looked at my dad and mom. They were silent, probably pondering what I'd said. Knowing their conservative Chinese ways, they would not likely reply until they had investigated what I had just told them. To help them understand what I meant, I suggested, "Why don't we give it a try right now? Let's pray for Blade together. You won't lose anything by saying a prayer for him. As a matter of fact, you may gain something. Should we join our hands and pray?"

They were a little reluctant to do this. I could tell from their facial expressions. But not having any valid reason to turn me down, they slowly took my hands and closed their eyes. Knowing this prayer might set my parents free from their anger toward Blade, I smiled and began to pray with them.

"Papa God, I come to You with my loving parents. Today, we want to pray for our enemy, the person who first got me into all this trouble. It's very hard for us to do this, but we must, because that's what You've taught us. Lord, give us strength to love our enemy. Please look after Blade and help him to become a better person. We pray for his salvation. If he hasn't known You yet, please make a way to reveal Yourself to him. For my parents, help them to forgive. Set them free from hatred, and let them taste the freedom that only You can offer. Provide us healing for our wounded hearts. Restore us individually, and as a family. In Jesus's name, we pray."

Bosco H. C. Poon

"Amen." Mom and Dad said it out loud together with me.

Without realizing it, I'd been working in the Mission chapel for two and a half years. Every member of the chapel team was like family to me. We'd see each other and work together every day. During that time, we'd seen each other through a lot of ups and downs. They always stood up to protect me because I was the smallest among them.

One time our chapel was opened for an incense sale. People from all different religions rushed in to stock up on their supplies. Towards the end we were getting really short of inventory, so we had to limit everyone still in the lineup to two tubes per person. One guy named Donald was making a big scene because I wouldn't let him buy more. He insisted on buying ten, but I stood my ground, telling him that I'd been told he could buy a maximum of two. I gave him two tubes and asked him kindly to be on his way because the lineup was long. Donald promptly launched into a profanity-ridden tirade and then stormed out. Afterward, he waited for me outside the chapel door with a small knife in his hand.

Dave saw him standing in the corner and warned me not to go outside. While Glenn and the other chapel workers stayed inside the chapel with me, Dave went outside to talk to Donald. After a long conversation, Dave went back to his cell to grab three tubes of incense to buy him off from the idea of stabbing me. I don't know if I would still be alive today without the chapel team.

Friday night was normally the movie night at Mission Institution. Everyone would save up money to buy junk food from the canteen for the movie. But one night I saved my money because my friends were throwing a farewell party in the chapel. My work release had lowered my security score, and because of that, the warden had approved my transfer to the minimum security prison next door. On my way there, I had a sudden flashback: I remembered the first time I'd walked that same path to the chapel. I was completely lost. I didn't know anyone, and I was extremely nervous. But since then, time had flown by. Now I knew most of the inmates, not only the ones who came to chapel but most everyone in the whole institution, except for those short-timers who came in and went out within a few weeks. I'd had the opportunity to counsel many of them. *What a turnaround in my circumstances*, I thought. I sure had changed a lot.

When I arrived at the chapel, I gave the secret chapel workers' knock on the door. Within a second, Rob opened the door for me. "There you are, big guy! We're all waiting for you."

"Hey, Rob, thanks."

"Come on in, Bosco! Dinner is about to be served." Dave was yelling from the back office while making some microwave popcorn.

"Buddy, here, take your seat." Glenn was setting the table.

"I hope you enjoy this meal," Jason said, as he poured some crystal mix juice into the plastic cups.

"After dinner we'll have some dessert as well." Danny was spooning out mac and cheese onto paper plates.

"Thank you for doing this, guys," I said as I sat down and took a sip of the juice.

"Everybody is here. Why don't we say grace and begin to eat?" Dave put a few bags of popcorn on the table beside the pizzas they'd prepared in their living unit's toaster. Frozen pizza was a special treat that we could get from canteen once in a while at the medium security. We said a prayer together, giving thanks for the food, and then dug in. This wasn't the first time we'd eaten together of course. On the contrary, we were pretty used to eating together in the chapel because of all the different programs that ran there. But tonight, there was an awkwardness in the air. Everyone was surprisingly quiet.

To break the ice, I asked how everyone was doing. Rob started to talk about the latest cross-stitch he'd been working on, as he was the cross-stitch master. In fact, he even taught me how to do cross-stitch. Glenn then joined the conversation and filled us in on the recent sports news. Jason told us about the latest book that he was reading, and Danny told us a new workout routine he'd been trying.

When it came to Dave's turn, he didn't say much. That was weird, because normally Dave would be the one who spoke the most—a trait that had earned him the nickname "motor-mouth." Something wasn't right.

As I thought about it, I realized that everyone sitting at the table was either a lifer or had been given a really long sentence like myself. In their years of imprisonment, they must have seen countless inmates move on and leave them behind. While celebrating with me that night, it must have triggered feelings of loss for all those friends who had left and a yearning for the day when they could enjoy their own "graduation" from Mission Institution.

Understanding that this might be why the atmosphere was so glum, I said, "Thank you for putting this together, everyone. It means so much to have you as my brothers in this place. I appreciate every single one of you. I wouldn't be who I am today without your help during all my time here. Rob, thank you for teaching me how to do cross-stitch. You were kind enough to help me with the paperwork to buy all the materials. You prepared my workstation in my cell and showed me stitch by stitch how to do my first one as a gift for my grandma. She loved it and has it framed in her room. Thank you so much for doing that." I gave Rob a toast with my cup of juice.

"Glenn, I always felt safe when I was with you. You're really tall. To me, you're like a gladiator. Whenever there was someone causing me trouble, just your presence was enough to intimidate that person into leaving me alone. Thank you for always making sure we're safe in the chapel." I gave Glenn a nod, and he smiled back.

"Jason, you had such patience for me. When I first had the idea of making a pair of ceramic dolls for my parents, you didn't even blink and said you'd help me. I had no clue what to buy at the hobby shop, and you showed me step by step what to do. Oh, and you stopped me from putting my hand inside the ceramics furnace! That saved me big time. The end result was amazing, and the thanks go to you. My parents love them." Jason laughed and told me not to worry about it.

"Danny, it's been so good working with you over the past year. You always have a different perspective on things, which has helped broaden my view. We may not see eye to eye with our theology, but we appreciate each other in the family of God. Your muscles really put me to shame, which just shows that I should be at the gym more often. Thank you for always staying behind to clean up with me." Danny raised his cup.

"Last but not least, Dave. Words cannot express my gratitude for our friendship. You were always there to help me out in whatever challenges I faced here. You listened to my stories and gave me godly advice. You always knocked on my door to check up on me. Sometimes it could be annoying, but I could sense God's love through your caring spirit. Through your work in this chapel I have seen you constantly helping others, and I'm one of the recipients. Thank you for your faithful service to the Lord. I have learned so much from you."

Dave tilted his baseball cap, cleared his throat, and replied, "And I have learned so much from you too, Bosco. You have grown so fast, it's hard to keep up with you. You're wise beyond your years. It's so obvious that God has His hand upon you. Like I said, I have no doubt that the Lord is going to use you mightily. It's very sad for me to see you leave us. You have been a great help to this chapel and all our ministry work. This place will never be the same without you. You'll leave a really big hole behind. We'll miss you. But don't get me wrong—we're really happy for you. I have mixed feelings, you know." Dave took off his cap.

With that I started to get emotional. "I just wanna say thank you to all of you. I'll remember all the things we've done together. I was very broken when I came, and you kept supporting me with endless encouragement. I didn't know my way around here, and you guys showed me the dos and don'ts. When someone wanted to push me around, it was you who stood up for me. You shared your food with me and looked after me in every imaginable way. You may not know this, but I see Jesus in you. I can't believe I'm about to move on. It's hard for me to leave here without you coming with me. I know there are some who have left Mission Institution and have forgotten you, but I promise you this will not happen to me. I will always remember you and keep you in my prayers. And if I get the opportunity, I'll make some videos out there and find a way to send them back to let you see the outside world. I'll remember you, I promise." I started to sob in front of them.

Ever since I was a kid, I always hated the feeling of saying goodbye, and this feeling was now overwhelming me. I just could not hold it in. I no longer cared about my image as the little tough guy, and so out came all my tears. One by one each man came to comfort me with a hug. Afterward, we managed to finish off the meal and enjoy an ice cream dessert they'd prepared. We talked for a little longer, reminiscing about some of the bigger events we'd put on together in the chapel. Looking at the photo collage on the wall, Dave said, "Well, we got some of your photos up there. At least we still have a memory of you here with us."

When I looked at the photos that had been taken by the inmate photographer, I couldn't believe how many events we managed to put on. I didn't know if I would get to attend another one before I had to go. Like Dave, my feelings were mixed. One part of me really wanted to leave the place, but the other part of me wanted to stay to enjoy the brotherhood in Christ I shared with these men. But I guess I didn't really get to choose. Such was prison life. When your time was up, you moved on. I just had to trust that God had a plan for me. All I could do was to follow His guidance one step at a time, and He would make my path straight.

This evening was so special for me. I would never forget the times I'd spent with these brothers.

> "Two are better than one, because they have a good return for their labor: If either of them falls down, one can help the other up."
> (Eccl. 4:9–10)

CHAPTER 18
A STEP CLOSER

"Poon to A&D, Poon to A&D!" I heard my name being called to "Admission and Discharge" first thing in the morning, just minutes after our cells were unlocked. Still in the middle of waking up, I yawned on my way out the door.

"Bosco, you hear that?" Dave opened his door as I was stepping out of mine.

"Arghh ... yeah, I'm going up right now," I said with resignation in my voice.

"You know what they're calling you up for, right?"

"No. What do you think it is?"

"It's 'cause you're probably leaving today."

"No way, really? Today? You think? Wow, I wasn't really prepared for that!" With this exciting prospect, I was now fully awake. For years I'd just heard others being called to leave, and now it seemed like it might finally be my turn. The whole thing seemed surreal.

"Well, let's go find out!"

"All right, all right, I'll see you in a bit." I hurried myself out of my living unit.

In order to get to the upper building where A&D was located, I had to pass through the middle post outside the kitchen. I didn't have many fond memories of this place—where the guards had constantly mocked me and called me Jackie Chan. I was fully expecting the usual dose of derision, but to my surprise, the guards were uncharacteristically nice. They didn't even search me on my way through the heavy metal door. *That was easy. Is it because it is really my last day here?*

With a great deal of anticipation, I entered A&D. "Hi, was I called up here?"

"Poon, come in! Here is some paperwork for you to sign. You're moving to Ferndale Institution today. You have two hours to pack your cell. Make sure to bring everything you need. If you leave anything behind, you won't be able to get it back. Here are some boxes for you. Come back up here with all your stuff when you're ready. We'll have to search through everything before we can transfer you. Understand?" The officer offered me a stack of empty cardboard boxes.

"Okay. Yes, I understand." I signed the sheets and grabbed the boxes.

My heart was beating like a rabbit's as I walked back to the living unit. Seeing the boxes in my hands, other inmates expressed their good wishes and vicarious joy—though some showed hints of wistful envy.

"Oh man, you're leaving us?"

"Come on, you can't leave us behind!"

"All the best, Bosco!"

"Take me with you, man!"

"We'll miss you, big guy!"

When I arrived my cell, Dave was standing at the door waiting. "So, you're leaving today." Dave tilted his baseball cap with a smile tempered by a sense of impending loss.

"Yeah, you were right. I'm leaving today."

"Well, let me help you with some packing. You don't have much time left. They will want your stuff soon."

"All right, thank you. I remember you helping me move in to this cell. Now you're helping me to move out."

One by one, I put my belongings into the boxes. On the wall, there were three calendars I'd collected from the Mission chapel. Volunteers had brought them in as Christmas gifts for the inmates. Since I worked in the chapel, I always got my first pick. I had actually treasured these calendars throughout the year because of the colour they added to my cold cell. The first one had photos of Vancouver scenery, the second one had flowers, and the third one was of Richmond City. They had allowed me to have a different view on my wall every month. Sometimes I would stare at the scenery in the calendars and imagine myself being there. There was a photo of False Creek in Vancouver that had really captured me. I spent hours imagining myself walking on the seawall by the water. This was one of the things I would do to kill my time during lockdown. After carefully taking them down from the wall, I put them in the box.

After putting my clothes into the last box, I was ready to go. Dave went outside to get me a dolly to carry everything on. Standing in the middle of my cell, I took one last look at it. Memories of all the challenges, struggles, and triumphs kept flooding back. Every morning, I pinched myself to make sure it wasn't just a nightmare. Every night, I prayed for the day I could leave. And that morning, my prayer was finally answered. With my eyes closed, I took a deep breath, then turned around and walked out.

"Thank you for everything, Dave. Take care of yourself, brother." I gave Dave a long hug.

"You too. We'll miss you here. Remember to write us. I'll be waiting for your mail." Dave gave me one last firm squeeze.

Outside my living unit, I took one long last look. I recalled experiences, some good, some bad, in every corner I glanced at. I couldn't believe it was really my time to leave. Pushing my boxes through the middle post, I made my way up to A&D. It was like a flashback: this was the place I'd reported to when I first arrived, full of fear and grief. But in the intervening time, I had become a totally different man. So many things had changed. I was leaving as a much happier and fulfilled person than when I'd come.

The officer took my boxes and did a thorough search. While he was taking care of that, I walked outside to gather my thoughts. As I looked down to the ally, I saw my nemesis: the dumpster. I remembered the night the garbage bag had broken open mid-flight as I was swinging it, covering me in the fetid juice of prison kitchen refuse. I would never miss a single moment of working in that kitchen. It had been the lowest point of my brief life. I was so glad I'd been switched to a job in the chapel. I turned to my right to look at my living unit through the fence. Dave and a few good friends were standing outside to bid me farewell. They waved wistfully to me, and I did the same. I felt like I was waving goodbye to family—it was the same feeling I'd had when I'd left the Supreme Court in shackles.

The officer broke my train of thought by calling me in to sign the last bit of paperwork. I was then transferred to Ferndale Institution in a correctional van. It was time for a new journey.

Oh man, where am I? I'd woken up from another nightmare. With my eyes half opened, I looked around. *Man, I'm still in prison.* Every time I woke up, I'd face the same disappointment. I'd believe for a brief moment that I was in the free world, but as I got my bearings, there I'd be, still in prison. But this time things were a little better. I was in a minimum-security prison. The bed was only tiny bit wider than my old one, but at least now I enjoyed the blessing of a wooden frame instead of the cold, squeaky, rusty metal kind at Mission. I felt more like a regular human being, sleeping in a regular bed. Looking out the window, I saw that the sun was just about to rise, which meant we would be leaving our living units for movement time soon. So I got up and headed to the washroom to brush my teeth before there was a lineup. But I had to do it quietly, since my roommate was still asleep. Walking down a hallway to a washroom felt so weird after being locked in a cell with a toilet and a tiny sink for over three years. I wasn't used to walking outside my cell to go to use the toilet.

Once inside, I looked at myself in a *real* mirror above the sink. I could see my reflection so clearly: every strand of hair, my pupils, and even the pimples on my face. In the reflection, I saw a shower right behind me. *Wow, what freedom!* After I was done, I walked to the kitchen to grab something to drink from the fridge. Everything felt old and familiar and yet brand new. I had the freedom to open a

Bosco H. C. Poon

refrigerator, to see the light inside, to pick something for myself, and to pour my own drink in a cup of my choosing. Staring at the couch and TV in the living room with a glass of milk in my hand felt so strange. It was just too normal for me.

    At Ferndale Minimum Institution (now renamed Mission Minimum Institution), every living unit had eight bedrooms, two washrooms, a laundry room, a living room, and a kitchen. There was a phone in the middle of the unit for the duty office to communicate with the inmates, and vice versa. It was a place to help us reacquaint ourselves with basic life skills before our reintegration. Every member of the unit was in charge of different household chores, from mopping the floor to cleaning the bathroom to taking out the trash. Everyone was responsible to do his own laundry and cook his own food. No more getting in line for precooked meal. A form with a list of food items was placed in the living unit. We were on a fixed weekly budget for food, so we had to be careful and think ahead for what we needed. The unit food order had to be handed in and picked up at a specific time at the institution kitchen on a weekly basis. The food distribution door only opened once a week, so if someone was too lazy to fill out the form, he would have to make do without food for the whole week. One solution was to go to the loan sharks, who had lived there long enough to accumulate food items they could lend out at interest. The other possibility was to go to the gambling table, where you could try your luck to make some quick money. None of these was a suitable solution for me, so I always made sure to fill out the form. However, my first week, I miscalculated a bit and ended up spending all my money on cereal, milk, and instant noodles. Consequently, I basically ate nothing but Cheerios and Mr. Noodles for the next seven days. The second week, I got eggs and broccoli but forgot to get cooking oil and salt. I had to borrow from my roommate, who was kind enough not to charge me interest. I didn't realize how institutionalized I had become.

    "Bosco, how are you adapting to this new place?" Father Mako was seeing me in his office inside the Ferndale chapel. Both he and Pastor Tom took turns looking after the chapels at Ferndale and Mission.

    "I'm still trying to get used to it. There's more freedom here, which is nice, but I'm having to relearn a lot of things. I didn't realize how lost I'd become when it comes to basic life skills. Simple things like ordering decent food on a fixed budget are a real challenge. Fortunately, I took notes from the shows on the Food Network while I was back in Mission and brought them with me, so at least I have some recipes to follow. But I don't have a job yet, so my weekly budget is quite tight. I have many questions about this place, but I don't know who I should speak to."

    "I understand. It's a transition period. Give it some time, and you will find your way. I'm going to introduce you to Teddy. He is one of our chapel workers here. I'm sorry I can't hire you at this chapel right at the moment. We only have two inmate positions here, and they are already taken. This is also a much smaller chapel than Mission's. But I'm sure there are different job openings you could look into. Since this is a minimum, the turnover rate is very high, so jobs become available more quickly. Most inmates are here for a relatively short time, so they get to get out within months or even weeks. Don't worry too much; you'll get used to this place in no time. I'll have Teddy show you around, okay?"

"Thanks, Father Mako. I appreciate your help. And you're right. Everyone in my unit has a very short sentence. One of them is even getting out in three weeks. Nevertheless, they manage to complain about everything. They have no idea how good they have it—I mean, having real food and a real washroom? I know the grocery selection is not like IGA or Superstore, but still. There are real eggs, milk, a few different kinds of meat, and veggies. Man, what luxury! I couldn't stand listening to their whining the other night, so I told them about our cells in Mission. They asked me the length of my sentence. I told them twelve years, and they were all shocked. Then clammed up and eventually went back to their rooms."

"Heh, yes, your sentence is quite long compared to the others here. But as you said, this place is way better than Mission. Your time here will be much easier. Oh, and speaking of which, there's Teddy now. Hey, Teddy, come on in; I want you to meet Bosco!"

Teddy was a five-foot, nine-inch Quebecois man in his early fifties with a muscular build and covered in tattoos. He walked into the chapel office and extended his hand to me. "Hi, Bosco. I'm Teddy."

"Hi, Teddy, it's good to meet you." I shook his hand.

"Teddy, Bosco just arrived here from Mission. He was one of my chapel workers there for the past few years. He's a very trustworthy young man. Would you show him around this place, introduce him to some of the people here? And please help him settle in." Father Mako smiled at Teddy.

"Okay, Bosco, come with me. I'll take you for a walk." Teddy spoke with a thick French-Canadian accent.

After saying goodbye to Father Mako, Teddy and I left. I hadn't yet had a chance to explore the full perimeter of Ferndale. It was a much bigger property than Mission, and different areas were in or out of bounds. Without knowing all the "dos and don'ts," since my arrival I'd just played it safe by staying in the comfort of my room most of the time.

"Bosco, you came from Mission, eh? I was there for a few years before I ended up in here. I was in the chapel quite a bit there too." Teddy led me to the trail surrounding the institution apart from the main road.

"Yeah, and I heard about you from Dave. The chapel crew back there told me a lot of stories from the past."

"Oh yeah, Dave. How is he doing?"

"He is doing fine. We worked together in the chapel a lot. We became good friends."

"I see. Very good. So, you just arrived? Have you walked the full trail around this place yet?"

"No, I haven't. I did a lot of reading in my room. I didn't know anyone here, so I didn't go outside much."

"Well, let's take a walk then. It's quite a place here. You'll like it way better than Mission. As you can see, all the units here are separated into two parts: the lower and upper district. All the newcomers like you are assigned to the lower one. You gotta share your room with somebody. But as you settle in, you can request at the duty office to move up to the upper units as vacancies become available. Up there it's all single rooms. In between the two districts, there's the gym and a recreation room with a pool table."

Teddy paused outside the gym. Looking through the fence I could see some parts of Mission Institution in the distance. I paused and wondered how Dave and the rest of the chapel crew were doing. I said a brief prayer for them. Teddy tapped me on the shoulder. I guess he thought I was daydreaming. We resumed our walk up the slope as he continued, "There's a big backyard, above all the units, like a park, with lots of trees and a big field of grass. This trail will lead us there. At dusk and nighttime, it's completely out of bounds. But during the day we can go up there. You can jog, read on the grass, or get a few friends together to play some soccer. I'm not a big fan of soccer, so I mostly stick to my workouts in the gym."

As we passed by the last house in the upper district, the trail led to the park. I saw enormous cedars at the very far end beyond the fencing. I walked toward the fence where it said "Do Not Enter" to take a better look. It was real West Coast rainforest, where bright green ferns, thick moss, and fallen timber covered moist, shaded ground. There was a chorus of birdcalls emanating from the woods. I had no idea this institution was built so close to nature. I wouldn't be surprised if there were bears or mountain lions back there from time to time. Since it was the beginning of spring, there were all kinds of plants and flowers decorating the trail: crocuses, dandelions, and young ferns. Someone had even planted a bed of tulips, my favourite flower.

After a ten-minute walk, we arrived at the other side of the park, where it met the sidewalk and the street. Through the wall of bushes, I could hear cars and people talking. Teddy then said, "We're just one fence away from the street. This is minimum security, the last stage before we go back out there. It requires a lot of self-discipline to stay here because you are constantly reminded of the free world. As you can see, you could scale the fences easily. It's more or less just a symbol, you know? Anyone could climb out, and we are right next to a regular civilian neighbourhood. But it's a test of sorts. If people want to escape, they can easily do so, but I wouldn't recommend it. Many have tried, but we are on top of a mountain, and it won't take long for them to catch you and put you back to a higher security prison. It's a privilege to stay here. It took me long enough to make my way down here, so I never want to go back up."

"You're not kidding. We're so close to the street. I can see cars, random people with their dogs, and even houses through the gaps in the bushes. I haven't been so close to anything normal in a long time. And here I am, just one fence away. I really am getting closer to freedom. It's so refreshing. Thank you so much for taking me through the park. I'm definitely going to make good use of it."

We walked out of the park towards the entrance of the institution, where the trail merged back onto the main road. After passing by the duty office building, Teddy showed me which unit he lived in and said, "If you need anything, you know where to find me. Besides Sunday afternoon, there are things going on in the chapel at least two nights a week. Come by and meet some people. Pay attention to the PA system. They'll make an announcement when the chapel is open."

"Oh, you mean the chapel here only opens twice weekly in the evening? What about other times? We used to run different chapel programs in the daytime in Mission."

"Sometimes, but not always; it depends. You see, people here have more opportunities than in the medium, so they're not always around. Many of them are on work-release programs outside and only come back at night. Some get extended leave to attend programs outside. Don't forget many are short-termers who will be gone in no time. So it would be hard to arrange something consistent in the chapel," Teddy explained.

"Oh, that is very different than Mission. I guess you're right. Okay then, I'll pay attention to the PA. Thank you so much for showing me around. I'll see you soon." I shook his hand and then headed back to my living unit. After my experience in the park, I took out my notepad to write to my parents and Dave that evening.

In Mission, each living unit had its own institutional parole office, but at Ferndale there was only one, located at the administration building beside the duty office. There was a timeslot in the afternoon on weekdays for inmates to line up to see their parole officers. It was first come, first serve, so I stood in line for over an hour for my first visit with my new IPO.

"Hi, Bosco, I'm Joyce. You have been assigned to me. Come on in." Joyce opened the main door and led me into her office.

"Hi, Joyce. It's good to meet you." I sat down.

"Okay, so I have been spending some time reviewing your file. I haven't read every single detail yet, but I have an overall impression. You have quite a long sentence. But you finally made it here, so that's a good sign. All the reports indicate your good behaviour and your consistent involvement with the chapel program. Now as far as I know, you haven't got a job here yet, have you?"

"No, I haven't. I have been looking around, but there aren't really any openings that suit my interest and expertise at the moment. I did, however, put in an application for the social program office clerk yesterday. I saw there was an opening, but I have to wait for the interview."

"Okay, I see. Let me take a look here ... based on your work in Mission, you were an inmate peer counsellor for quite a few years. So I suppose you have all the skills to deal with conflicts and crisis then, do you?" Joyce was looking at my file on her computer screen.

"I did peer counselling for inmates on a regular basis. There were many occasions when I had to deal with unexpected anger and outbursts right on the spot, yes. So in that sense, I do have the skills that you described."

"I see. Well, there is an open spot for a counsellor. Seems like you fit the criteria. It's a volunteer position, but the nice thing is that you'll get to move into the very top unit with the largest rooms in the institution."

"Very top, you mean the one right by the park?" My heart skipped a beat.

"Yes, that would be the one. But there's a catch, Bosco. It's not a normal unit. It's the special-needs unit. Inmates assigned there all have some sort of mental illness. They are medically monitored, checked regularly, and issued proper medications. There is already one inmate counsellor living there. We're hoping to have two inmates who can both deal with crises when they arise. One really isn't enough."

"Oh, so that's the cost of living next to the park. Can you tell me, how serious are their mental illnesses?"

"It's hard for me to say. I don't know the details of their psychological issues, but since they are in minimum, it means they are fairly well controlled and their mental health is more or less stable. We understand that it's not the most glamorous job. So if you take that position, the staff here will do their best to provide you assistance. Just call us from the unit or come to the office anytime you need us. You'll gain trust and credibility among the management, which will benefit your parole application in the future. You don't have to answer me now, but you can consider this option."

"I understand." I pondered for a moment, thinking how I should respond. Then the teaching of God's Word popped into my head: *Whoever wants to be greatest in the Kingdom of Heaven has to become the servant of all.* I sensed God's will in this, so I replied, "I was trained for peer counselling for a reason. My faith taught me to help those who are in need. If there's a need in that unit, and if I'm a right candidate, I'm open to giving it a try. Hopefully I can help maintain the balance there. I'm new here, so there are many things that I have to learn. I hope you guys can have patience with me."

"That's a great response. With that attitude you'll be a perfect fit. I'll put in a note for the duty office to contact you for the move. Just go there and speak to them, say, tomorrow. They will help you with the rest. And as for your clerk application, I'm sure you'll get hired. With your work history, they will be happy to have you there." She was typing while talking to me, "Okay, just let me finish this email ... done. The duty office is notified. Well, it was good to get to know you a bit today. Thanks for coming by. I promise I'll study your file more, so next time I see you, we can speak more specifically about the steps for your reintegration, okay?" Joyce got up from her chair and walked toward the door.

"Thank you for your help today. I look forward to seeing you again. Take care." I followed Joyce out of the administration building. With a sense of curiosity, I walked up to the last unit at the top of the slope. From the outside, it looked the same as all the other ones. I stared at it for a bit, wondering what was waiting for me inside.

"But the LORD said to me, 'Do not say, "I'm only a youth"; for to all to whom I send you, you shall go, and whatever I command you, you shall speak.'" (Jer. 1:7 ESV)

CHAPTER 19
A BITTERSWEET GOODBYE

The flicker of the living room TV lit the hallway with a faint blue-white light as I stumbled toward the washroom. I'd been woken from my sleep by something or other. I saw Nick from the back.

"Hey, buddy, why are you up so late?"

"I am, y'know, channelling to my other world so that I can rearrange the events of *this* world's dimension," Nick replied, trance-like, his eyes fixed on the static of an empty channel. White noise played in the background. Nick was a 300-pound African-Canadian who lived next to my cell but was part of the special-needs unit. He did indeed require special care. He would stare at the TV static for hours on end. He explained to me once that he believed he was able to enter another spiritual realm through a portal hidden in the static, not unlike the way Neo could travel between two worlds in the movie *The Matrix*.

"I understand how important this is to you, Nick, but it's getting late, and the guards will do their rounds very soon. They would want you to be asleep in your room by now. Why don't we head back there?" I tried to cajole him back to his room. At a minimum-security prison, we were allowed to move around within the unit after lock-up time. However, guards didn't like us staying up all night, especially in the living room.

"No, I can't go back now. I'm in the middle of giving commands to all the great religious people. I am the Creator who created Jesus, Buddha, and all the gods that you people worship in this dimension. They all listen to me!" Nick was not willing to leave his important mission quite yet.

"That must be a very serious business, Nick." In my head I was trying to determine the right way to navigate his religious delusions without triggering his anger. Then an idea came to me. "Ah, since you're talking to all of them, wouldn't it be more fitting for you to speak to them from your throne? After all, a throne represents power, and your throne is in your room—the chair that you always sit on, right? That belongs to you. This chair is for common use. Everyone can sit on it. Just saying." I had worked on finding creative ways to keep peace on the unit, as this was one of my duties as the peer support provider.

Nick's eyes grew big as he looked straight at me. "Oh man, you're so right! How can I speak with authority if I'm not on my throne? This is crazy! Okay, I'm going right now!" He flew back to his cell and shut the door behind himself.

Finally, I thought to myself. After shutting off the TV with the remote control, I shuffled back to the washroom. That very moment, two guards came into the unit to check up on us. "Poon, you're still up!" Gary went into the hall and looked inside each cell through the window on the door.

"Yeah, I just woke up from a dream and needed to use the washroom," I replied politely.

"No trouble tonight, right?"

"Nah, everything is good. A quiet night."

"Good, good. All right, have a good night." Gary and the other guard checked off the list on their clipboards and walked outside.

It had been about four months since I'd been moved to this unit. After my conversation with Joyce, I was called to the duty office within a few days. I was issued a set of keys for my new cell, number 108, and its mailbox. No longer would my mail be handed to me by guards at the duty office. I would be picking it up myself like a regular civilian. I was able to take more ownership of my life. There was a chapel there too, and I made a number of friends after the first service—a few of them even lived in my unit. The other peer support worker, Tony, helped me tremendously in my transition to this new living environment and also acquainted me with the peculiarities of each member of the special-needs unit, giving me advice on how to manage their unique challenges.

While there were many wonderful things about Ferndale, there were difficult things that happened there as well. People were still from a very rough background, and sometimes tempers would boil over. Many inmates there relied heavily on medication in addition to peer support, counselling, and social workers. Sometimes their moods could change drastically after a change in medication or missed dose. When this happened, the usual outcome was arguments and, occasionally, physical altercations.

"I have had enough of you!" Jody abruptly stopped cutting his apple on the kitchen counter and turned the paring knife toward Edmund.

"What? You want a piece of me? Come on!" Edmund readied himself in a fighting stance.

"Guys, guys! Stop it! You're gonna hurt yourselves!" I was trying to intervene from a distance.

"I'm gonna cut you in half!" Jody yelled.

"Come on! I'll beat the sh*t out of you first!" Edmund was ready to throw a punch.

"Hey, hey! Put the knife down! There's no need for that here. Come on, guys! There's always another way to solve a problem. Violence is not the way!" I tried to talk some sense into them.

"Yeah guys, stop it! If the guards see this, we'll all be grounded. Come on, just chill!" Nick tried to help.

"Listen guys, the guards are coming to do a round very soon. You know that. Look at the clock. If they see this, all hell will break loose. Both of you will get shipped back to maximum in no time. Come on. Think about it. Maximum, man! No cooking a good meal for yourselves, a tiny cell, full-day lock-ups. Think about it. You don't want that. It's not worth it. Put the knife down." I was trying to calm them down while praying fervently in my heart.

Jody paused for a bit and then slowly put the knife down beside the sink. I then continued, "Jody, that's good. Just take a deep breath. It's okay. You can do it. Let's all take a break. Edmund, why don't you come with me for a walk in the park? It's beautiful outside, and I want some company."

The tension slowly eased from Edmund's face and his arms fell to his side. He looked to the ground for a moment, and then turned to me. "All right, let me go get my jacket." He walked out of the kitchen.

"All right, everybody, everything is back to normal. Everything is fine. Let's put this behind us and carry on our normal business." I walked over to Jody and patted him on the shoulder. "It's okay buddy. We all have bad days. You just need some rest."

"Nah, man, I'm losing control. Maybe it's my medication. I think it's better for me to check in to higher security."

"You're doing fine here. If it's the meds, then let's talk to the doctor. I can go to health care with you if you want to. You don't have to check in."

"You don't understand. I have serious problems. You saw what just happened. It's better for me to be locked up." Jody went back to his cell with his head down.

I took a walk with Edmund afterward, allowing him to vent steam. In prison, most inmates were, in some measure, emotionally unstable—some more, some less. I was only able to maintain my emotional stability because of my faith. Without Jesus's promise of a brighter day, I would probably have gone crazy long before my transfer to minimum. Since Edmund was a believer, I prayed with him before we headed back to our unit. He seemed a lot better after our prayer.

Upon our return, we found out that Jody had reported the incident at the duty office and turned himself in. He would be shipped to a higher security immediately. That was the last time I saw Jody. He was one of the many inmates who were being torn apart by a terrible combination of mental illness and the stresses of imprisonment. His cell remained empty for two weeks before a new inmate was assigned to it.

Bosco H. C. Poon

Ring ring, ring ring. I went to pick up the common-use phone in the middle of our unit. "Hello."

"Hello, Bosco. It's Father Mako."

"Hey, Father Mako, how are you?"

"I'm good. Thanks for asking. I uh … I just want to inform you that I've received a call from your parents. And it's about your grandpa."

"Oh boy, what is it? I've worked with you long enough to know that you don't just contact an inmate about their family for no reason. Don't tell me. Is it what I think it is?"

"Bosco, I'm sorry. Your grandpa has passed away."

"No, no, no …" My heart sank with this bad news.

"I understand how hard it is for you. We'll do our best to assist you during this difficult time. You have our full support. Pastor Tom has already started the process of applying for a compassionate pass so you can attend the funeral. The warden will make a decision within the next few days. It's very likely that you'll be granted the pass. Now, I can help you make a phone call to your parents if you can come down to my office now."

"My goodness …" I covered my face with my left hand. Holding off my tears, I continued, "Thank you, Father Mako … I, uh, I need a moment to collect myself. I'll call my parents with my phone card in a bit."

"All right, Bosco. You do that. Listen, I know it's hard for you. If you need anything, just let me know, okay? Pastor Tom will come in tomorrow. He will keep you posted on any news regarding the funeral arrangements."

"Okay. Thank you."

"Take care, Bosco. Your family is in my prayers. I'll talk to you soon." I heard the click as Father Mako hung up the phone.

My mind was filled with disbelief. For years I'd seen inmates get called to the chaplain's office to receive the news of a family member's death. I guess it was some manner of denial, but I never really considered the fact that my turn would come. A.C.'s murder was already devastation enough for me. I was just getting over that loss. Now I had to face another death, and this one hit me even harder. I was very close to my grandpa. But when I was free, I was too busy doing my own thing and didn't pay him enough attention, and I regretted this so much during my incarceration. For this reason, during my many prayer times in my cell, I asked the Lord if someday I could cook for grandpa or take him out for walk after dinner. I prayed that he would be able to attend my wedding after my release. All those were pipe dreams now. It was very hard for me to accept that I would never be able to make up for all the lost time.

God! What's going on? Why did my grandpa have to die while I'm still in here? I did not get to reunite with him in the outside world. Why did You take him from me?

Dozens of questions filled my mind as I went back to my cell to weep. After letting all my tears out, I took my inmate phone card and left my unit. I walked towards the public phone station outside the activity building, but I didn't want to make the call. I was afraid to hear the news from my parents.

I slowly inserted the phone card, and a few seconds after punching in my passcode, my call went through.

"Hello? hello?" My mom answered the call.

"Mom, it's me."

"Oh son, oh son ..." My mom started to sob. That was the exact sound I did not want to hear.

"Mom, is it true? Grandpa?"

"Yes, it is, son. He passed away at 1:05 p.m. today." Mom continued to sob. She blew her nose and continued, "But it's okay, son. He is with the Lord now. A few days before he passed away, I saw a white light beside his bed, and I recognized it was Jesus. At that moment, I knew He was coming to receive Grandpa."

"What? A white light?" This caught my attention.

"Yes, a white light in the shape of a man. I saw it! It lasted for a few seconds, then disappeared. Even though I should have been afraid, I was very calm. I didn't know why, but I just knew that was the Lord, and I knew Grandpa's time was up."

"Wow. So now you've seen the white light too!"

"Yes, son, I did and I am certain your grandpa is with the Lord now. Right before he passed away, he raised up both of his frail hands as best he could. He looked like he was worshipping. Then he breathed his last breath."

"Wow, really? So he is with the Lord. Then this is not too bad after all. Being in heaven is a beautiful thing. I'm so happy for him."

"Yes, it is, son. I cry because I miss him, but inside I rejoice, because he doesn't need to suffer from pancreatic cancer any more. He couldn't eat, and he'd become so gaunt. It hurt me so badly every day I visited him in the hospital. Son, this is a relief for him."

"I guess it is. One side of me is happy that he has finished his race, but the other side of me is so sad because I wanted to have the opportunity to treat him as he deserved. I never paid him enough attention when I was free, and I've been waiting for the day I am released so that I could do something good for him." I started to break down.

"Son, I understand. Son, don't beat yourself up. You have done something amazing for him. Something more than any one of us out here could do for him. You have told him the truth and led him through the sinner's prayer through your letter. The courage you showed has inspired us all. Do you know that he cut that prayer out from your letter and placed it in his wallet? He brought that prayer with him wherever he went. Son, he is now with the Lord because of you." My mom tried to comfort me.

"I, uh ... I, uh ... I miss him ... I wasn't there for him before he went." I was still sobbing.

"I know, son, I know, and your grandpa understood your situation. Just a few days ago he said that both you and him were enduring a trial. His was cancer, and yours was prison. He was so encouraged by the way you have faced your trial, and he wasn't afraid of his. Son, you've done a lot more for him than you think. Even though you're not physically here with us, you're a blessing to us all."

"Really?" I wiped my face with my T-shirt. "Thanks for that, Mom. I get it, and I understand. I guess I just need to grieve. But I understand what you just said. I do. Anyway, I'll be fine. Oh, by the way, Father Mako said I have a good chance of getting a compassionate pass to attend the funeral. Are you guys arranging that now?" I began collecting myself.

"Yes, we're arranging it right now. It's going to be this Saturday, the 5th. We'll let Father Mako or Pastor Tom know all the details. Don't you worry. We're in contact already."

"Okay, I'll let you know once I receive any updates about the pass. I better go and put some money on my phone card right now because I won't be able to reload it for two more weeks. I will probably need to call you more often than usual for the next little while. Please take care, Mom. Say 'Hi' to Dad."

"Okay, son, I will. Take care of yourself too. Love you. Goodbye." Mom hung up.

After the phone call, I felt a lot better. That evening, all the memories I shared with Grandpa flowed unceasingly through my mind. I didn't sleep too much. In my small spiritual journal, I wrote,

June 2, 2010 Wed.
My LORD, thank You for receiving my grandpa and welcoming him home. He has finished his race today. You came to receive grandpa @ 1:05 p.m. LORD, one part of my heart is aching, yet the other part is rejoicing. This feeling is so weird. Please continue to take good, good, good care of him.

Grandpa, can you hear me? Do you know, Lup Lup loves you very, very, very, very, very much! I miss you. Please wait for me in Jesus's presence. When I see you again, I want a big hug.

God, please grant me this petition. My whole family needs You; please be with us, please.

"Bosco, we're almost there." After an hour and a half drive, Pastor Tom broke the silence.

"Oh man, it's time." My heart was heavy—very heavy. I didn't talk much throughout the ride. Normally I would be very happy to be in the outside world, even for a brief time, but that was not the case on this occasion.

Risen From Prison

"And here we are." Pastor Tom made a right turn into the parking lot of Richmond Funeral Home. Stepping out of the car onto the soil of Richmond brought memories flooding back: from winning my first record label contract with Warner Music Taiwan to walking in the malls with my girlfriends to having countless bubble-tea meetings. But all that was gone now. I had been in many places in this city before, but never had I been to that particular place, and I wasn't sure that I would enjoy my visit.

I followed closely behind Pastor Tom through the front entrance, and we stood in the middle of the main hall looking for clues to where my grandpa's service was to be held. At the end of the hallway, I saw my grandpa's name, "Ho Yung Kong," on the stand. *So here it is: Grandpa.*

The moment I entered the room, I saw that everyone was facing my grandpa's body, on top of the casket at the front that all the seats were facing to. As Pastor Tom and I broke the silence in the room by our footsteps, everyone turned toward us. Uncle Chris and his family came to give me a hug. I walked toward my parents and gave them a hug. Then I walked to my grandma, who had been staring at my grandpa the entire time, and hugged her from behind. She said to me calmly, "Oh, Lup Lup, you came." From the tone of her voice, it didn't seem as if she remembered that I'd come from prison. But I couldn't blame her. She'd just lost her lifelong friend. I couldn't even imagine what was going on in her head.

Among the people who came to attend the service were some of my music friends, some prison ministry volunteers from different churches, and some Chinese Christian Mission Canada volunteers. I went to give all of them a hug and then walked up to the front and took a long look at my grandpa's body. He was very good-looking that day, dressed in his best suit. There was makeup on his face to make him looked warmer and more alive than cold and dead. I touched his ice-cold hand, and tears instantly burst out from my eyes. This was kind of a psychological confirmation that he was really dead. Knowing I still had a service to host, I sucked my tears back and turned around. After taking out my notes from my jacket pocket, I addressed everyone. "Thank you for coming to attend my grandpa's funeral. The service is about to begin, and I'll be your host alongside Pastor Tom today. It's not going to be a very formal service. It's going to be family style. Is that okay? So we can just relax."

Pastor Tom then said, "Yes, everyone. First, we want to welcome you to the memorial service of Mr. Yung Kong Ho. This is a difficult time for your family, who has lost someone so dear to them. So we want to extend our love and care toward all your family members during this grieving period. At the same time, our Christian faith reminds us that death is not the end. So while we mourn today, the other side of us should be full of hope, because our Saviour has conquered the power of death. Let us not lose hope, and remember the beautiful gift of eternal life that Jesus Christ has given us." He continued with a prayer and then opened the floor up for anyone who wanted to share their thoughts about Grandpa. After a few people shared, I went up.

Bosco H. C. Poon

After clearing my throat a little, I said, "I had a very close relationship with my grandpa. I lived with him and my grandma from the time I was a child. He taught me a lot of things. I still remember how he taught me to speak and how to ride a bike. Those memories are so precious to me. He was an honourable man. I knew how hard he worked for his family, raising my mom and my three uncles. He loved to read and was always seeking knowledge. Even though only his left eye functioned, he would still read every day. He couldn't hear much because of his hearing loss. So when we spoke to him, we either had to yell or remind him to turn on his hearing aid. It was difficult for him to hear me over the phone when I called from prison. Every time he would end our conversation with 'Grandpa is getting old. He can't hear you. So I'll just pass the phone back to your mom.' Oh, how I miss him."

I paused for a moment, holding back my emotions, and continued, "There's a time for everything, and a season for every activity under the heavens: a time to be born and a time to die. This is a natural cycle for us. As we mourn for the death of my grandpa today, I want to encourage you that this is not the end but the beginning of the next chapter for him. There is life after death. That's the promise of the gospel of Jesus Christ. For God so loved the world that He gave His one and only Son, that whoever believes in Him shall not perish but have eternal life. I'm happy to let you know that, together with my parents, we helped him to receive Jesus as his Saviour in the past few years. Therefore, we are confident that today he is with God in paradise. And we should rejoice for that. That's why we've called it a celebration of his life. The beauty of our Christian faith is that while in this world we have sorrow, our spirit can rejoice because of the promises of God." I was trying hard to lift the atmosphere in the room while hoping to share the gospel with some of the people at the service who did not know Christ Jesus.

After all those who wanted to share had taken their turns, Pastor Tom led us to the next part of the service. "For the next part, we would like to dedicate flowers to Mr. Ho. Please bring along your roses one by one and put them on his chest. You can say something to him while you do that. If there are any last words you want to say to him, take this time to do it. Say it out loud or say it in your heart. It's up to you. Take this time and cherish this moment. We're not in a rush, so take your time."

People came up one by one as I walked out and sat down on the last row of seats. Some spoke out loud to say their last words, while others remained silent or cried. The whole atmosphere became very heavy with tears. My mom broke down bitterly as she put her rose on Grandpa's chest. Grandma was too short to reach above the casket, so Uncle Chris helped her with her rose. She just stood there looking up at Grandpa. The way she looked at him showed she didn't want to let him go. Not a word came from her mouth, but the way she was staring at Grandpa spoke a thousand words. I will never forget that moment.

After letting everyone else take their turn, I walked up slowly with my rose. I looked at Grandpa from head to toe very carefully. Knowing that this would be the last time I could see his physical body, I was trying hard to remember the moment.

Risen From Prison

As I put down my rose to pay my respects, I said to him, "Grandpa, I miss you. I'm so sorry that I wasn't there when you left us. I'm so sorry that I lied to you for so long. I'm so sorry that I got myself into such a mess and wasn't there for you when you needed care the most. I'm so sorry!" I lost control and knelt down before him. "Grandpa, I want to repay you for all the care you gave me ever since I was a little boy. When I was growing up, I never gave you the attention you deserved. And now it's too late. It's just too late. I'm so sorry!" I fell on the side of the casket, crying in sorrow, "I had nothing to give you besides pointing you to Christ. When I had nothing left, God came to me. I really have nothing else to give you but Him. That's all I have now. By giving you Him, I have given you my all." I wiped my tears with my sleeves. "Grandpa, do you know? I love you. I love you so much!" I kept weeping in great sorrow. A few people came to help me up and sit me down on a chair while I continued to cry.

Pastor Tom waited for me to calm down a bit before leading everyone into the last part of the service. "It's normal to get emotional when we're saying our last words to our loved ones. It's even harder for Bosco, because he is in prison and didn't get the opportunity to say his goodbye properly. But I think you can all see his heart. You see how real God is to him, and that's what he wanted to pass on to his grandpa. As Bosco said earlier, there's life after death. As we feel a great loss today, let us remember that Grandpa's story doesn't end here. As believers in Christ, we have hope even in our death. Even so, we have to go through this grieving process. It is absolutely essential to our recovery. It's normal and healthy. But we take heart in the hope of Jesus, and because of Him we aren't just stuck in our grief. First Thessalonians 4 tells us this: 'Brothers and sisters, we do not want you to be uninformed about those who sleep in death, so that you do not grieve like the rest of mankind, who have no hope. For we believe that Jesus died and rose again, and so we believe that God will bring with Jesus those who have fallen asleep in him.' Our hope in Jesus is that even if we die, we'll rise again in our new body with Him. He has conquered death. Your grandpa's testimony in coming to accept Jesus and receiving eternal life directs us to a God who loves us so much that He would die for us. If we are believers, we'll see Grandpa again. Let us look forward to our reunion one day. We will see each other again in the presence of God. Shall we pray together?"

After the closing prayer, the funeral came to an end. Everyone stayed around for a little bit to comfort one another. I gave Grandma a long hug before I left. Then Pastor Tom drove me back to Ferndale Institution.

I locked myself in my cell for the whole evening, not wanting to talk to anyone. The image of Grandpa in his suit kept playing over and over in my mind. I looked out the window into the dark sky. While I was reflecting on what happened that day, a thought came to me: "You did great, son."

I looked to the left and right and didn't see anyone. *It's that still small voice again. Is God trying to talk to me? Or it was just my imagination?* I closed my eyes to meditate on what I had heard, wanting to double-check with my spiritual ears to see if God was indeed talking to me. After spending ten minutes in silence, I saw someone in white light standing before me in a vision. He said to me, "Don't be discouraged; you've helped your grandpa. You did the right thing by having the courage to tell him the truth."

"I did? Well ... it was actually You who pushed me to do it."

"You listened and did it. You did great."

"It was so hard though."

"But you did it. And led him to salvation."

"Is he?"

"Yes, he is with Me right now. Don't you worry. I'll take good care of him."

"So you knew it all along that he was gonna go before I got out?"

"Did I not ask you what would happen if he died during your imprisonment? And did you want to let him die with your lies?"

"So You knew."

"You made the right choice not to let him die with lies but with the truth."

I did not answer.

"Son, remember this. Your mistake led you to prison, and you're very ashamed of that. But this lesson is transforming you into a better man. Now you've learned to stand up for what's right, even if everyone is against you at the moment. Your character is being shaped. Your relationship with Me is getting stronger every day. And that is becoming a life-changing power. If you look at it carefully, that power has been affecting and impacting the lives around you in abundance. This is just the beginning."

I pondered what I just heard.

"I'll continue to be with you to the very end of the age. Have faith." The white light slowly disappeared, and I felt into a deep sleep.

> "This means that anyone who belongs to Christ has become a new person. The old life is gone; a new life has begun!" (2 Cor. 5:17 NLT)

CHAPTER 20
TELLING MY STORY

In prison, I often listened to Praise 106.5, a local Christian music station, on the radio. One day, there was an interview I was really excited to catch. Brian Doerksen was being interviewed about his new DVD and the different stories of God's grace he had included on it. The reception was always poor from prison because Praise 106.5 is broadcast out of Washington State, and this was especially true during bad weather. Normally, the static was pretty distracting, but for some reason, that day I could hear everything perfectly. When Brian mentioned a story of a prisoner who was still incarcerated, I knew he was talking about me. Just before my grandfather had passed away, by God's grace I had been granted permission to have my testimony recorded by a Christian organization. It all began with a conversation.

"Bosco Poon to the chapel. Bosco Poon to the chapel." I heard Pastor Tom calling me over the PA system. Naturally, I was a little worried by the apparent urgency, so I headed to the chapel in a hurry. I was prepared for bad news about my grandpa and hoped it was not about him.

Slightly winded as I came through the door, I saw Tom on his computer. "Come on in, Bosco!" he called.

"Hi, Pastor Tom. How are you?"

"I'm doing great; thanks for asking. Have a seat."

"O … kay." I sat down.

"I have some news for you. Don't worry. It's nothing bad. It's actually great news."

"Oh, what is it?" I was curious, and a little relieved.

"You know Brian Doerksen? The worship leader who comes to share his music with us every once in a while?"

"Yes, of course. I have two of his CDs."

"Well, he is making a new DVD. And he wants to have some testimonies included on it. He thought of you and wondered if it would be possible to get you out of prison for a few hours so he can get your story on camera. This is definitely not possible for people in medium, but since you're now in a minimum, it's much more likely to get approved. I wanted to know if this is something you'd be interested in."

"Wow. Is this for real?" I had a hard time believing what I'd just heard.

"Yes, this is a rare opportunity. The fact that Brian wants you to share your story means you must have left a remarkable impression on him during his visits."

"Really? He wants me to share my story and he will put it into his new DVD?"

"Yes, that's exactly what he wants to do. From what I understand, he will also have several others share their stories as well. It's going to be a collective of grace stories."

"Interesting. But do you think this is doable?"

"Yes. I believe it's doable. If you are interested, I can start the paperwork to get you a pass to the event. I can act as your escort. It's more likely for the management to approve it that way. Now because you will be recorded, you'll have to sign a waiver to allow the production to use your recording. This is a great opportunity for you to bring God glory by pointing others towards Him."

"Right ..." I pondered for a moment and then replied, "Yeah, I think I'm interested. I mean, if I can point more people to God, I'm all up for it. That's what I've been doing all along, and I'll continue to do it for Jesus."

"That's great, Bosco. That's the attitude all Christians should have. There's power in our testimonies. People are better able to relate to God through our stories. I pray that you'll be led by the Holy Spirit to freely share about your journey with God. Okay then, I'll prepare the paperwork. That's all I need from you for now. I'll let you know more details within the next few days."

"All right, thanks, Pastor Tom. Please keep me posted."

"I sure will. Have a great day!" Pastor Tom gave me a big smile as I got up from his desk.

On my way back to my unit I was full of excitement for what lay ahead. It had been a while since I'd stood before a video camera. Just thinking about it brought back all kinds of memories. *Speaking in public for a recording—I haven't done that for a while. Will I be able to do it?* I played different scenarios in my head over and over, trying to figure out what I wanted to say. In my previous life, when I was preparing for a music competition or performance, I would practice in front of the mirror and film it with a camcorder. Then I'd study the footage and make adjustments until I thought things were perfect. For those times when I had the budget to practice at a dance studio, I would have a coach to help me with choreography. I spent countless hours with a choreographer named Raphael at Studio One Richmond in preparation for the music contest hosted by Warner Music Taiwan. I recorded every single session and played it over and over at home, trying to perfect every move. This was how I had managed to get first place and score the record deal that went with it.

This time, however, I was struggling a great deal because I had no way to practice. Without a camcorder or a coach, I couldn't really figure out what I was supposed to say or do or which parts needed improvement. On top of that, my confidence had shrunk dramatically during my time in prison. I felt inferior to people in the outside world and had forgotten how to carry myself. All I really knew to do was pray and trust that God would guide me along the way.

> **"When you are brought before synagogues, rulers and authorities, do not worry about how you will defend yourselves or what you will say, for the Holy Spirit will teach you at that time what you should say." (Luke 12:11–12)**

"Bosco, please come in and let us take a photo of you." I was led to a room after my arrival to the filming location. A photographer directed me to a seat in front of a backdrop. "Just sit still and look into the camera."

"What? I need to take a photo? I don't know if I look good enough." I hesitated because of my drab blue outfit. It's all I had access to in prison. I made the most of my faded jeans and turned the collar up on the long-sleeved golf shirt I had on. It was the best I could do under the circumstance.

"You're about to go into a video recording, and you're worried about not looking good enough for a photo? Don't worry. You look fine. Come on, sit up straight, and look at the lens."

"Well, I guess you're right." I sat straight.

"Good. One more, and ... you're done!"

"Is he done? Good, he is up next." A lady came in and let us know they were ready for the recording.

"Well, Bosco, are you all set?" Pastor Tom greeted me with his wife, Linda. "Let's walk over together."

The filming of Brian's DVD, called *Level Ground*, was held in a high-ceilinged meeting place that could hold about two hundred. It was decorated as a big country-style living room with area rugs throughout for people to sit on. It wasn't a really big place, but since I'd been trapped in an institution for so long, it seemed enormous. As Tom and I passed through the entrance, we were directed to sit among the audience. I felt very uncomfortable surrounded by all these normal people from the outside world, especially by women, since I hadn't interacted with any for a long time. The lights were very bright, it was warm, and I was nervous.

There were two stools positioned in the middle of the room, and folks of all ages were seated around on the wooden floor. The cameramen and technicians adjusted their equipment as Brian walked up to one of the stools. Then he leaned forward and spoke closely into the microphone. "Bosco, are you here, my friend? Come on up." Pastor Tom and Linda patted my shoulder. I took a deep breath and walked towards him.

Walking through the crowd, my heart was beating fast and my palms were sweating. As I got myself up onto the empty stool, I wiped my hands on my jeans. The stage lights coming from all directions made it difficult for me to see. I wasn't used to this kind of bright light after being locked up for years. I closed my eyes for a moment. *Come on, stay cool. This is not the first time you've been under the spotlight. I can do this. I can do all things through Christ who gives me strength.*

I had been telling my family and friends about my transformation for years, and I was constantly sharing with the other inmates, too. But talking about it in such a public setting, admitting my wrongs, and being vulnerable in front of a large crowd *and* in front of a camera: this was a first. My biggest concern was that my English was still very heavily accented. In high school I often had to repeat myself, and sometimes this was still the case. I was afraid the audience wouldn't be able to understand a word I said. But looking at it as a God-given opportunity, I just rolled with it.

Talking myself out of my fear, I looked straight at Brian, who was now sitting right across from me. He turned to look at all the cameramen and gave them the signal. The cameras began rolling. Brian looked off in the distance. "Wow, this is … this is a miracle." His gaze came back to me.

"It is." I smiled back.

"It's an incredible miracle. Here we are. We're sitting having a conversation."

"Absolutely."

"You're still in the middle of your sentence. This is your first time out—not with a guard—very first time out. Bosco, I met you the first time about three-ish years ago. I was doing a little concert at the prison. You came up to me after the concert"—Brian laughed—"and you were talkin' … music business. Like you were gonna hook me up. And I'm thinkin' to myself, 'I don't know if this guy gets why I come into prison.'" The audience broke into spontaneous laughter. Brian continued, "I wouldn't come into prison to further my music career—to get 'hooked up for the biz.' I'm there because I see Jesus."

Brian continued, "Describe for us what your life was like before you encountered the grace of God."

"Wow. I was a slave. I was bound by the depravity of the world. I was a slave to self-ambition, fame, materials, and sex. When you turn on your TV, you see all these commercials, you see all these shows, music videos, showing us all these beautiful celebrities wearing their fancy clothes, cruising around in their unbelievably expensive vehicles, having all-night-long parties at the pool house or club with a soccer team of sexy ladies in bikinis. Wow, I thought that was life. I thought that was happiness. I thought by chasing after all these things I would eventually find happiness and make my mama proud. You know, we are powerful people, Brian; by willpower we can do many things that can last for a period of time. But without God, we can never accomplish the godly things that can last for eternity. By pursuing my 'superstar dream,' I got a chance to experience so many different things. I got to know all the behind-the-scenes procedures and connections. I worked so hard, from a high school grad living in a small town to a Chinese-English rapper who had my own music crew, dealing with agents and record companies in both Asia and North America. But the reality was, I wasn't happy at all. I was living in a world of uncertainties. I was building my whole kingdom on shifting sand. And when an earthquake came, my whole kingdom collapsed.

"In the first chapter of Proverbs, it says 'do not give in to the enticement of sinners, 'cause they will drag you down to hell.' And that was exactly what happened to me. I listened to some bad peers and made some bad decisions and got myself involved into some illegal activities that involved human lives. There are consequences for our actions. For me, it was a twelve-year sentence, a hundred and seventy grand in lawyer's fees, separation from all my loved ones, and a total loss of my dream career, freedom, dignity, and confidence."

"Wow, I mean …" Brian paused for a bit, then asked, "So … so, what turned it around?"

"You know, to tell you the truth, prison is not a pretty place. It is a place that is full of broken hearts, failures, hatred, and shame. What has been done cannot be undone. I can't go back in time and change things, but I can do things today to change my future. I have a Christian background, but it's just that I never really practised it out there. So at the very beginning of my sentence, I chose to find out who is this Jesus that all Christians put their faith in. I was brutally honest with God. You know, I just told Him that, you know, You are not my first priority. In my secular mind, back then, I was … all that I was caring about was my girlfriend at the time, my career, and my family. But I would love to put Him above all things. I asked God to show me how.

"I didn't get an answer instantly, but He did indeed show me, through my experiences behind bars and through His Holy Words. For the first three months in prison, I was earning one buck per day, and then five bucks afterward. I was saving up that money with sweat and tears, and when it slowly accumulated to around four hundred bucks, I sent it all to my girlfriend, whom I loved so dearly. Not too long after that, on my first birthday in prison, I found out that she was going out with another guy. A dude picked up her phone and told me that she was not available while I could hear her voice in the background. My heart was broken into a million pieces. And I was so alone that night. Everything that I built myself in my life, I lost. It was so painful.

"Then a Bible verse came to me. In the last verse of Matthew, Jesus says, 'I am with you always, to the very end of the age.' A couple weeks later, during my evening prayer, Jesus appeared before me in a great white light. He extended His hand into my chest and lifted up my heart. He opened up my spiritual ears and said to me, 'I will rescue you.' So God literally came down to my level and showed me His grace.

"Since that day I have been talking to Him daily. He has taught me so many things and has promised me things that I cannot fathom. God can turn ashes into beauty. He picked me up piece by piece and formed a new me and turned me into His soldier."

"As you look forward now for the rest of your life, what do you want to do with this grace?"

"You know, Brian, we are living in a fallen world. Anyone who doesn't believe in the devil, just turn on the news and you can see how corrupted the world has become. In prison, I have seen so many very ugly depravities. I have seen people being stabbed, raped, threatened, sucked into the drug world. I can turn a blind eye and pretend I didn't see anything—just do my time. But the Holy Spirit just continues to push me out of my comfort zone to be a support for those who are in need in prison. And together with the chapel group, we go to the outcasts to give them the hope of the gospel. We protect those who are in danger, and we encourage those who are sick. I just appreciate the privilege to be a part of the prison ministry team and to learn how to be at the forefront to fight against the devil. God came down to us and showed us His grace, but we are required to do one thing—that is to respond with actions. I have seen so many people come to Jesus, give Jesus their lives verbally, and then do nothing afterward. In John 5, verse 8 and 14, Jesus said to the leper, the paralyzed—"

At this point I transitioned to a rap I had prepared in advance. "Being paralyzed 38 years—stayed on the side—thirsty, in fear. Didn't realize salvation is near. Put yourself together. Wipe those tears. If you wanna get well, gotta get help. Don't just sit there listening to fairy tales. Chuck the old self in the junk mail. It's time to change within yourself. Don't just talk all the talk. Get on the floor to walk. Nothing gonna change till you act on the walk. Believe it or not, to unlock the lock, simply have to fully depend upon the Rock. First take your first step, then take your second step, next thing you're walking forward step by step. Even when the devil sets you back, with Christ nothing can ever hold you back. Get up, pick up the mat, start to walk. Get up, pick up the mess. Stop the talk! Get up. Pick up the mat. Start to walk! Get get get get get up!"

As I finished, everyone in the building was cheering. I knew the delivery of my rap wasn't the best because I'd become a little rusty in jail, but people cheered all the same because they knew the God I was speaking about and were overjoyed at the transformation that Jesus had made in my life.

Knowing that I had to give a more proper closing, I continued, "Before we have a true relationship with Jesus Christ, we are all spiritually paralyzed. If we truly want to be healed and made whole, we have to pick up that stinky old mat we've been sitting on for ages and start walking. Let's use our actions to show our God that we truly want to follow Him and that we appreciate His love. My grandpa is in the hospital right now, not knowing if he will ever come out. There is one thing I know, and that is where he is going, 'cause he's come to have a relationship with Jesus because of my testimony in prison.

"Six years ago, I made some bad decisions, and the consequence was the devastation of many. Today, I choose to follow my God and love Him wholeheartedly, and the consequence of it is the salvation of my loved ones. If God can set me free for couple of hours to testify of His power, how much more He can use each and every single one of you, free men and women, to prosper His Kingdom. So let us lift up our hearts, pick up our mats, and follow Jesus. And let's give Him some praise!"[3]

With that I raised my hands in clapping and praise to God, and to my joy and surprise, everyone else joined in. As the cheering continued, the interview ended with an important word from Brian. He said that all of us, no matter how sinful and depraved we are—Jesus changes us when we come to Him. But He doesn't do so in order to turn us into someone totally different. That is, He doesn't take away our giftings, interests, and passions. Rather, He redeems them. We are the same people, but we are not the same people. We are the same people, but we are made new. As a believer, I still loved rapping, but my rapping was now directed to the purpose for which it was intended.

After the recording, I had to leave with Pastor Tom right away. Before I went off, Brian prayed over me along with all the audience. It was an amazing experience. Never had I imagined I would be granted a pass to leave prison to record my testimony. Once again God showed me He could open any doors according to His will. Since then, telling my story has become a regular part of my life. I wasn't doing it to draw attention to myself but to point others to the Lord Jesus, the Saviour who rescued me from the pit. From the bottom of my heart, I wanted everyone to find hope in Him.

---

[3] Brian Doerksen, "Level Ground | Grace Story | Bosco Poon," video, 14:05, Sept. 8, 2010, https://vimeo.com/14807786.

CHAPTER 21
THE NEXT CHAPTER

"Bosco, my daughter wants me to give you this." Pastor Tom handed me a business card.

"Oh, thank you. What is this?" I looked at it. It said "Knotty Boy Lock Shop & Salon."

"She remembered a conversation she had with you during one of her visits to prison as a volunteer—that you wanted to get dreadlocks one day. She found this in her drawer and wanted you to have it. She recommends this salon in Vancouver."

"Oh wow, that's … how thoughtful of her. Please give her my thanks. I *do* want to get dreadlocks when I get out. But who knows when I'll get out? I have a long sentence."

"Well, just keep it with you. When you get out, you'll know where to get your dreadlocks." He smiled.

"Yeah, thanks."

I had kind of forgotten the prayer I'd prayed about getting dreadlocks as a sign of my commitment to God. It had been a long time, and so much had transpired since then. I hadn't given it too much thought because I had no idea when I would be released, though, to be clear, I had every intention of fulfilling my promise. Staring pensively down at the business card, I couldn't help but wonder if my time in prison was almost up. *Is this a sign from God?*

Bosco H. C. Poon

I sat impatiently fidgeting while waiting to be called up by the panel. The silence in the hearing room made me nervous. I hadn't been in a courtroom for a good long time. Not being accustomed to all the procedures, I wondered about everything that was happening and sat nervously watching the two parole board members furtively whispering to one another. Flipping through a stack of papers on the table, they finally called me up to the seat in the middle of the room directly facing them.

A hearing officer documented everything being said. Sitting next to me was my IPO, Joyce. It was November 26, 2010. As my parole hearing began, the panel read the details of my file from my index offence and forward. They read out the police report of my crime and the decision of the judge. When they had finished, they looked up and began their questioning.

"Mr. Poon, do you understand the seriousness of your crime?" one of the two national parole board members asked with a fairly severe tone.

"I do, and I now understand the impact it had on the victim, his family, and society. This is why I received a 12-year sentence." The board members seated in front of me would determine my fate, so I had to be respectful and thoughtful in my responses so as to convey that I understood the damage I'd done and that I had truly changed.

"Why did you do it? Why did you want to hurt your victim?"

"I ... to be honest ... I never wanted to hurt the victim. I didn't know him personally, and I didn't have any ill wishes towards him. I got involved into this crime because of my own naivety, lack of assertiveness, and the misplaced loyalty to the peers who'd protected me from bullying in high school. When they first came up with the idea, I thought they were kidding. At the time I thought that letting them use my parents' house was really just a matter of doing them a favour. As for the promise they made to pay me $10,000 rent—I never really expected them to follow through. But I was open to the idea that if they did, I could make some quick cash. I was motivated by greed, but I never wanted to hurt anyone.

"In the middle of the whole affair, I tried to convince my co-accused to release the victim multiple times. But, of course, they didn't listen. From my perspective, my involvement was minimal. However, I remember that during my sentencing, the judge told me even though my participation was limited, my provision of the house was a crucial contribution to the success of the kidnapping. For this reason, I was treated similarly to the others.

"At first, I didn't understand. I thought it wasn't fair. But seeing how much my loved ones suffered over time, especially my parents, I gained some important insights. I realized how much the family of the victim must have suffered when *their* son was gone, particularly since they didn't even know if he was alive. Prison is a scary place. I felt so lonely and helpless here. That also gave me insight into how lonely and helpless the victim must have felt. This helped me see the impact of my foolish decisions. Without my parents' house, the kidnapping might never have happened. Unintentionally, I brought tremendous harm to the victim and his family and, in return, harmed my loved ones, too."

I paused for a bit, then continued, "When I fully realized what I had done, I felt very sorry for the victim. There was a program called Restorative Justice from the chapel. I participated in this program, wanting to reconcile with the victim and to give him my apology through a letter. Unfortunately, the staff told me the victim couldn't be located. So he never received my letter. I just hope he will someday know that I'm truly sorry for the pain I inflicted on him."

"So, tell us, what have you done to change?"

"I understand that what I have done cannot be undone. I take full responsibility for my wrongdoing. There is no way I can go back in time to change the past. All I can do now is learn from my mistakes and work on my weaknesses, and I have been doing that to the best of my ability. Since my imprisonment began, I've tried my best to get involved in as many programs to better myself as I could. I distanced myself from negative influences and dedicated myself to the chapel work and peer counselling. I'm continuing these efforts at this institution where I'm a mentor to inmates who have mental health problems.

"I used to be impulsive and self-centred, and I lacked any kind of discernment. I did not think carefully, and I did not consider the consequences of my actions. I've learned and I've changed. Now I always try to put myself into other peoples' shoes first before making a decision. Would my actions or words harm the other person or build them up? While in prison, I have been trying my best to contribute to the building of a better society. That's what I want to do when I rejoin the outside world. I want to become a law-abiding and constructive citizen. I hope my institutional records for the past four years show that what I am saying is true."

The board members turned to my IPO. "What would you say to that?"

She gave her report. "Mr. Poon has done well during his incarceration. While he initially found adjustment to prison life difficult, he worked hard to make things better. He actively sought ways to improve, such as the chaplaincy programs. As he said, when he was at medium security, he was a peer counsellor. He spent a great deal of time helping other inmates. Now here in minimum security, he's continued his involvement in mentoring by helping the prisoners with mental health problems. Besides the voluntary programs he took in the chapel, he completed the moderate intensity Integrated Correctional Program Model, and the report was positive. His institutional behaviour has been consistently good. He has gone as far as he can while incarcerated. The next logical step is day parole, and I'm supportive of that."

The board members were talking among themselves and writing things down. They asked me a few more questions. I answered them the best I could, with honesty and sincerity. When they were finished with their questioning, the hearing officer told us to wait outside the building so they could deliberate on their decision.

Once outside, I looked up to the sky. Trusting in God's plan for me, my heart was at peace.

Bosco H. C. Poon

"You did well. I think you have a good chance," Joyce said to me.

"My lawyer told me something similar about my trial. But it was different that time because I was guilty and was trying to fight against justice. This time I admitted my wrongs and did my best to be honest. I *do* hope you're right."

"The best thing you can do in a parole hearing is to be honest. That's what the board is looking for. It's not the easiest thing to do, but you did it."

"Yeah, and there's no point in hiding ... besides, I'm monitored 24-7. The truth will come out no matter what, and I've been doing my best to become a better man. That's the truth."

It was ten minutes before we were called back into the room by the hearing officer. As I sat back down in the same seat, the board gave me their final decision: "Mr. Poon, you were an integral part of a very serious crime. Your contribution caused significant psychological harm to the victim and his family. However, the board notes you have no prior criminal record, with a history of good institutional behaviour. You also have distanced yourself from negative influences and have completed the relevant programming. Listening to you speak, we see that you have gained insight. Given the support of your institutional parole officer and your clear motivation to reintegrate into society as a law-abiding citizen, the board concludes that your risk on day parole is not undue at this time. Day parole is therefore granted."

Granted ... granted ... GRANTED! I could hardly believe what I had heard. It was the word I'd been longing to hear for four years. After serving about one-third of my sentence, I was granted an early day parole. That meant I was allowed to serve the rest of my sentence in the outside world under conditions, curfew, and proper monitoring. Even though the duration and extent of my travel would be limited, it was a big step toward freedom. I was ecstatic!

After thanking the board and Joyce, I quickly left the hearing building and ran back to my unit to let everyone know the good news. That evening, all my friends came over to celebrate with me, including everyone from my unit whom I had been mentoring. We all chipped in to cook. After dinner, I took some time to talk to everyone. I divided my food and supply evenly among my neighbours, so no one would have to fight over my stuff when I was gone. I left some of my belongings to a few guys, thinking that it would benefit them more. Knowing I was heading back to the free world made that the happiest evening of my imprisonment. I could finally get back to my family and loved ones.

"Poon to A&D, Poon to A&D!" Admission and Discharge called me bright and early that morning. It was still dark outside because it was late November. With my eyes half opened, I put on my jacket and walked over.

Upon arrival, an officer told me I was scheduled to leave that very day for a halfway house in Vancouver. He gave me the option to order a taxi or call someone from the outside to pick me up. Without hesitation, I told him I'd call my parents. He said I had until 4 p.m. to arrive and report to the halfway house. My community parole officer would sign me in when I got there. My curfew was 9 p.m. to 7 a.m., meaning I had to stay inside the halfway house between those hours. I hurried to the phone station, and I made a call home.

"Dad! I can leave today!" I yelled into the phone.

"What? Today?" Dad wasn't sure if he'd heard me right.

"Yes! Today! I can leave prison now! Come pick me up!"

"Oh my ... Mom, our boy can leave prison today! We can go pick him up now!" Dad yelled to my mom with his hand over the receiver.

"Okay, Dad, I gotta go pack up. Meet me at the main entrance."

"Okay. We'll need at least two hours to get there."

"I know. This will give me enough time to pack up my stuff. See you in a bit. I love you, Dad! Can't wait to see you!" I hung up and ran back to my unit full speed.

Standing at the door, I looked into my cell with mixed feelings. I had a hard time believing that I was really leaving. For years, when I woke up each day, I would pinch myself to make sure that prison life wasn't just a nightmare. Every day I prayed for the day I could get back to my family. That day, my prayer was finally answered. I closed the door behind me, knelt down on the floor, and started to cry. *This day has come. I'm leaving this place. Finally ...*

While I put my belongings into cardboard boxes issued by A&D, all the memories of the past four years flooded back. I remembered the first time I wrote a letter to my parents with a tiny pencil and single sheet of paper, the first phone call I made to the outside world, the first time I got sick, the first time I was yelled at by a guard, the first time I witnessed a fight inches away from me, the first time I picked up the Bible and had no clue where to begin reading, the first time I tried to write in my spiritual journal (which later on became a daily habit), the first song I wrote in my cell, and the first Christmas I spent in prison. And there was much more: my first birthday, my first open visit with family and friends, my first step into the chapel, my first Alpha class, my first counselling session with an inmate, my first time praying over someone, my first time visiting others in segregation, my first time dealing with inmates with mental illness, the news about A.C., and finally the very sad news about Grandpa. I remembered every friend I'd crossed paths with in prison, every walk I had on the field, and all the times sobbing behind closed doors. A lot had happened during my incarceration. And this chapter of the journey was coming to an end.

If you asked whether I would remove this part of my life if I had it to live over again, I'd probably say "No." It wasn't because I enjoyed prison life. As a matter of fact, I hated every second of it and constantly regretted the impulsivity that landed me there. But the experience changed me into a new person. The suffering I endured produced character in me that would never have come about on its own. Paradoxically, through losing all my privileges and freedom, I learned the secret of contentment. I was forced to look deep inside myself, to put things into a proper perspective, and to understand what kind of person I really was and what I wanted to become. The things I used to strive for weren't necessarily good for me, and I lacked the ability to discern right from wrong. Consequently, I brought harm to many people, including myself.

At the darkest point, when I'd lost all hope, I found God. Actually, it was Him who found me. Jesus was the most valuable of all gains from this difficult chapter of my life. Connecting to the Creator who had made me allowed me to discover my purpose—something I'd had no perspective on before. My relationship with God helped me to sleep at night, knowing that I could lean on Him for help with all my problems. Compared to my former life of sleepless anxiety-filled nights when I'd worried so much, I now lived in relative serenity. While the world told me I had no future, God assured me that I could hope in Him. When I wanted to *give* up, He told me to *look* up. When I didn't think I deserved a second chance, He reminded me that He died to give me a chance at a new life, and because of this I was forever changed. Everything that I've experienced through this journey is beyond my wildest imagination.

After I finished packing, I still had some time left. Taking advantage of my last hour, I decided to walk the perimeter of the property one last time. As I passed by the gym, I paused to look at Mission Institution in the distance through the chain-link fence. All of a sudden, I longed to see all my old friends there. *Guys, I'm leaving today. I wish you could hear me. Thanks for everything. I'll never forget the times that we spent together.*

When I was ready to leave, I said a prayer before I walked out my unit. After signing all the paperwork at the duty office, the officers said goodbye to me and told me they didn't ever want to see me again—in the nicest possible way. As I stepped outside, I turned back to look one more time. *I'll never forget you. Thank you for all the lessons you've taught me. I'll take everything I've learned with me. I'll do my best to be a blessing for the good of this world. I'll fight against the darkness with all my strength for the rest of my life. It's time for me to close this chapter and leave you behind. Time to go now ... goodbye.*

After closing my eyes to take a deep breath, I turned around and walked out toward the main gates. I could finally step outside those walls and enjoy freedom once again. Full of anticipation, I walked out of prison with great joy in my heart and stepped into the next chapter of my life. *Freedom, here I come!*

"Now the Lord is the Spirit, and where the Spirit of the Lord is, there is freedom." (2 Cor. 3:17 ESV)

Little did I know that I have been risen from prison for a reason. My work for the kingdom of God was just getting started the moment I stepped outside those gates. I was yet to experience many more things that were way beyond my wildest imagination. The ongoing story is to be continued in the outside world.

"I was as moved by Kevin's devastating and glorious story as I was by his manner of telling it ... *Dancing on a Razor* is humbling and beautiful."
—**Steve Bell**, singer-songwriter, author

"This is a remarkable book! ... Kevin reveals how he was in the battle zone between Heaven and Hell and what it is really like to enter into the pit of hopelessness. Yet God never forgets about him."
—**Rev. Dr. Alistair P. Petrie**, executive director of Partnership Ministries

"Kevin White walks readers through the dark worlds he's known, ultimately to find the most radiant of lights awaiting at the end of each one."
—**Tim Huff**, author, speaker, social-justice worker

"Get this book not only for yourself, but buy copies for your friends. It may just save their life. This is real!"—**Barbara Yoder**, apostle, Shekinah, Ann Arbor, MI

"*Because God Was There* will take you deep into the spiritual realm. This book should be in every counsellor's office."—**Moira Brown**, TV and radio personality

"What a story! This book should be turned into a movie."
—**Steve and Sandra Long**, senior leaders, Catch the Fire, Toronto

"A manual to lead you from tragedy to triumph."
—**Barry Maracle** (Mohawk), Desert Stream Ministries

"A must-read for every person who has ever experienced trauma or hurts in life, especially Indian residential/boarding school survivors."
—**Dr. Gerard and Peta-Gay Roberts**

"This down-to-earth book will bring hope, encouragement and fresh vision."
—**Mary Audrey Raycroft**, international speaker

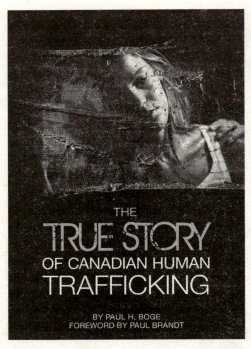

"This powerful book shines a light on the very dark, insidious reality of human trafficking here in Canada. It could happen to anyone and presents a risk to all. This is a clarion call to action."
—**Hon. Peter MacKay,** former cabinet minister, partner at Baker & McKenzie LLP

"Thank you, Joy Smith, for giving Canada a reality check on the horrific crime of human trafficking. We are grateful that because of you, Canada is a safer place for women and girls!"
—**Diane Redsky**, executive director, MaMawi Wi Chi Itata Centre Inc. & project director, National Task Force on Human Trafficking of Women and Girls in Canada (2011-2015)

"This story as seen through the eyes of survivors will be an educational tool for Canadians. We cannot get enough education and awareness on this poignant issue."—**Scott Kolody**, assistant commissioner, RCMP Manitoba

"Powerful and devastating! This book is a must-read for all who care about the safety and well-being of our nation's children and the systemic, malevolent sickness that targets them."—**Steve Bell**, singer-songwriter, author